Sir Charles Raymond of Valentine House, Baronet

Sir Charles Raymond of Valentines and the East India Company

Georgina Green

Hainault Press

© Georgina Green 2015

All rights Reserved. Except as permitted under current legislation, no part of this work may be photocopied, stored in a retrieval system, published, performed in public, adapted, broadcast, transmitted, recorded or reproduced in any form or by any means, without the prior permission of the copyright owner.

ISBN   978-0-9507915-2-4

Hainault Press
24 Henry's Walk
Hainault, Ilford
Essex IG6 2NR

CONTENTS AND TABLES

ACKNOWLEDGEMENTS

PREFACE by Professor Margot Finn

INTRODUCTION

Notes on dates, currency and abbreviations used

PART 1. LIVING BY THE SEA

The Raymond family in Devon

Hugh Raymond (1674 – 1737) and the East India Company

Charles Raymond at Sea

Purser of the *Dawsonne*

Third Mate of the *Princess of Wales* 1732/3

Captain Charles Raymond

Wager voyages 1734/5 and 1737/8

The *Wager* and Anson's voyage

Wager voyage 1740/1

Marriage to Sarah Webster

Captain Raymond's last voyage, *Wager* 1743/4

Risk and Reward

The Finance of sailing for the East India Company

PART 2. FAMILY, FRIENDS AND FELLOW CAPTAINS

Upton and Ilford

Valentine House

Ilford's evolving network

Charles Raymond as a Principal Managing Owner

Risk and Loss

EIC Ships which did not return home in the seasons 1727/8 - 1789/90

Woodford's East India connections

Charles Foulis (*c*.1714 – 1783)

Robert Preston (1740 – 1834)

Pitt Collett (*c*.1729 – 1780)

Pinson Bonham (1724 – 1791)

v

Sir Charles Raymond of Valentines and the East India Company

PART 3. CITY GENTLEMAN ~ BUSINESSMAN, BANKER AND BARONET

Early City interests
Free British Fishery
Sun Fire Office
Scotch Mines
South Sea Company
Governor of the Hospitals of Bridewell and Bethlem
Valentine House and park
The gardens, plants and birds
Other property in Ilford
Family weddings
Later City interests
Banking
Politics
East India Company
Sir Charles Raymond's ship *Valentine*
More Family Matters
Broadstairs
The last years

CONCLUSION

THE PORTRAIT OF SIR CHARLES RAYMOND

APPENDICES

1. Family of John Raymond
2. Family of Hugh Raymond
3. Family of Charles Raymond
4. Family of Sarah Raymond (née Webster)
5. The Crabb – Boulton family
6. Cargoes
7. Summary of journeys made by Charles Raymond (speed and distance)
8. Careers of Charles Raymond, William Webber, John Williams, Henry Fletcher, John Pelly, Pinson Bonham, Charles Foulis, Robert Preston, Pitt Collett
9. Principal Managing Owners for 5 or more voyages, 1750/1 – 1779/80, in 5 year periods
10. Extracts from EIC Court Books showing some charterparty entries, 1766/7 and later seasons
11. Poems by Lady Sophia Burrell

INDEX

TABLES ETC

	Page
Percentage of crew dying on voyages of the *Wager*	29
The Career of Raymond Snow	33
Principal Managing Owner for 10 or more voyages, 1747/8 – 1787/8	47
Details of seven ships managed by Charles Raymond, 1758/9 season	48
Ships which did not return home in the seasons 1727/8 - 1789/90	52

ILLUSTRATIONS

	Page
Sir Charles Raymond © see page 129	ii
Crest of the East India Company © The British Library Board, L/MAR/B/549A (1746/7, image is from the front page)	ix
Valentines Mansion at Ilford, 17 April 2011 © Georgina Green	xv
Map of the East Indies drawn by T. Jefferys, from the *Gentleman's Magazine*, Vol.18 p.251 (1748) © London Metropolitan Archives	xviii & xix
A Map of the County of Devon by Benjamin Donn, 1765	xx
An East Indiaman *c.*1720 by Peter Monamy © National Maritime Museum, Greenwich, London	5
Picture of Madras Roads (South East View of Fort St George) Madras Oriental Series II no.7 by Thomas Daniell and William Daniel © The British Library Board, Tab.599.a.(2) Plate VII	9
East India House as Charles would have known it © London Metropolitan Archives	14
Captain Raymond's journal of the *Wager (1)* February 21st and 22nd, 1736 © The British Library Board, L/MAR/B/592A	18
Marriage of Charles Raymond and Sarah Webster at St Stephen's Walbrook, 22 January 1742/3 © London Metropolitan Archives	24
Captain Raymond's journal of the *Wager (2)* January 1746 © The British Library Board, L/MAR/B/592D	27
Spanish 'Pillar dollar' silver coin dated 1736 © Georgina Green	30
Map from *The Environs of London* by the Rev. Daniel Lysons Vol.4 (1796)	38
Marriage of William Webber and Elizabeth Webster at St Mary le Bowe, 15 February 1755 © London Metropolitan Archives	41
Valentine House, 1799 from a copy of *The Environs of London* by Rev. D. Lysons Volume 4 (1796) © London Metropolitan Archives	42
Highlands, 1798 from a copy of *The Environs of London* by Rev. D. Lysons Volume 4 (1796) © London Metropolitan Archives	42
East Indiaman *Dutton* (1781) taking a pilot off Dover by Robert Dodd © National Maritime Museum, Greenwich, London	49

Sir Charles Raymond of Valentines and the East India Company

Drawing of an East Indiaman from the journal of the *Suffolk* 1755/6 © The British Library Board, L/MAR/B/397D — 52

The Hunt Mickelfield Memorial in the churchyard at St Marys, Woodford © Georgina Green — 55

The bell donated by 'Lady Elianor Rowe' in 1668 at St Mary's, Woodford © Georgina Green — 55

Picture of Harts House, Woodford, from the *Gentleman's Magazine* 1789 — 57

The Memorial to Charles Foulis erected by Robert Preston at St Marys, Woodford © Georgina Green — 61

The cup presented to John Allen © National Maritime Museum, Greenwich, London — 64

Journal of the *Grantham*, 19 January 1750 © The British Library Board, L/MAR/B/617K — 71

East Indiaman *York* and other vessels by Thomas Luny, 1788 © National Maritime Museum, Greenwich, London — 74

Extract from a map of London by John Rocque, 1769 © London Metropolitan Archives — 78

The Mansion House, 1754 © London Metropolitan Archives — 80

The Godfrey Memorial in the churchyard at St Marys, Woodford © Georgina Green — 83

Engraving of *Southwark Fair* by William Hogarth — 89

Valentines from *A New and Complete History of Essex by a Gentleman*, Vol.IV — 90

Plate made for Sir Charles Raymond in China *c.*1760 © Georgina Green — 92

Wright's Compleat Collection of Celebrated Country Dances both Old and New that are in Vogue, with the Newest and best Directions to each Dance ye whole Carefully corrected Voll 1st *c.*1750, courtesy of the English Folk Dance and Song Society — 93

Black Hamburg Grapes © Georgina Green — 96

'Snake-eater' Reproduced by kind permission of the Royal Society from their *Philosophical Transactions* Volume 61 (1771) — 98

Cranbrook House, 1798 from a copy of *The Environs of London* by Rev. D. Lysons Volume 4 (1796) © London Metropolitan Archives — 100

The Mausoleum at Highlands (undated) from a copy of *The Environs of London* by Rev. D. Lysons Volume 4 (1796) © London Metropolitan Archives — 100

Lady Sophia Burrell (Private Collection) — 104

Captain Henry Hinde Pelly © Trinity House — 115

The Pump Room, Bath, in the year 1784 with the Characters of that Day © Victoria Art Gallery, Bath and North East Somerset Council/ Bridgeman Images — 120

Porcelain fragments from the wreck of the *Valentine* © Georgina Green — 144

ACKNOWLEDGEMENTS

The records of the East India Company can be seen at the British Library's Asia, Pacific and Africa Collections Reading Room. I would like to thank many people who have assisted my research there, but particularly Margaret Makepeace for her help and encouragement. I'm also very grateful to the clerks and archivists over the last 250 years who have preserved these records for us today!

I would like to thank Jean Sutton and several others who are working on aspects of the East India Company who have given me assistance.

The team at the 'East India Company at Home 1757-1857' project at University College London have helped me greatly and I would like to thank Professor Margot Finn and Dr Kate Smith who inspired me to write up my research and whose help has been invaluable.

Thanks also to Philip Winterbottom of the Royal Bank of Scotland who has answered many questions and provided much encouragement since I started my research.

I would like to acknowledge the assistance given me by John Farrant, who was researching the history of the Burrell family when I started my own research (see Sussex Archaeological Collections 139 (2001) pp.1-17).

Thanks are also due to many librarians and archivists at scattered locations across the south of England who have helped me in various ways.

I would like to thank many relations and friends who have listened patiently while I have been working on this research since 2001 and particularly Linda Rhodes, Claire Dyson, Joan Westover and Joy Blake for their support in the later stages of the work.

But I am most grateful for the help and encouragement given to me by Richard Keen who dived to find the wreck of Raymond's ship *Valentine* which was lost off Sark (Channel Islands) on 16 November 1779. Without his help and support this book would not have been written.

Georgina Green, 17 March 2015

Sir Charles Raymond of Valentines and the East India Company

PREFACE

Meticulously researched, Georgina Green's *Sir Charles Raymond of Valentines and the East India Company* offers readers a detailed biography of a successful eighteenth-century sea captain whose Oriental fortune laid the foundations for domestic comfort and commercial achievement at home in Georgian England. Tracing Raymond from his family home in Withycombe Raleigh, Devon, to Ilford in East London via India, Green situates her protagonist within the trans-oceanic reticulation of networks that established and maintained social, political and economic life in eighteenth-century Britain. At once global and local, Raymond's story illuminates the key developments that underpinned not only the making of the British empire in Asia but also shaped business innovation, civic politics, sociability and philanthropy in English parishes.

As was typical of his time, Raymond's story was a family story. A key theme that emerges from Green's study is the extent to which his career relied upon (and fostered) the ties of kith and kin. Raymond's initial connection with the East India Company (EIC) came via his uncle, Hugh, himself Captain of successive Company vessels; Hugh Raymond's own relationship with the EIC likely derived from the family of his wife, Dynah.

It was avuncular patronage that enabled Charles Raymond to make his first voyage to India as purser of the *Dawsonne* 1729/30 when not yet seventeen years of age. This initial voyage was followed by selection as third mate on the *Princess of Wales* 1732/3, which sailed from Bombay along the west coast of India. Raymond first served as Captain in 1734/5 (aged only twenty-one), commanding his Uncle Hugh's East Indiaman the *Wager*. He made a second voyage in this ship as Captain in 1737/8. Raymond's command of the rebuilt *Wager (2)* in 1740/1 was followed by his last voyage—the *Wager (2)* sailed to and from India in 1744/6. Green rightly underlines the high risks and the high profits of Company trade in this era; 15% of the crew on Charles Raymond's four Indian ships died during the voyage, but their captain garnered perhaps £1million in present-day money from each of his later voyages.

From serving as an East Indiaman captain, Raymond in the later 1740s turned his maritime attentions to managing voyages for the Company in the capacity as a Principal Managing Owner (PMO). Three themes already evident from his seafaring years emerge clearly from Green's analysis of this phase of his life: the importance of family ties, the risk of conducting business with 'the East', and the potentially high rewards enjoyed by men who took those risks. For forty years, from 1747-1788, Raymond helped organise the lucrative transport of the Company's trade with India and China, playing a decisive role in the maritime networks that saw woollen cloth, lead and other English exports reach Asian markets in exchange for exotic cargoes of tea, porcelain, cotton and silk. His role in this aspect of trade, as Green's statistics demonstrate forcibly, was decisive. In all, from 1747-78 Raymond served as PMO for 113 EIC voyages—just over 12% of all East Indiamen that sailed in this period (excluding voyages on the Company's own ships). Some years saw this contribution rise even higher; in 1758-59 Raymond was PMO for a third of the ships chartered by the Company to carry goods to the East. Risk was endemic to these ventures, but Raymond enjoyed remarkable good fortune as a PMO. About 7% of East Indiamen failed to return to England between 1727 and 1790, yet of those ships for which Raymond was PMO only three failed to return—the *Ajax* 1758/9, *Lord Clive* 1766/7 and *Valentine (2)* 1776/7. (The travails of the *Valentine*, wrecked off the coast of Sark, are documented in the book with scrupulous attention.) Such luck, further bolstered by the support of Raymond's extended family network, helped build new wealth that was soon translated into new levels of domestic comfort.

Raymond was related by family and/or marriage to many of the other men who served the EIC as PMOs, an association that illustrates the extent to which the development of the Company's commercial and political empire rested on the ties of domestic social life. Marriage and domesticity, indeed, are vital components of Raymond's life-story. In 1743 he married Sarah Webster in the City of London, and took up residence at Wellclose Square, a hub of both his own clan and that of his new in-laws. Upon retiring from the sea Raymond moved his family to Upton, east of the City and near West Ham, although business in the City required his continued residence in London during the week. The year 1754 saw Raymond purchase Valentine House in Ilford, previously the residence of a Company colleague. Ilford emerged in this period as a nodal point of the EIC's maritime business, a geographical hotspot complemented by the presence of a major cluster of Company men in nearby Woodford. Green's book gives rich detail of Woodford men such as Charles Foulis (*c*.1714-1783), Robert Preston (1740-1834), Pitt Collet (*c*.1729-1780) and Pinson Bonham (1724-1791). Growing increasingly wealthy from his Company business, Raymond substantially extended and rebuilt Valentine House in 1769. Insurance records adduced by Green provide a clear indication of the extent to which Raymond's Asian profits were transformed into English domestic comforts. His refurbished mansion was insured in 1769 for £2,000; its contents— insured for a mere £500 in 1755—were now valued at £2,000 as well. Chinese armorial porcelain with the Raymond family arms (luxury ware accessible only by families with close Company connections) now entered the Raymond home in Ilford. Raymond's gardens likewise benefitted from his privileged access to the flora and fauna of Asia: it was Raymond who engineered the first arrival in England of a secretary bird, in 1771.

Sir Charles Raymond of Valentines and the East India Company

The year 1771 was also a key year in Raymond's civic life, for it was the year in which he became High Sheriff for the County of Essex and a Master Keeper of Epping Forest. His creation as a baronet in 1774 confirmed his civic reputation. Raymond's contributions to philanthropic endeavour pre-dated (and likely helped to foster) his civic profile; he had become a Governor of the City of London's Bridewell and Bethlem Hospital (Bedlam) already in 1749. Raymond's East Indian fortune was clearly vital to his development into a man of civic substance, but Green's book also demonstrates the extent to which this Asian fortune fed into business developments more often understood as being English, or British, in character. In 1750 he was elected to the General Court of the Free British Fishery; in 1756 Raymond became one of the twenty-four managers of the Sun Fire Office; in 1757 he was elected a Director of the Scotch Mines; and in 1766 Raymond became a Director of the post-Bubble South Sea Company. 1771 (the year of his appointment as High Sheriff) saw Raymond together with four other men become a founding member of a new City bank, Raymond, Williams, Vere, Lowe & Fletcher, a predecessor of the Royal Bank of Scotland. Like Raymond's earlier maritime ventures, the new bank's personnel and finances were enmeshed in his family and Company networks through both lineal descent and marriage. In their first year of trading, its partners became founding partners of the first bank established in Manchester. Thus the tentacles of empire extended into England's emerging industrial heartland.

Readers of Georgina Green's book will encounter Georgian Britain in the round. Trade, politics, marriage, culture, business, sociability, neighbourhood and material life were intertwined in the life of Sir Charles Raymond, just as they were woven through the foundation of Britain's Indian empire. What better way to understand them than through this rich and rewarding Company biography.

Margot Finn
Professor, Modern British History
University College London

7 May 2015

INTRODUCTION

In 1754 Charles Raymond, a retired East India Company (EIC) captain, bought Valentine House in Ilford, Essex, as a home for his wife and young family. He had been born in Devon and through family contacts had worked his way rapidly through the ranks of the EIC to captain a ship on his third voyage to India. Less fortunate young men undertook several voyages before achieving a captaincy and without family contacts it required a significant payment to the owners. However, the potential benefits from legitimate private trade were enormous and the majority of captains retired from the sea very wealthy men. But not many of them achieved the high level of financial and social success attained by Charles Raymond once he settled back to life at home.

Charles became a major figure with the Company in London, managing many voyages for ships carrying cargo home from India and China. In doing this he worked alongside several men he had known when they were also captaining ships for the Company. Some became friends and business partners. Some married into his family circle and came to live near Charles in Ilford. This book is much more than the narrative of one man's life. All those who feature in this book led interesting lives but it is their inter-relationships which makes the story of interest to those studying the history of the EIC and London life in the eighteenth century. By highlighting these inter-connections and the complex network of family, friends, business partners and other colleagues in the City, this book offers new insights into the workings of the EIC and other City institutions. Many men are mentioned in passing but they too add to the whole tapestry of life played out on board ship, at the shipyards by the Thames, in City boardrooms and Essex homes.

London and its environs are the setting for the later parts of this book. Many of the EIC administrators and officials who became rich through Asian trade retired to country estates, often to the west of London. Having survived the heat, disease and the wars of India, or used their skills in diplomacy in China and other far-flung settlements, they were content to live out their lives in comfort. Some became Members of Parliament and involved with political life, but they were free from both the perceived and real dangers of service in the East. Retired captains, on the other hand, thrived on taking risks. Many preferred the cut and thrust of the City, gambling their fortunes as the Merchant Adventurers who financed the earliest voyages to the Eastern Seas had done in the early 1600s. Without the personnel who manned their ships and the men who financed their voyages, there would have been no need for the army of clerks and officials who worked in London and abroad as administrators of the East India Company.

Sir Charles Raymond of Valentines and the East India Company

The country air but also closeness to their shipping interests by the Thames attracted Charles and others involved in similar business interests to settle to the east of London, in Ilford and its neighbouring villages of Woodford, Wanstead, Chigwell and Loughton. This is not a history of the East India Company, but the Company is the setting for the stories of these relations and friends: their adventures at sea and family life at home are a large part of this book. Similarly the contacts made by Charles during his life at sea rippled through his later life as an influential figure in the City.

Sources

Rich evidence of the lives and activities of those connected to the EIC remains in the archives of the Company held at the British Library in London. The magnificent collection of material includes printed books and original documents such as ships' journals and management paperwork from London and overseas settlements, from 1600 until the late nineteenth century. Handling the journal written by a captain describing his voyage 250 years ago is an immense privilege and joy. Unfortunately some sections of the material were discarded in the mid-nineteenth century and the archive is not complete. More remains for the period after 1760 than before it when Charles was at sea. However, it is amazing that so much has survived and this invaluable material enables researchers to glimpse facets of the lives of the men who worked for the Company so long ago.

In contrast, the private correspondence and archives of the Raymond family have not survived. Knepp Castle in West Sussex was purchased by Sir Charles Raymond in 1787, less than a year before he died, and it has stayed in the family of his daughter, Lady Sophia Burrell, until the present day. However, little in the way of family material survived a fire in 1904, so it has not been possible to use private letters to add colour to the facts from other sources.

Ilford in the eighteenth century was a small village in the parish of Barking and has, until now, been considered a poor relation of the affluent communities which flouted their success with prestigious houses in Woodford and Wanstead.[A] The research included in this book challenges that perception by revealing new evidence of Ilford's importance in the Georgian era. When Victorian 'progress' reached Ilford many grand residences were swept away, leaving Valentine House and park as sole survivors of the eighteenth century. Woodford and Wanstead managed to resist the march of developers a little longer and more traces of the stately and affluent past remain to be discovered by those who look around them there.

[A] Ilford, Wanstead and Woodford now make up the London Borough of Redbridge.

Valentine House was built in 1696-7 as a home for Elizabeth Tillotson, widow of the Archbishop of Canterbury, John Tillotson. She was not wealthy and her home was a modest building where she could bring up the children of her daughter who had died. In the following two hundred years it was home to a number of interesting people: Robert Surman, a banker who had been deputy cashier of the South Sea Company and was disgraced when the 'Bubble' burst, lived there from 1724 to 1754; he sold it to Charles Raymond; and in Victorian times it was the home of Dr Clement Mansfield Ingleby, a noted Shakespearean scholar, and his wife, who inherited Valentine House from her uncle Charles Holcombe, an industrialist.

Valentines Mansion at Ilford, 17 April 2011

During its occupancy as a private residence it was referred to as simply 'Valentines' or 'Valentine House'. In 1912 the then Ilford Urban District Council (now the London Borough of Redbridge) purchased the house, which was used as council offices for much of the next eighty years. It was the council who renamed the building as 'Valentines Mansion'. From 1993 the building was left empty. Due to public pressure, and thanks to the Heritage Lottery Fund, the house and gardens were both given a major restoration in 2007-8 and are now used by the community. Set in a Rococo garden and wider park, Valentines is a beautiful oasis in the East London suburbs, not far from Gants Hill underground station (Central line). The final accolade was when Valentines Mansion and Park was the venue chosen for Her Majesty the Queen to meet the people of Redbridge on 29 March 2012 as part of her Diamond Jubilee tour.

Structure

This book is divided into three parts which explore the theme of risk and reward throughout Charles's life. The first examines Charles's childhood and family connections to show how the networks established within the East India Company framework enabled trusted family members to work together for the benefit of them all, across the eighteenth century. The six voyages Charles undertook will be examined, the financial aspects explored and the personal risks outlined. When he married Charles was shown living at Wapping, but soon after retiring as a captain he moved to a more salubrious home at Upton (West Ham).

Part two turns to examine Charles's shipping interests once he had retired after a relatively uneventful career as a captain. It demonstrates how Charles continued his involvement with the EIC through managing ships and investing in voyages. Although he no longer exposed himself to physical danger at sea, he risked his wealth and reputation in the City. Meanwhile he settled permanently at Valentine House, a modest villa where he could relax with his young family in the country but be close to his City interests. Part two continues by demonstrating the variety of risks faced at sea by examining the adventures which befell some of his friends and neighbours. Extracts from ships' journals will be used to illustrate the dangers they faced. Alongside these stories of personal risk and financial loss, statistics will illustrate Charles's involvement and investments and his importance as a leading member of the EIC shipping lobby where he managed ships alongside these friends and neighbours as they, in turn, retired from the sea. One group clustered around Charles in Ilford while a second group was centred nearby in Woodford Green. They were a vital part of the EIC's vast enterprise. Without men such as these to command their ships and finance the voyages, there would be no trade!

The final part of this book looks at the work undertaken by Charles in the City of London, both with the EIC and in other areas. He played a significant part in City life as a Director of the Sun Fire Office (insurance) and in other City institutions. It is clear he was a respected member of the City's business community. His three sons-in-law come into the story and a conjectural account of life at Valentines has been sketched from the fragments of information gleaned. In later life Charles became a respected banker and he was created a baronet in 1774. Further aspects of City life conclude the story. Ironically, although he continued to risk his fortune investing in EIC shipping throughout his life, it was in banking that Charles made his most significant financial loss, shortly before he died.

See www.valentines.org.uk (a website set up by The Friends of Valentines Mansion in 2001) and www.valentinesmansion.com (the official website set up by LB Rebridge in 2009). The two are complementary, the first including much of the history of the house and about the restoration, the second with details of all forthcoming events and activities, and information about hiring the house.

NOTE ON DATES

In 1752 the Gregorian calendar replaced the Julian calendar in England. Previously the New Year was recorded as at the first of April, so that a baptism on 28 March 1741 might be followed in the parish register a few days later by one on 2 April 1742. The dates given in this text are modern equivalents, whenever possible. However, the date a ship sailed is given as 1741/2 to indicate the winter in which the ship left the Thames.

NOTE ON CURRENCY

As a rough guide, amounts given in this book have been converted as x 200 in the early 1740s and by using the Bank of England calculator from 1750 to get a present day (2013) value.

For a more accurate amount see the Bank of England website

http://www.bankofengland.co.uk/education/Pages/resources/inflationtools/calculator/index1.aspx e.g.

£1000 in 1750 was worth £193,470 in 2013

£1000 in 1788 was worth £131,560 in 2013

ABBREVIATIONS USED IN TEXT AND REFERENCES

BL – British Library

EIC – East India Company

NA – National Archives

PMO – Principal Managing Owners

Sir Charles Raymond of Valentines and the East India Company

*Map of the East Indies drawn from the latest discoveries
by T. Jefferys, Geographer to His Royal Highness the Prince of Wales,
from the Gentleman's Magazine, Vol.18 p.251 (1748)
© London Metropolitan Archives*

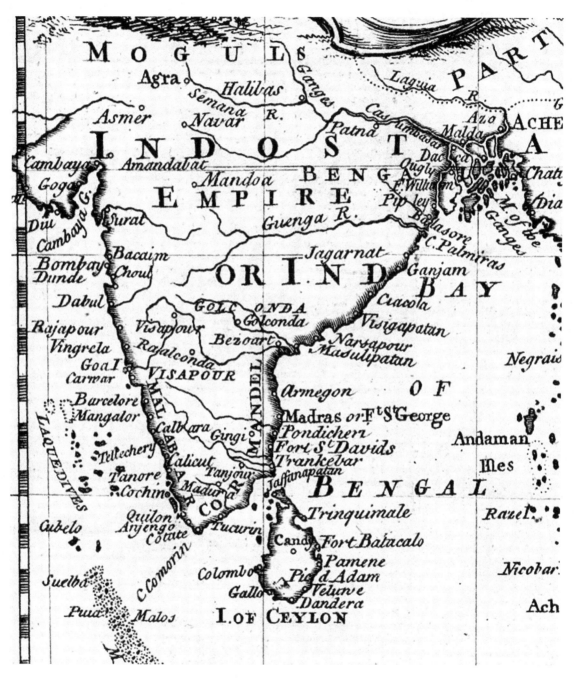

India enlarged from the Map of the East Indies in 1748 shown opposite

A Map of the County of Devon by Benjamin Donn 1765

1. Charles Raymond's sister married John Penneck of St Thomas's, Exeter.
2. William Webber was christened at Clyst Honiton, just north of Sowton
3. Charles's mother was the daughter of Samuel Tanner of Clyst St Mary and she married John Raymond at Farringdon.
4. Charles's family lived at Marpool Hall and he was christened at Withycombe Raleigh

PART ONE – LIVING BY THE SEA

Sir Charles Raymond, Baronet, was born in 1713 at Withycombe Raleigh, Devon, which was described in 1850 as 'a pleasant scattered village, with several handsome villas, a mile or two outside Exmouth'.[1] Now it is part of the town but it is still possible to find some remnants of the old village where Charles Raymond was born and brought up. The village had been given that name because of an association with the Raleigh family going back into the Medieval period. Sir Walter Raleigh was born at Hayes Barton, an ancient timber-framed house, in an isolated position on the high plateau above the sea inland from East Budleigh. Living there in a rural spot with farmland and heath all around it is easier to imagine Walter becoming a farmer than a sailor. The magic of the sea seems to have lured young Charles just as it had done young Walter a century and a half earlier.

It is a long way from Withycombe Raleigh to East London, about 220 miles. However, Charles Raymond travelled much farther than that before he settled at Valentines in Ilford where he lived from 1754 until just a few years before he died in 1788. His travels took him to India six times, on ships commissioned by the East India Company (EIC), and it was his association with that Company which enabled him to die a very wealthy man.

The Raymond family in Devon

The Raymond family had long connections with Withycombe Raleigh and the Exmouth area, Charles's grandfather being described as 'John Raymond Esq of Marpole'. Another reference says 'Their house, the capital messuage of the reputed manor of Rill, was occupied by them over 130 years – "the Old Manor House" in North Street, Exmouth.' A house with that name is still standing at no.13 North Street. It is a Grade II listed building and the specification mentions that the name was given to the building in the nineteenth century, though it is 'probably originally an early eighteenth century brick house but now with stuccoed façade'. Perhaps it was rebuilt by a later owner, Sir John Colleton, who lived there for a number of years before he died in 1754. We cannot be sure this was the location where Charles was brought up, but the area is very different now. A car park and several roads cover the land between The Old Manor House and the River Exe, but in Charles's youth the estate extended right down to the waterside.[2]

John Raymond (1668-1725), the father of Charles, was one of eight children. He was the eldest son and so presumably inherited the family property from his father. He seems to have been a man of considerable status, respected by the local community.

Sir Charles Raymond of Valentines and the East India Company

There is some evidence which suggests he owned ships and had mooring rights at Dawlish Warren on the opposite, more sheltered, side of the river estuary.[3] The attractive town of Topsham, still a popular harbour today, was a major centre in the eighteenth century for the export of the woollen cloth made in the Tiverton area.[4] Perhaps John Raymond's ships were employed in taking the cloth to London. With waves washing the rocks at the bottom of the garden, it would have been almost inevitable that Charles played about in boats as a youngster.

Charles's mother, Anna Maria, was the daughter of Samuel Tanner of Clyst St. Mary. They married on 15 January 1703 at Farringdon (both neighbouring villages between Exmouth and Exeter) and their first child was a daughter, also named Anna Maria, who was nearly nine years older than Charles. Another daughter and two sons were born and died as infants before Charles came along. He was baptised on 23 April 1713 at Withycombe Raleigh [5] and was their last child. On 12 September 1716, when Charles was three, his aunt Isabella (another of the daughters of Samuel Tanner) married Samuel Newte of Tiverton at Withycombe Raleigh. The little boy may have been excited by the event but would never have thought that one day Isabella's grandson would marry his daughter.

Hugh Raymond (1674 – 1737) and the East India Company

Since the original foundation by Royal Charter on 31 December 1600 when 218 men of the Merchant Adventurers were given exclusive rights to trade with the East Indies (meaning at that time South-East Asia) the EIC had grown into a major financial force in the City. It had established its own fortified bases abroad: Surat, Bombay, Madras and Calcutta grew from settlements founded by the Company.

Hugh Raymond was a younger brother of Charles's father John, having been christened on 30 January 1674 when John was five. It is not clear how he first came to serve with the EIC as his early career is not recorded, but his rise to captain may have been as a result of his marriage to Dynah, daughter of Captain Samuel Jones of Stepney. The will of her mother Amy Jones (senior),[6] widow of Captain Samuel Jones, makes it clear that the family was very closely involved with the EIC. Not only did Dynah marry an EIC officer but her sister Sarah married EIC Captain Matthew Martin while another sister, Amy, was the wife of Captain James Osborne who also served on East Indiamen.[7]

The will of Amy Jones (senior) also explains that her daughter Dynah and Captain Hugh Raymond had five children: Amy, Dynah, Jones, Bridget and Susannah, who were therefore Charles's cousins. No record of their marriage has so far been found, but

Living by the Sea

Amy was their first child and she was born before Hugh sailed on his first voyage as Captain of the *Duchess* 1700/1 in January 1701.[8]

Hugh also captained the *Duchess* on her next two voyages, 1702/3 and 1706/7, and then became captain of the *Bouverie* 1709/10 visiting Madras and Calcutta. In 1710 he upset the inhabitants of Madras by capturing a friendly brigantine flying Moorish colours, believing she was a French spy ship.[9] The previous year his brother-in-law, James Osborne, had been captured by the French when captain of the *New George*, so maybe he wasn't taking any chances. As a captain, Hugh had a significant entitlement to engage in private trade and he seems to have retired from the sea a wealthy man when he returned home in September 1712. He soon started to invest in ship building and managing voyages for the EIC.

One of the ships Hugh managed was the *Dawsonne*, captained by John Raymond, who died at sea in April 1719 leaving his possessions to his cousin Amy Raymond of Stepney.[10] It is possible that John was the son of Hugh's brother Charles who was baptised at Withycombe Raleigh on 19 January 1672. He is the only brother not buried as a child or traced as an adult, unless he was the Charles Rayment who married Mary Upuy on 1 December 1690 at St James, Dukes Place, London.

Earlier, when Hugh Raymond was sailing as Captain of the *Duchess,* the administration of the EIC underwent substantial change and a new United Company of Merchants of England trading to the East Indies was created. The Bank of England had been founded in 1694 and the financial world was changing too. The War of the Spanish Succession cost the country dearly. By 1710 the National Debt was enormous but a scheme put forward by a small group of astute politicians and businessmen gave the government a wonderful solution to all its problems. The formation of a new company with sole rights to trade in the South Seas (much as the East India Company had been doing in Asia so successfully) could in one stroke write off the debt. The unfunded government securities (£9,000,000) would be exchanged for shares in a new joint stock company - and so the South Sea Company was born.[11] It seems that from the very beginning this was a scam planned by this small group who involved other (non-political) businessmen to be Directors, most of whom were unaware that there was anything dubious going on.

Hugh Raymond became a Director of the South Sea Company in February 1715 and it seems his role was to provide ships for the trade which the South Sea Company was entitled to undertake. In 1717 he built the ship *Royal Prince* for the Company, named after its Governor, the Prince of Wales. Hugh's brother Baynham Raymond was the captain and the ship sailed off to South America in 1718, but war with Spain halted any serious trading and Baynham died at sea. His will was made while riding at anchor in the Port of Vera Cruz in the Gulf of Mexico.[12]

Sir Charles Raymond of Valentines and the East India Company

In 1717 Hugh bought Saling Hall (near Braintree) in Essex as his country seat,[13] but he also had a home at Marine Square (later renamed Wellclose Square) in Wapping. Although Wapping was densely populated by people engaged in many trades associated with ship-building, there were also some good residential areas, like Marine Square, for the affluent gentlemen who managed the various industries or captains home on leave.[14] He became captain (1715) and then colonel (1720) in the Tower Hamlets Militia and it is interesting that in later years the records of the EIC refer to him as Col. Raymond rather than Capt. Raymond.

By 1720 Hugh Raymond was a very wealthy man and was also a Director of Chetwynd's Insurance (later the London Assurance) along with several other Directors of the South Sea Company.[15] He appears to have been unaware of the fraudulent activities of its leaders until the 'Bubble' burst at the end of 1720. Many people, from the King down, lost a great deal of money and Parliament set up a Committee of Inquiry which met in the South Sea House, sitting for fourteen hours a day. Their first report showed there had been complete disregard for sound financial practice and blatantly corrupt dealings.[16]

During the summer of 1721 the financial affairs of each of the Directors and officials of the South Sea Company were examined and a decision was made about how severely they should each be penalised. The inventory of Hugh Raymond's property makes interesting reading.[17] It shows EIC shipping investments and partnerships, loans to his captains as Bottomree Bonds, investments in cargoes of *Marlborough, Dawson,* and *Bouverie* sent to the East Indies, and 'Adventures' including cargoes of the *Boston Galley* and *Dunwich* Merchant ship both sent to Guinea. Hugh was also part owner of five smaller vessels, which could have been part of a family fleet at Exmouth. He had other assets too. By 1721 Hugh's wife Dynah had died, but he had purchased jewellery for his daughters including a diamond buckle and earrings worth £800 for his eldest daughter Amy. He had interest on £10,000 India Bonds and £12,000 bank stock for his widowed mother-in-law, Mrs Amy Jones, with additional investments for Mrs Lydia Raymond (widow of his brother Baynham). In fact, Hugh Raymond had assets totalling £92,708, but he was treated leniently and forfeited only half his estate.[18]

In 1725 Hugh's eldest brother, John Raymond, died and was buried at Withycombe Raleigh. As John's only surviving son, Charles became his heir, but was only 12 years old - the same age as Hugh when his own father died. The only other surviving child was the first born, Anna Maria (baptised 22 June 1704) who later married John Penneck of St.Thomas's Parish in Exeter on 3 January 1731.[19]

Hugh and his sister-in-law must have agreed that a career in the East India Company would be suitable for young Charles and just before his seventeenth birthday he sailed

Living by the Sea

as purser of the *Dawsonne* 1729/30 on a trip to Madras and Bengal. This position allowed a young man of a good family to find out what a voyage was like and to learn about the administration of the ship.

An East Indiaman c.1720 (starboard-bow view) by Peter Monamy
© *National Maritime Museum, Greenwich, London*

Charles Raymond at Sea

Purser of the *Dawsonne*

By 1730 the East India Company was governed by a committee, or Court, of twenty-four Directors who owned substantial Company stock, and who met at least once a week to discuss the affairs of the Company. In addition, sub-committee meetings meant that being a Director entailed a significant commitment of time, but gave the post-holder considerable power. The Company employed many clerical staff and their diligence in keeping good records enables us today to learn much about their activities.

The EIC did not own any of the ships which carried their cargo but used ships, called East Indiamen, which were built by groups of owners.[20] One of them, who was not necessarily the major investor, acted as the Principal Managing Owner (PMO) for the group. Most of the investors were just passive backers. The Court decided which ships to employ for their voyages each year and to which destinations each should sail. It was therefore a rule that a Director could not be the PMO of a ship employed by the EIC. For each voyage a legal agreement, or charterparty, was signed by two representatives of the investors in the ship (the first being the PMO) to confirm the arrangements for the voyage. This protected both the Company and the investors. The second signatory was often someone older, with considerable experience and financial resources, who could support the younger PMO. The owners had control of the navigation and management of the ship and were responsible for engaging the crew and supplying provisions, but its carrying capacity was controlled by the charterer, the EIC.

The Essex Record Office at Chelmsford has some papers of Samuel Braund, who was PMO for several voyages in the 1750s. The charterparty document for the East Indiaman *Boscawen* which sailed in 1756/7 [21] for 'Coast and China' is twelve printed pages, slightly smaller than A3 size, with a standard text and gaps to fill in the necessary details for each individual voyage. For example, the dates when it would be ready to sail, the tonnage it was to carry outwards for the Company, the amount that each must pay in demorage (i.e. from the Company to the owners if they caused a delay, or vice-versa), how much gun-powder she should carry, the freight allowance home, the provision for passengers, etc.[22]

The charterparty agreement for the 1729/30 voyage of the *Dawsonne* to Madras and Bengal was signed by Hugh Raymond, Charles's uncle, and Hugh's son, Jones Raymond, Charles's cousin.[23] Hugh invested in many ships which sailed for the EIC in the 1720s and 30s and had extensive contacts within the EIC circle. This was the fourth voyage made by the *Dawsonne*: the first voyage in 1719-20 had been captained by John Raymond (probably a cousin of Charles), but he died on the voyage, in April 1719.

Living by the Sea

Charles must have been on board a number of smaller ships before stepping aboard the *Dawsonne* for the first time, but no doubt he had a thrill at the thought of the new life ahead of him. An East Indiaman in the middle of the eighteenth century was usually about 499 tons, 105 feet (32 metres) long but rounder in shape than the sleek navy ships as it was designed to carry cargo, rather than for speed. The bottom of the ship was the hold, approximately 14 feet (4.3 metres) deep, above which were two enclosed decks with about 5ft 10 inches (1.8 metres) headroom. The lower deck was mostly for storage while the upper was living quarters for the men who ate and slept between the guns (cannon) which were used for self-defence and in ceremonial salutes. The top deck was open to the elements and there could be chicken coops and livestock penned here. At the back of the ship (stern) there was a raised area (the roundhouse) above the 'great cabin' with its row of windows. This was the quarters of the captain and any passengers of quality or status in the Company and the officers. Each ship had three large masts and could use twelve to fifteen sails of various sizes. A new ship of 499 tons built in the 1740s might cost £4,000 - £4,500.[24]

The journals of many voyages undertaken by ships for the East India Company are held at the British Library and are a wonderful source of information. Reading them provides an insight into the way of life on a ship. The speed in knots is recorded for each hour of day and night while on the voyage. Every day the weather is noted and the course is shown frequently. It was not until the 1760s that longitude could be established accurately, after John Harrison invented the clock which was reliable at sea over a long period of time. This was not introduced routinely for East Indiamen until late in the eighteenth century.[25] So in earlier years there are details of all land marks seen which might help in building up better charts when the ship returned to London.

Throughout the eighteenth century there were periods of war and periods of calm in Europe, but in the Eastern seas there was always the added risk of piracy. A century earlier the Dutch had fought a brutal battle to secure their cargoes of precious spices. But in 1730 the English and Dutch were working together to ensure that ships from the newly formed Ostend Company, which sailed for the (Austrian) Hapsburg Empire, did not take their trade.[26] The Ostend ships were manned by experienced and ruthless seamen and carried officials skilled in the politics of trade in the East. It had taken many years for the EIC to establish bases in India, and the rights to trade, but the Ostend ships could easily secure cargoes with sufficient inducement. What we might call bribery was the accepted means of working with the rulers and their representatives in India by all European agents.

Charles would have been on board the *Dawsonne* for several weeks before she finally left sight of England, about the time of his seventeenth birthday. He had signed on as

Sir Charles Raymond of Valentines and the East India Company

purser, which in the Navy was a very onerous position, responsible to the Admiralty for provisioning the ship, ensuring that foodstuffs were properly stored and distributed, purchasing additional provisions as necessary and available, and making detailed accounts of all expenditure.[27] However, if wages are an indication, it seems the role of purser in the EIC did not have such importance and that it was mainly a clerical post which assisted the captain in maintaining correct records of men and stores. It was a means by which an inexperienced young man, with the right connections, could start his career at sea.

The captain, Francis Steward, was newly appointed, having served as chief mate on the previous two voyages of the *Dawsonne*. He would have been greatly indebted to Hugh Raymond for this promotion and only too willing to support Charles and teach him all he needed to know. When the *Dawsonne* had reached the end of her life Francis Steward became captain of the *Godolphin* for three more voyages, under the management of the Raymond family.

Although the captain was in command, the first mate was the chief officer who effectively supervised the ship on a day-to-day basis. Under him were three or four other mates and should the captain or any of the mates die, it was usual for the next in line to be promoted. Gabriel Steward (the captain's brother) [28] had been promoted to second mate for the voyage of the *Dawsonne* so no doubt he also willingly helped Charles in learning about life at sea. Other officers included a surgeon and up to six midshipmen (another post suitable for a young gentleman hoping to make a career at sea). The chief tradesmen, like the carpenter, the caulker (who made the ship water-tight) and the gunner, were given a high status and usually had assistants. There were something like sixty seamen and at time of war the ship may also have carried soldiers of the East India Company.

As a young man, James Main (who was at that time gardener to Gilbert Slater of Knotts Green) made a voyage on the East Indiaman *Triton (3)* in 1792/3 to collect plants and he later wrote about his experiences:

> The north-east breeze, or rather gale of wind, which wafted us from England, carried us to the equator, which we crossed (with all the usual and ridiculous formalities) . . . Here we were becalmed for a few days; and here the heat was oppressive, usually from 85 to 90 degrees of Fahrenheit. . . . A calm on the line, in the middle of the Atlantic Ocean, the clear blue sky thinly sprinkled with white tufty clouds, the blazing sun, the sea as smooth as glass, forming a mirror eighty miles in diameter, without an object on its surface to attract the eye, save, perhaps, the sudden lunge of the dolphin in pursuit of the flying fish, which rise in shoals before him, or occasionally the heavy form of the stupidly audacious and prowling shark by the ship's side; all these circumstances, seen and felt for the first time, can scarcely be described in sober prose. They are most interesting to every mind

Living by the Sea

previously acquainted with the theory of geography, meteorology, astronomy, and navigation: and, besides the daily occurrences among a jovial and healthy crew, made our little floating world far from being either an irksome prison, or disagreeable abode.

In the case of the final voyage of the *Dawsonne* 1729/30 the journal has not survived. But the voyage was unusually long. Normally an East Indiaman would leave English waters early in the new year and return about eighteen months later, but the *Dawsonne's* crew were paid for a voyage from 10 February 1730 until 15 August 1732 (thirty months). It has been necessary to look at the journal of another ship, the *Derby* (also managed by Hugh Raymond), to understand why.[29]

It is likely the *Dawsonne* arrived at Madras around the end of May 1730 and the extreme heat would have been quite an experience for young Charles. All East Indiamen anchored some distance out to sea as there were three bands of high waves which had to be negotiated by everyone and everything which needed to go ashore. It seems this was either exhilarating or terrifying, depending on the state of the sea and the age and sex of the person concerned.

Picture of Madras Roads (South East View of Fort St George) Madras Oriental Series II no.7
by Thomas Daniell (1749-1840) and William Daniel (1769-1837)
© The British Library Board, Tab.599.a.(2) Plate VII

Sir Charles Raymond of Valentines and the East India Company

James Main continues:

> Our approach to the Indian coast was most interesting, and any one who considers the length and difficulties of such a voyage must be astonished at the accuracy with which the ship was navigated to her anchorage before the landing place at Madras . . .

> Madras has no harbour, but has an open roadstead on an extended level shore, covered chiefly with groves of cocoa-nut trees. Landing through a heavy surf is not a pleasant matter to a timid stranger; for though there is no serious fear of loss of life, there is every chance of a good ducking. The skill and amphibious character of the poor naked creatures, who guide the large tub-like boats on the tops and in the shallow valleys between the impetuous waves, is our security; and they seldom fail in taking advantage of a careering wave to land high and dry upon the beach. [30]

Having unloaded and completed their business in Madras, the *Dawsonne* proceeded to Calcutta where conditions were very different. Far from the sandy beach protected by sand bars, the approach to Calcutta was up the heavily silted Hugli River. Many ships stopped at one of the smaller ports, such as Kedgeree, near the mouth of the River, to await a pilot who could guide them up the channel towards Calcutta. As they approached the town they passed a sandbank named 'James and Mary' after an East Indiaman wrecked there in 1693, while the settlement was developing. [31]

The business of unloading the cargo was carried out and the ship thoroughly cleaned. Then in October orders were received that the *Dawsonne* was to spend a year guarding the Hugli River and protecting other shipping from the threat of the Ostend vessels, which explains the unusual length of the voyage. Captain Steward sailed the *Dawsonne* to Rogues River and took turns with the captain of a Dutch ship to take charge, hoisting the pendant to signify that he was the Commodore on the thirteenth day of each alternate month. Each time an East Indiaman passed by in the Hugli River this was noted in the journal and seven guns were fired in salute. In February 1731 an Ostend ship was reported in the area so troops from the EIC were taken on board as reinforcements. In September a detachment of soldiers was despatched to assist the Governor's boat which had been stopped at Rankafulla.

Apart from that, their year was only disturbed by matters which although routine would have taught Charles a great deal about seamanship. The simple task of keeping the ship and men safe was not easy in waters which were so silted, in a ship manoeuvred by sail. Their companion guard ship, the *Derby*, lost two men when one of their smaller boats (a yawl), bringing men back from shore leave, clipped the side of the ship, started to fill with water and they accidentally let go of a rope cutting themselves adrift. The captain of the *Derby* immediately launched another boat (the pinnace) to assist them but two men were drowned. On 22 October 1731 the *Dawsonne's* longboat was sunk in similar circumstances and a seaman drowned. At least ten men died during the year on guard

Living by the Sea

duty, most probably due to the fever and dysentery which took so many lives in the humidity of Calcutta. The *Dawsonne* was lucky that none of its officers died on the trip, but in August 1731 Gabriel Steward, second mate, left the *Dawsonne*, transferring to another East Indiaman, the *Drake,* to fill the office of chief mate. (The *Drake* had left England a year earlier than the *Dawsonne* and had visited several ports on the east and west coasts of India as well as the Persian port of Bandar Abbas. Her chief mate and the third mate both died in August 1730, so when the second mate died on 11 July 1731 in Calcutta the captain needed help. Several other senior personnel were seriously ill and the fourth mate died two days after Gabriel Steward was transferred.) [32]

On 10 October 1731 the *Frances* arrived to relieve the *Dawsonne* allowing her to return to Calcutta to prepare for the voyage home. It is likely she was loaded with cotton materials, raw silk, salt petre, red dyewood and other goods, as well as their private trade. She probably left Calcutta in January, called in again at Madras and then made her way home to arrive back in the Thames in mid-August 1732.

Charles arrived back in London having experienced (and survived) life in Indian waters and having learned a great deal about the day-to-day running of the ship. Other young men from a similar background may have followed a similar 'apprenticeship' or joined the crew as midshipmen, learning about seamanship rather than the management aspects of the ship. They might hope to progress through the ranks as fifth or fourth mate on their next voyage, but Charles was fortunate that his family connections helped him more swiftly up the career ladder. Next he needed to learn more about seamanship and Hugh Raymond was able to arrange this, happy to nurture his nephew so that Charles would be fully trained to become a captain and play a leading role in the family shipping business. Meanwhile Hugh's only son, Jones Raymond, was learning how the East India Company worked in London and assisting his father in managing ships. [33] He became a Director of EIC serving for much of the period from 1734 until 1757 and was able to promote the family interests at the EIC Court.

While he had been away, Charles's mother, Anna Maria Raymond, had died and was buried at Withycombe Raleigh on 27 October 1731. The previous January his sister, also Anna Maria, had married John Penneck of St Thomas's parish in Exeter so there was little reason for him to journey down to Devon before his next voyage. He inherited considerable property in Devon when he came of age but between voyages he probably lodged with his uncle, Hugh Raymond, and his family at Wapping. [34]

Sir Charles Raymond of Valentines and the East India Company

Third Mate of the *Princess of Wales* 1732/3

Charles Raymond's next voyage was as third mate on the *Princess of Wales (1)*,[35] again thanks to his family connections. The previous voyage of the ship (to China) had been the subject of an enquiry at East India House. While the *Dawsonne* was on guard near Calcutta, Thomas Gilbert, captain of the *Princess of Wales* and Charles Small, captain of the *Lyell* were both implicated in a scandal and threatened with legal action by the Court of Directors. The main culprit was James Naish, who was the principal supercargo, or chief buyer, for the EIC at Canton. His was a very responsible role and he had abused his position. It appears that Naish was cheating the Company over the price of tea at Canton and making a profit for himself. He had also illegally taken out great quantities of silver and other treasure which he traded in China for gold and other valuable goods which he then smuggled back home to avoid paying duty. The goods were brought back to England in the *Princess of Wales* 1729/30 and *Lyell* 1729/30 and transferred while the ships were at Spithead to the *Louisa* and *Romney,* both Men of War.

On 23 July 1731 Hugh Raymond, PMO for the ship *Princess of Wales,* was called before the EIC Court. A clause in the charterparty was read to him 'for the Captain to deliver in upon Oath a true full and perfect account of all the Bullion and other goods received in, and delivered out of the ship, if required' and he was told that Captain Gilbert had refused to give the oath which rendered the owners liable to a severe penalty. Hugh Raymond agreed to do his utmost to persuade the captain to give the Court all the information they required. Eventually Captain Gilbert did reluctantly admit to the Court that eight or ten casks of silver to the value of £5,000, belonging to Mr Naish, were brought on board his ship at the Downs and taken to Canton, and that 365 pieces of gold were brought back for Mr Naish but he didn't know the value. It was delivered via Portsmouth to Mrs Hester Naish and her receipt was produced at the EIC Court.[36]

In the event it was agreed to prosecute Captains Thomas Gilbert and Charles Small on the grounds that 'they clandestinely and illegally took out great quantities of silver and brought back great quantities of gold'. However, after a short break both resumed their career captaining ships for the EIC. Edward Gilbert (brother of the captain), second mate of the *Princess of Wales,* prevaricated when questioned and Joseph Wood, third mate, also gave unsatisfactory answers to questions and both were dismissed the Company's service. It appears this ruling was enforced.[37]

So for the next voyage of the *Princess of Wales* (1732/3) the charterparty was signed by Sir John Lock, with Hugh Raymond as the second signature.[38] It is likely that this was to appease the East India Company and that Hugh Raymond did in fact manage the

Living by the Sea

voyage, while Lock was one of several investors. Lock had been the second signature on the charterparty agreement of the previous voyage.

Serving as third mate on the *Princess of Wales* 1732/3 enabled Charles to learn about navigation and seamanship. The captain was Robert Mead who had previously served as chief mate of the *Dawsonne*, while Gabriel Steward was the chief mate. Charles would have known them both from his previous voyage as purser and was again in reliable hands. Unlike the other five voyages made by Charles, this was not planned as a straight-forward trip to Madras and Calcutta, but involved calling in at various ports around the west coast of India. They left in March 1733 calling at Sao Tiago (Cape Verde Isles) and Johanna (Comoro Islands north of Madagascar) by which time several of the crew were ill with scurvy. They reached Bombay on 27 August having spent a total of 149 days at sea, travelling at an average of four knots. Their best days were 8-9 June when they averaged nine knots, a fortnight before they rounded the Cape of Good Hope. On these two days they travelled 216 and 217 miles, whereas on average they did not manage a hundred miles. On 1 July they lost a significant part of the topmast but managed to carry out repairs while continuing the voyage.

The *Princess of Wales* stayed at Bombay for thirty-six days and then travelled down the coast calling in at Goa, Tellicherry, Cochin (Kochi) and Anjengo (near the southern tip of India) where they stopped for eleven days. This had been the scene of a terrible massacre of Europeans by the local people in 1721, just twelve years earlier.[39] They then travelled back north via Cochin, Callicut, Tellicherry, Annanore, back to Tellicherry, and then returned to Bombay where they stopped for twenty-three days. The journey involved taking various necessary stores to the settlements and collecting cargo, mostly pepper. The Malabar coastal waters were hazardous not least because of the threat of attack from a fleet of small ships under the command of the local Angria family who controlled the forts along the coast. Although they twice saw 'sails' and got ready for an engagement, the ships proved to be friendly, or they moved away, and the *Princess of Wales* was not attacked by Angria's fleet.[40]

On their journey home they spent 168 days at sea, travelling at an average of 3.6 knots per hour. Casting out the log-line to establish the speed (by the number of knots tied in a rope passing the stern in a given time) and lowering the lead-line to establish depth, would have become routine. Charles was able to learn about the use of instruments for navigation as well reading such signs as changes in the colour of the sea, the cloud formations and seeing birds other than those expected in mid-ocean. The threat from Angria had given him experience of preparing for an attack and the routine of 'saluting the fort' at their destinations had taught him about firing the canons. Charles now had the knowledge he needed to command a ship himself.

Captain Charles Raymond

While Charles was at sea, Hugh Raymond acquired a new ship which he intended for his nephew. It was rated at 490 tons, had thirty guns and was expected to have a crew of ninety-eight. Charles was still only twenty-one when he was proposed as captain of the *Wager* early in 1735. It may seem foolish to consider using such a young and inexperienced man as the captain of a new ship – but Hugh was no fool. He must have had great faith in the ability of his nephew to trust this huge investment to his command. The EIC would not risk their cargo in a ship unless they had confidence in the captain. In 1765 the Company brought in a ruling that a captain had to be at least twenty-five years old.[41] It was established practice that once the Court of the East India Company had used a vessel, the ship and its commander could expect to be regularly employed by the Company. Hugh was now approaching sixty, but assisting Charles to the top of the ladder would ensure a secure future for his nephew who could trade in India on behalf of the whole family. Without his uncle's help, a new captain could expect to pay the owners of his first command a great deal of money.

East India House as Charles would have known it © London Metropolitan Archives

Living by the Sea

It was not certain that any new ship would be accepted by the EIC and it helped to have contacts within the Court of Directors. Hugh's son, Jones Raymond, served as a Director from 1734 to 1757 (except for statutory breaks) and as he bowed out his cousin, John Raymond (son of Baynham Raymond), was elected to the Court in 1757 to safeguard the family interests.[42] Jones and John were the only sons of their fathers; neither married and neither went to sea, but both continued the family connections with the EIC.

Hugh Raymond offered his new ship, *Wager*, to sail for the EIC on 30 August 1734 but while twenty-one ships were tendered for the coming season, only thirteen voyages were planned. The Directors each indicated which thirteen ships they preferred and the *Wager* was not chosen. It had been the joint thirteenth choice with the *Scarborough* (which was also managed by Hugh Raymond) and had lost out on a second ballot. Hugh then wrote to the Court, reminding the Directors of an agreement made two years previously when he had taken responsibility for the finance of this new ship to assist them in a potentially embarrassing situation. A week later the EIC Court decided an additional voyage was necessary, and so the *Wager*, Captain Charles Raymond, was added to their fleet. The charterparty agreement was signed by Hugh Raymond with Captain Richard Mickelfield.[43] This had been a very rapid rise to the top and Charles must have felt very proud on 21 September 1734 when he joined the other captains for the season to take the Company's oath against trading contrary to their regulations.[44] It seems Charles must have been a young man of great capability and assurance.

The position of the captain was one of great status not only on board his ship and in port abroad, but also at home. He commanded the ship, but it was run on a day-to-day basis by the chief mate. It is likely that Hugh and his captain selected the officers together, so Charles sailed on the *Wager* with John Hume as chief mate, Edmond Doran as second mate and Joseph Sherrer as third mate. Hume had previously been chief mate on the *Harrington* while Doran and Sherrer had served with Charles on the *Princess of Wales*. At this time the crew of an East Indiaman leaving England would total about a hundred men, with maybe twenty more signing on later in the voyage. On average fifteen men would die and ten men would leave the ship abroad, either they 'ran' (and therefore did not get paid) or with permission of the captain. The journal always refers to the crew as 'the people' and it seems generally the EIC treated its employees with some respect. Unlike sailors who served in the Royal Navy, they were not 'pressed' into service but chose to sign up as crew on East Indiamen.

On the first voyage of the *Wager* 1734/5 [45] Captain Raymond was beset by illness and sixteen men died. The fourth mate John Biss 'ran' while the ship was at Madras in July 1735 and Hume and Doran died at Bengal in September 1735. It was a sad captain who

Sir Charles Raymond of Valentines and the East India Company

wrote on Saturday 17 April 1736 'At 2PM departed this life Mr Joseph Sherrer Chief Mate, who came out of England Third with me, so that I've now but the fifth mate remaining that came out with me.' This was Gilbert Slater who served as third mate on the next voyage of the *Wager* under Captain Raymond. Slater went on to become a captain and ended his days as a PMO for the EIC and Deputy Master of the Trinity House, living at Stepney.

John Scroggs, gunner, and John List, cooper, had also died in October 1735 while the quartermaster Robert Deere died three months later. Doran, Sherrer, Scroggs, List and Deere had all served previously with Raymond on the *Princess of Wales*.[46] Captain Robert Mead also died at sea while captain of the *Princess of Wales* on her next voyage. On 19 March 1736 he 'departed this life having laboured under a long lingering consumption'.[47] Perhaps the cramped quarters of these senior officers in their previous voyage meant the health of the others was weakened by the illness of Robert Mead, an illness often referred to as 'the spitting disease'. Death was an ever-present risk men were prepared to take in return for the potential rewards of a good voyage.

However, Charles survived and completed his first voyage as captain successfully under these extremely difficult circumstances. On the plus side, Richard Darling had served as captain's steward to Robert Mead on the previous voyage of the *Princess of Wales* and he supported Charles in that capacity for all four of his voyages as captain of the *Wager*. A new member of the crew, who also served on all four voyages of the *Wager*, was Josiah Hindman. He started as purser, served as purser again, then as second mate, ending as chief mate. He took over as captain of the *Wager* when Raymond retired and became the managing owner of the ship.

This first voyage of *Wager* 1734/5 was fairly routine. The cargo on such a voyage to India was made up of woollen 'broad cloth' or 'long ells', lead, maybe copper items, ironmongery such as guns, essential items for the maintenance of their own ship and for use in India etc. However, the value of the cargo out was worth much less than the cargo home, so on 5 February the captain received on board 62 chests of the 'Hon. Company's treasure' (silver coins). They then anchored in the Downs (between Deal and Ramsgate, the usual place where ships congregated waiting for good weather to start their voyage) awaiting their final instructions, sailing a few days later. South of the equator they sprung the topmast and lost some of the rigging but were able to repair the damage. All East Indiamen carried a spare mast and other timber and a quantity of spare sails, so that the carpenter and sail maker could carry out their duties at sea.

On 15 June the captain's journal reported 'This morning Richard Martin Seaman being detected of the Theft of a Guinea in money, a gold ring, two pairs of Silver buckles, two pair of shoes and severall other things I thought on the morning to bring him to

Living by the Sea

Examploary punishment; but contrary to my expectations, he's not to be found which appears he has avoyded both the Shame and Punishment by throwing himself overboard.' Punishment on East Indiamen does not appear to have been frequent or unduly harsh, but Charles would have remembered an incident on the *Princess of Wales* when on 4 May 1733 the captain wrote in his journal 'This morning, in a consultation with my officers, brought Thos Pickett [seaman] to the Jeers and whipped four and twenty lashes for thieving.'[48]

On 10 July the *Wager* anchored near Madras and, as was customary, they saluted Fort St George with twenty-one guns and nine were returned. They sent most of the treasure ashore along with what cargo was destined for Madras and some private trade. They then received other goods on board and set about filling up with water before sailing on to Ballasore. Here they took two pilots on board to guide the ship up the Hugli River towards Calcutta.

Having reached their destination they began to strip the ship, taking down the rigging, caulking and generally making the ship good for her return voyage. Nearly every day some items were taken ashore, and later their return cargo of salt petre, bales of material, turmerick, redwood etc. was loaded. Meanwhile the journal records the loss of life among the crew. Towards the end of December they began to negotiate their way back down the Hugli to Ingerlee where more cargo was loaded. On 25 January 1736 they started their journey home, calling in at St Helena three months later.

While here Charles heard the shocking news that the *Derby* had been captured by Angria (referred to in his journal as 'Augary the Pirate') on 26 December 1735, near the Malabar coast. The *Derby* was another ship managed by Hugh Raymond. She had sailed in company with the *Dawsonne* on the first voyage made by Charles, as purser. Angria did not usually attempt to capture such a large armed ship as an East Indiaman but in this case *Derby* was surrounded by nine smaller ships at 5am. After twelve hours fighting, with the mizenmast, mainmast and much of the rigging destroyed, seven men killed and many wounded, they submitted. In all, 115 of the crew were taken prisoner by Angria and once they had unloaded the cargo from England, they were kept in irons on very meagre rations until the EIC Governor in Bombay could assist them.[49]

Wager left St Helena on 10 May and nearly lost another member of the crew. On 14 June 1736 the journal recorded how in reasonable weather 'the Boatswain's servant fell from the Mizen top but received no other damage than dislocating the joint of his Great toe.' He had a miraculous escape! However, he was among sixty-two men who were discharged from the *Wager* on 16 July 1736 while it appears she was in the mouth of the Thames. There is no mention of this in the journal but perhaps the men were pressed for

Sir Charles Raymond of Valentines and the East India Company

Captain Raymond's journal of the Wager (1) February 21st and 22nd, 1736 two fairly typical days mid-voyage. The columns show 24 hours from midnight with the speed in knots © The British Library Board, L/MAR/B/592A

18

Living by the Sea

the Royal Navy. Most of the crew were paid for 18 months and 8 days but the sixty-two who left early were paid for 17 months and 11days.[50]

Charles returned from this first voyage as captain to find that his uncle and mentor Hugh Raymond had very recently died, on 10 July 1737. The second voyage of the *Wager* was therefore under the management of John Raymond (cousin of Charles, son of Baynham Raymond) and Francis Salvador.[51] The latter was from a wealthy Sephardi family which had come to England from Holland towards the end of the seventeenth century, and he managed many voyages for the EIC, often in association with retired Captains Richard Mickelfield and Thomas Hunt.

The second voyage of the *Wager* 1737/8 [52] was fairly routine although they anchored in Table Bay (South Africa) for ten days. Having collected more water they continued to Madras, arriving on 13 July, and then travelled on to Calcutta as before. The names given to places which were passed conjure up a romantic journey: the Black Pagoda, Point Palmires, Ingerlee, Kedgeree, the Diamond Sand, Mayapore Creek, but noting them in the journal with details of their bearing (e.g. 'At 7AM anchored in 23 fathoms Jackarnat Pagoda NW½N and the Black Pagood NNE dist of shore Abt 4 or 5 leagues') was significant. EIC clerks back in London collated any new information about rocks or sandbanks and passed it on to assist future navigation. This was invaluable to a captain sent across seas he had not visited before. Captain John Prince of the *Latham (2)* 1769/70 [53] had written notes provided by the EIC in London at the end of his journal, for his use on the voyage:

Remarks on Rocks, Shoals and Islands said to be seen, some of which are not in our draughts. [shoals in this context means sandbanks]

To the eastward of the Cape of Good Hope, Lattitude 38° 29' So.

A shoal 25 degrees to the Eastward of Cape of Good Hope, found 3 years successively by three different ships, one (and I believe all) the ships were Dutch. I believe it was discovered since the year 1730. It is above water.

Kismas or Christmas Isle lies S ¾ W from Java Head distance 227 miles, is so high as to be seen 10 leagues off, no breakers off it, and is supposed to be a bold island; abundance of birds about it. [10 leagues = approx. 30 miles]

Directions for St.Helena

If a ship should be under a necessity of coming into St. Helena Road from the westward, I believe it may be done at any time and commonly with great ease but care must be taken to avoid a Ledge of Rocks which lay between Horsepastures Point and Lemon Valley. These rocks lay midway between this point and the western point of Lemon Valley, and run about a quarter of a mile and better from shore (as near as I could when upon 'em in a boat). Just opposite to them on the shore is a piece of ground different from the rest. It looks like mould and rocks fallen down from the rest above, being loose and not so compact and close as the rest of the bank, and a little to the Eastward about halfway between the Rocks and Lemon Valley Point, is a large Rock close in shore is a good mark for being past the danger (when you are abreast of it) and for hauling up.

The captain also noted every other East Indiaman which he saw. If another ship was lost these notes might prove useful in trying to establish the fate of that ship.

The return voyage of *Wager* 1737/8 was also fairly routine, leaving India on 6 February 1739 in company with the *Duke of Cumberland*, and calling in at St Helena on 20 May, where they stopped for eighteen days. From St Helena they travelled in company with *Nassau*, *Scarborough*, *Princess Mary* and *Cumberland*. Keeping together slowed them down but was good protection if there was a threat of war. When they had been at sea for several months the news that war had actually broken out might not have reached the captains. When they arrived in the Downs on 27 August they 'Found riding here 9 of his Majesty's ships with Admiral Balchen who hoisted the Red flagg at the foretopmast Head on board the *Russell,* saluted him with 9 guns he returned 5. Came in here the *Nassau & Cumberland* our Consorts. The Lieut presst 30 of our men. at 9AM weigh'd [anchor] Mr John Bell our Pilot being come on board & at 3PM anch'd in Westcot Bay.'

The mention of Admiral Balchen is interesting. Five years later, as senior admiral in command of a large combined fleet of seventeen British and eight Dutch warships, he was on board the Royal Navy's flagship *Victory*. Over 1,100 men were also on board and because this was such a prestigious ship, it included a good number of the younger sons of the gentry. On 3 October 1744 the ships were caught in a ferocious storm approaching the English Channel and dispersed, but soon newspapers were reporting the safe return to Spithead of various ships in the fleet. By 12 October concerns were expressed that the *Victory* had still not returned and on 15 October the *General Advertiser* said 'There is yet no news relating to Sir John Balchen in the *Victory*, which greatly encreases the pain of the Publick for his safety.' Within a few days it was reported that wreckage had been washed ashore in the Channel Isles of Alderney and Guernsey and it was assumed the ship had been wrecked on the Caskets rocks.[54] Early in November a special pension was granted to Lady Balchen and in May 1746 a monument to Sir John Balchen was unveiled in the north aisle of Westminster Abbey. Sadly, by this time her son had also died, while in command of the Royal Navy ship *Pembroke*.[55]

Living by the Sea

Fortunately, the loss of the crew on the second journey of the *Wager* was below average. A total of 109 men signed on, with ten dying and five leaving the ship on the journey. None of the officers died but the second mate 'ran' almost a year after leaving England while they were preparing to return home from Calcutta.[56] The very next day William Webber was signed on as a new third mate. It has not been possible to trace any previous service, nor any earlier passage to India by William Webber, so it seems likely he was already on board the *Wager* as a 'guest' of the captain. It is also worth noting that on the previous voyage, when so many of the officers died, only one man was signed on abroad as a replacement. This was a new chief mate, just after the deaths of Hume and Doran.[57]

William Webber had been christened on 30 January 1713 at Clyst Honiton in Devon. He was therefore born less than three months before Charles Raymond, about eight miles away from his childhood home at Withycombe Raleigh, and it is possible they were cousins.[58] William Webber went on to serve as third mate of the *Wager* 1740/1, under Captain Charles Raymond, chief mate on *Prince William (2)* 1743/4, (taking over as captain when Captain Thomas Langworth died on 29 December 1744, just as they were leaving Calcutta) then as captain on her next voyage. There is no doubt that the assistance given by Charles Raymond helped him very swiftly up the EIC ladder. He retired in September 1761 after three voyages as captain of the *Harcourt* and later became a Director of the EIC. His life was further inter-woven with that of Charles as will be seen later.

The *Wager* and Anson's voyage

It was usual in the eighteenth century for a ship to make four voyages before being replaced, due to the detrimental effects of sailing in warm waters. However, the *Wager (2)* was commissioned after just two voyages. The crew was discharged on 12 October 1739 and payment of £4,500 to the owners was agreed on 21 November.[59] This is not the only payment they received from the EIC but it was the major settlement and the date was significant.

On 21 November 1739 the Royal Navy purchased an East Indiaman, Charles's ship *Wager*, to join the small fleet gathered to sail under the command of Captain George Anson. The plan, backed by Admiral Sir Charles Wager, was to sail around Cape Horn, plunder the coasts of Chile and Peru and capture the Spanish galleon which crossed from Manila to Acapulco with a cargo of silver, suggested to be worth up to £2,000,000.

Not everyone at the Admiralty and in the government was enthusiastic for the venture but in 1740 seven ships were allocated and Anson set about preparing for the voyage.

Sir Charles Raymond of Valentines and the East India Company

Unfortunately the necessary stores were in short supply and it proved difficult to get a full complement of seamen and the required soldiers. It was normal practice for the officers to set sail with a crew of men, many of whom had been pressed into service, but Anson's crew consisted of many older and sick men who were not up to the rigours of the voyage. In the event, the voyage was one of both disaster and triumph. Of 1,900 men who set sail, 1,400 died of scurvy or other disease, or starvation. Anson's determination and fortitude made him a national hero as although only one ship, the *Centurion*, returned home in 1744, he did capture the Spanish treasure galleon.

The *Wager*'s function was to act as an armed support vessel, and an Indiaman was ideally suited for this, being effectively the transporter of her day. She carried military stores, guns and merchandise to trade at the coastal towns in order to curry favour with the locals. However, the *Wager* was wrecked on 14 May 1741 off the coast of Patagonia, Chile, and the story of what happened to her crew is amazing. Although some mutinied, a few rowed 2,500 miles to eventually reach England. The place where the ship was wrecked is now called Wager Island, in the Gulf de Penas.[60]

In 2007 an expedition was put together to try and find the wreck, diving from this remote island. In spite of fairly detailed accounts of the location, after a month the team were no nearer finding the wreck. It became apparent that a series of earthquakes had changed the coastline far more than had been realised. It was quite by chance that some timbers from the ship were recognised in the bed of a stream just a few metres from the diving team's campsite! Now the site has been located there may be a further study of what remains of the wreck.[61]

The rebuilt ship, called *Wager (2)*, was of similar size to the first ship, so Charles would have felt immediately at home. He would have spent much time at the shipyards, checking on the ship, engaging his officers, and generally ensuring everything was completed to his satisfaction for the next voyage. The charterparty agreement was signed by John Raymond of London, Merchant (Charles's cousin) and Joseph Tolson of London, Mariner, on 13 February 1741.[62] Joseph Tolson had served as Captain for the *Heathcote* East Indiaman for eight voyages between 1708 – 1733 and seems to have been a member of the Raymond circle. The charterparty for Tolson's last voyage was signed by Hugh Raymond and his son Jones.[63]

The third voyage of the *Wager* 1740/1 [64] also seems to have been relatively unremarkable. They were delayed until 22 April 1741 so that when they left Portsmouth to negotiate the Channel with a Royal Navy escort they were part of a large convoy of over forty ships. However, they completed the journey without calling in anywhere for water so managed to reach Madras by mid-September. They left India early in February,

Living by the Sea

stopping at the Cape and St Helena on the way home, reaching the Downs on 6 September 1742. There was one serious event recorded in the journal, on 27 May 1741 when they were in mid-Atlantic (north of the equator), which is worth noting:

> Hott sultry weather & for ye first & latter parts Fair with light winds, the other Cloudy intermixt with hard Squalls.

> About eleven it began to Thunder and Lightning much & continued till the morning between two & four of the clock it was ye most violent I e'er saw between which hours it split our Main topmast & topgallantmast all to peices striking splinters off them, three or four foot long and one that hung at the mast ten foot long. It likewise threw several peices out of the Mainmast which seem'd to be all on Fire, for a considerable time and had it not been for the Providence of God in sending us whole clouds of rain, at that time, must certainly have all perished, by the ships being burn'd. It knocked down several of our men on ye Deck some of which remained speechless for a considerable time. It likewise killed a Hogg on the Deck striking another at ye same time down the Main hatch way & splitt a stantion [stanchion or supporting pillar] on the Quarter deck leaving such a smell of Sulphur as creats great sickness to the stomach & lowness of spirits throughout all the ships company.

The threat of fire was always a danger, particularly with gunpowder on board. Many years later, a couple of days before reaching Madras on 21 August 1783, the journal of the *Earl of Oxford*, Captain John White, PMO Sir Charles Raymond, reported: 'Before 1PM perceived the *Duke of Kingston* to be on fire. Immediately hoisted out our boats, and sent them to the relief of the objects in distress. Every ship did the same. She burnt until 5PM when she blew up. Upon a division of the people saved, were received on board 81 persons, viz: 55 military, 5 cadets, and 21 of the ship's company.'[65] The *Duke of Kingston,* Captain Justinian Nutt, had been managed by John Raymond, but it is likely Charles had invested in the ship. Sadly the journal of the *Earl of Oxford* states that 65 people were lost in the disaster including the chief mate, surgeon and purser.

Marriage to Sarah Webster

While he was at home after his third voyage as captain, Charles attended to more than just the requirements of his fourth voyage. On 22 January 1743 he married Sarah Webster at the beautiful Wren church of St. Stephen's, Walbrook, in the City of London.[66] She was just twenty-one, he was approaching his thirtieth birthday.

Sir Charles Raymond of Valentines and the East India Company

*Marriage of Charles Raymond and Sarah Webster, at St Stephen's Walbrook,
22 January 1742/3 © London Metropolitan Archives*

Sarah was the daughter of John Webster of The Rookery in Bromley, Kent. He had owned considerable property but died on 24 November 1724, less than three years after Sarah was born. The Rookery estate passed to the custodianship of his executor William Guy, a salter of Wapping, in trust for the benefit of his children John, Sarah, Thomas, Robert and Elizabeth (who was born after her father had died). John was not married to the mother of these children, Judith Cooke, but went to great lengths to ensure that his children inherited what would have been their right had their parents been married.[67] It appears that John was forty-one when his first child (by Judith Cooke) was baptised on 20 November 1720 and she was aged twenty-five. It has not been possible to discover why they did not marry. However, on 16 August 1726 William Guy married Judith Cooke at St Clement Danes church in the Strand.[68] There were soon more children in the family, but sadly most of them were buried as infants and only Ann (baptised 27 July 1734) and Mary (baptised 30 September 1737) were still alive when their father died in 1755.

William and Judith used The Rookery as their country home (this is now the site of Bromley College of Further & Higher Education on Bromley Common).[69] It was very close to the Langley Park estate at Beckenham which had been purchased by Hugh Raymond and had become the home of his daughter Amy, Mrs Peter Burrell. It seems likely that Charles would have known William Guy, who was a contractor with the East India Company for many years, supplying their ships with provisions,[70] and perhaps they met socially if Charles visited his cousin at Langley Park. Having met and taken a fancy for Sarah, a young man of Charles's talent would soon have found ways of courting his future bride.

Living by the Sea

After their marriage Charles and Sarah lived at Wellclose Square which was a popular area for captains, close to their work but away from the waterside slums. It was a hub for both the Raymond family and Charles's in-laws, the Guys. Hugh Raymond had lived here around 1720 when it was called Marine Square. William Guy is first shown in the land tax assessments in 1742 at 'Square south east'. In 1747 and 1748 Captain Raymond was shown at 'Square south west' but in 1749 his house was empty.[71] William Guy later moved to the east side and both William and Judith Guy were shown as living at Wellclose Square when they died in 1755 and 1759.[72] Before his marriage to Judith Cooke, William Guy was described as 'of Goodman Fields'[73] which was at that time a residential area like Wellclose Square. Captain John Pelly, who sailed in command of the *Prince of Wales* in the same seasons that Charles was at sea in command of the *Wager*, lived at nearby Mansell Street. This still exists (near Tower Gateway and Aldgate) but it is hard to imagine it was also a prestigious address in the mid-eighteenth century.[74]

John Pelly was the son of another EIC captain of the same name who had been helped in his career by the Colletts of West Ham and Barking, the family of his second wife, Grisel. John Pelly junior had been nurtured in his career on ships captained by his father. Yet despite being two years older than Charles, he did not take over as a captain until 1740/1 when his father retired, and he continued at sea doing a further voyage after Charles had retired. He married Elizabeth, daughter and heiress of Henry Hinde of Upton and Aveley (north of the Thames, near the Dartford Bridge) on 20 January 1735/6 when she was only eighteen or nineteen and he was still serving as first mate under his father. It seems very likely that Elizabeth and Sarah would have met if William Guy had worked with the Pellys in provisioning their ships. Elizabeth Pelly's first baby was a girl named Elizabeth but by the time Sarah and Charles were married she had given birth to, and buried, three more infants.

Barely nine months after Charles and Sarah's marriage the parish register of St. John's, Wapping, records the burial of Anna Maria Raymond of Wellclose Square on 12 October 1743. No baptism is recorded which suggests that she died within hours of her birth. Perhaps the two wives, soon to be left at home while their husbands were at sea, took comfort in young Elizabeth Pelly and a baby brother John who was born earlier in 1743. Sadly John died when five years and four months old and was buried at Barking with his siblings.

Sarah Raymond was to suffer the loss of other children once Charles had returned from the sea: Anna Maria (2) died aged 13 months in August 1748 and Anna Maria (3) died in April 1749 just 17 days after her baptism.[75] By this time they were living at Upton and the events are recorded in the registers of All Saints church, West Ham. It was not

25

Captain Raymond's last voyage, *Wager* 1743/4

On 25 January 1744 Mr Francis Salvador and Captain Joseph Tolson signed the charterparty agreement for the next voyage of the *Wager (2)*.[76] In February the *Wager* was at Gravesend, in March in the Downs and from 12 April – 27 May she was in Portsmouth Harbour, finally leaving in convoy with four other East Indiamen and a Royal Navy escort to see them through the Channel. A few days later the captain received a signal from the commodore warning that '3 sail of French Privateers of 70 guns' had been reported in the vicinity, but they were not seen by the convoy.[77]

The *Wager* stopped for water in Table Bay (South Africa) in mid-September but their delayed start meant the winds and current were against them as they tried to reach the Coromandel coast (the south east coast of India). Many of the crew were becoming ill with scurvy and so the captain held a consultation with all his officers as to their best course of action. The journal for 4 December 1744 records that 'we think it our Duty to advise ye bearing away for Batavia as ye safest port we can proceed too. And we are the more incouraged in urging this our opinion by considering that ye Hon. Masters which we serve allways desire the welfare of their seaman and not their lives should become a sacrifice to a triffling expence that may accrue to the owners.' The journal entry was signed by all the officers to show it was a joint decision. By 18 December 'A great many of our people fell down of the Scurvy, many of which I fear I shall loose if we do not get quickly to port' and they must have been very relieved when they arrived at Batavia (Jakarta) on 26 December. Here they took on water and fresh food and repaired the ship, waiting for an English privateer to accompany them through the 'Streights of Sunda' to Bengal. They finally arrived in the Hugli River on 31 May 1745, a year after leaving home.

Once moored near Calcutta, the men were employed in transporting their cargo to the Company warehouses and repairing the ship as usual. Rigging was replaced and new anchors obtained. By July the weather was hot and cloudy with a great deal of rain and a number of the men became 'exceedingly sickly' and seven died during the month. Charles must have had a heavy heart when he wrote in the journal 'The 10th died Mr Thos Webster, Purser, of a Malignant fever' as this was his brother-in-law. It seems that Thomas was having his first experience of the sea in the position that Charles had filled on his first voyage, fifteen years earlier.

Living by the Sea

Ship Wager at Anchor in Bengall River

Wednesday the 1st Janr. to Sunday 5	Winds and Weather as before Receiv'd on board 3A6 Bales & Some Rattans Imploy'd in Stowing them Anchor'd here the Dolphin and Medway prize
Monday 6 to Wednesday 8th	Receiv'd on Board 18A Bales A Leagers Ships Anch 7 Tons of water & Stow'd the Same
Thursday 9th to Wednesday 15th	Fair weather Receiv'd on Board 80 Bales and 10 Tons of water Saild hence ye 10th. The Edgbaston Dolphin & Prize Salam Son Madrass
Thursday 16th To Monday 20th	Nerly Winds & Fair weather Receiv'd on Board AO Bales, & discharg'd all ye Lascars being 30ths I have been oblig'd to keep my own People being So Sickly that they could not perform their Duty Anard Staves & could be ready for Sailing in 3 Days would they think proper to Despatch me which they might do if they please
Tuesday 21 to Saturday 25th	Little or nothing to do but to take on Board Trifles Son ye Voyage the 21st Arriv'd the Scarborough Capt Westcott After being a 12 month from England who Brings us News of four more of ye Company's Ships at Madrass two of which are order'd here. The 2Ath Same on Board to prepare Sou Sailing
Sunday 26 to Friday 31	Fresh Northerly winds Receiv'd on Board all ye paper Lumber & Live Stock Son ye Voyage the 31st my Charter Party being expir'd I enter'd a protest against the Honble Company & their Governour & Councillor not Despatching ye Ship. the 30th paid own small Bower Anchor & sent to Ingellee Son another & there Drept down. Sweep'd a whole Day for ye Anchor but could not Sish him pass'd by ye Kent Capt Robson From Madrass
Saturday 1 Feb.	Winds & weather as before Saild hence the Jenney a Country Ship
Sunday 2	Light Breezes & Fair Weather Receiv'd on Board on Board an Anchor weighing 27 C I have lost A Anchors sin'e my Arrival

Captain Raymond's journal of the Wager (2) January 1746 showing the last days at Calcutta © The British Library Board, L/MAR/B/592D

Sir Charles Raymond of Valentines and the East India Company

In October they started to load stores and their cargo which included large quantities of salt petre, 30 tons of red wood, 300 bags of cowrie shells and a large quantity of material. They stayed in the vicinity of Calcutta for thirty-six weeks. Towards the end of that time the men had little to keep them occupied and the captain was quite agitated at not being allowed to sail. '31st January, my Charter Party being expir'd I enter'd a protest against the Honble Company & their Governour & Council for not Despatching ye ship.' The reason for the delay became evident when on 7 February Charles welcomed aboard 'the Hon Thos. Braddyll Esq, late Governour of Bengall who goes home as Passenger' and was then able to sail for England. They stopped at St Helena for eighteen days and then travelled in convoy with five other East Indiamen and two Royal Navy ships, arriving in the English Channel in August 1746. Governor Braddyll and the other gentlemen passengers went ashore at Deal and were saluted with twenty-one guns.[78]

Thomas Braddyll had served as Governor of Bengal since 9 May 1739. On returning home he contracted to purchase Luxborough, in Chigwell, although he died before the transaction was completed and was buried at Woodford on 5 December 1747. He left £70,000 (approx £14m. in today's money)[79] to his brothers and sisters. His brother Dodding Braddyll served as a Director of the EIC for at least twenty years before his death a year later. He was also buried in the family vault at St Mary's, Woodford.

A year later, on 12 August 1747, Joseph Salvador and Joseph Tolson signed the charterparty agreement for the third voyage of the *Wager (2)*, with Captain Charles Raymond as commander. However, on 28 October Charles Raymond sent a letter to the Court setting out his ill state of health and asking the Court to approve Josiah Hindman for commander of the *Wager* in his place. Other captains gave a variety of reasons to the Court for declining a voyage after the charterparty agreement had been signed, so it seems likely the illness was genuine. It is unfortunate, but hardly surprising, that the letter has not survived as it would be interesting to know the nature of his illness. Be that as it may, on 18 November 1747 a new charterparty was signed for the *Wager*, by Charles Raymond and Joseph Tolson, with Josiah Hindman as Captain.[80]

Josiah Hindman had served on all four previous voyages of the *Wager*, as purser twice, then second mate, then chief officer. His uncle Thomas Hindman had sailed as captain on four voyages at the same time as Charles, but they left in different years and it is unlikely they were more than acquainted before they retired. However, when Thomas Hindman died in July 1748 he named 'My beloved friend Charles Raymond Esquire' as one of his executors. Perhaps this shows his gratitude that Charles had nurtured the career of Josiah, the son of his late brother James Hindman.

Living by the Sea

Risk and Reward

Compared with some of his fellow captains, the four voyages of the *Wager* under Captain Charles Raymond were relatively uneventful, but even so 15 per cent of the crew who left England died. Mostly this was due to the diseases encountered, scurvy on the voyage or dysentery (often referred to as 'the bloody flux') in port, but also to accident both at sea and in port. The table below shows the mortality statistics for the four voyages of which Charles was the captain. (Others who joined the ship abroad did not always complete the voyage, but adding them below would distort the figures.)

Ledgers		Left England	Died	%
L/MAR/B/592G (1)	Crew of the *Wager 1734/5*	94	16	17.02
L/MAR/B/592H (1)	Crew of the *Wager 1737/8*	103	10	9.71
L/MAR/B/592-I (1)	Crew of the *Wager 1740/1*	114	14	12.28
L/MAR/B/592J (1)	Crew of the *Wager 1743/4*	91	20	21.98
	TOTAL	402	60	14.93

This is too small a sample to be statistically valid, but it indicates the risks to the crew from a routine voyage. Many men died on their first experience of the East but surviving the first voyage did not mean a man was immune to disease. John Phillips served as seaman on *Wager* 1737/8, midshipman on *Wager* 1740/1 and fourth mate on *Wager* 1743/4 only to die of a malignant fever on 19 July 1745 in Calcutta; John Wilkinson was a seaman who also acted as a servant to Captain Raymond on all four voyages of the *Wager* but after thirty-six weeks at Calcutta he 'died of a flux' on 7 February 1746, just a couple of days before they started on their voyage home. Add to this the fact that approximately 6.5 per cent of ships did not return home and it can be seen that survival over six voyages was in itself something of an achievement.

Nobody was immune to the risks and the captain sometimes died too. Joseph Tolson's nephew Jonathan Cape worked his way up on the *Heathcote* from second mate on the 1723/4 voyage, to chief mate for three voyages under the captaincy of his uncle. He then took over command of the *Heathcote* 1736/7 and for the three subsequent voyages. The charterparty for the last voyage, *Heathcote (4)* 1746/7 was signed by Francis Salvador and Joseph Tolson.[81] Sadly this ship was lost in the Bab el Mandeb (between the Red Sea and the Gulf of Aden). Although Jonathan Cape and Charles Raymond were captains at the same time, their voyages were made in different years so their cycles would have made it difficult for them to have become close friends. However, Joseph Tolson lived at Wellclose Square [82] and Charles and Jonathan Cape must have been well acquainted. By the time news of his death reached London Charles and

Sir Charles Raymond of Valentines and the East India Company

Tolson were working together as PMOs and Charles must have been saddened by the death of the captain.

> *Silver 'Pillar dollars', such as this dated 1736, were taken on board East Indiamen to assist in paying for the goods brought back home. It was salvaged from the wreck of the Dutch East Indiaman* Rooswijk *which sunk on the Goodwin Sands on 9 January 1740 at the start of her voyage to Indonesia. These Spanish dollar coins, with a value of eight reales, were known as 'pieces of eight' and were the world's first global currency.*
>
>

The Finance of sailing for the East India Company

At the time Charles was at sea the captain's salary was £10 a month, the chief mate was paid £5, second mate £4, the carpenter earned £3 10s a month, third mate, purser and surgeon were paid £3 and so on. Midshipmen and seamen were all paid 23s per month. When Charles made his second voyage as a captain on the *Wager* 1737/8, the crew were paid from 5 February 1738 to 12 October 1739 when they were discharged, so the captain earned £202 6s 8d for 20 months and 7 days. However, there were sums deducted for his various legal and other expenses, so his 'take home pay' was £181 15s 5d.[83] For his last voyage Charles was paid for 30 months 27 days, the longer voyage earning him a 'take home pay' of £248 6s 7d.[84]

However, an officer's salary paled into insignificance, compared to the opportunity for lucrative private trade. All members of the crew were entitled to bring back their own private trade goods, the space allowed depending on their rank.[85] The success of this 'privilege' must have been dependent on the financial investment available and the ports

Living by the Sea

visited for trading. For his first voyages Charles had worked with his uncle Hugh Raymond who may have provided additional capital for private trade, both as a loan to Charles and as his own investment. Hugh died in July 1737 and, as already stated, the charterparty for the second voyage of the *Wager* was signed by Charles's cousin John Raymond and Francis Salvador.[86] In December 1737 Charles Raymond signed a bond with Edward Radcliffe of London which seems to have been a loan for £2,520 to be repaid within thirty days of his ship returning to the River Thames.[87] It is possible Charles was working in a syndicate with John Raymond and others, and had a part-share in the ship, as well as other investors in his private trade. After each voyage Charles had a larger amount of personal capital to invest in goods he could sell in India (he never went to China), in business dealings there, and in goods to bring back home.

The private trade goods brought back to England by the crew were usually sold 'at the Company's Candle' where the final bid before the candle was extinguished was accepted, rather like e-bay today. The owner would be entitled to payment for the private trade he brought home, less duty. Alternatively, it could be claimed by the owner after the value was noted and duty paid. He might also have a share in the gold or diamonds brought home on his ship.[88]

It is clear that a captain could receive payment for a number of different reasons, quite apart from his wages (for example, payments from passengers for their berth and food). As well as the private trade goods sold in London, he might have deposited money with the company abroad as a result of his private dealings there. A bill of exchange or certificate was then presented to the Court which honoured the payment to him in London. Trying to extract reliable information about the financial affairs of a particular individual from the Court Books is not possible without additional supporting paperwork. Although some payments are listed, few give a reason for the payment, and they are listed together with many other payments agreed by the EIC Directors which could include, for example, £41717 11s 11d to Robert Man Esq for His Majesty's use, £25,122 to the Governor of the Bank of England,[89] regular payment from £5,000 to £200 to Henry Crabb, paymaster and clerk to the Shipping Committee, and £4 charity paid to a widow.

Although this may not be the complete picture, it appears that from his second voyage as captain Charles was paid £3,000 by the Court to honour deposits in Bengal, and £2605 1s 5d for his 'Private Trade touching on goods sold at the Company's Candle', plus a further £ 494 1s 3d. This was a total of approximately £6100 as against his salary of £248 6s 7d. The total in today's terms was approximately £1.2m. However, some of this would have been used to repay the bond with Edward Radcliffe.[90]

31

Sir Charles Raymond of Valentines and the East India Company

There was also the question of illegal income from smuggling which became a more common occurrence a little later in the century.[91] There is nothing to suggest that Charles was involved in anything like this, although he would have been aware of an incident where two colleagues were challenged on returning from their voyages. They had sailed in the same season as Charles's third voyage as captain of the *Wager*, all three ships arriving back at the Downs in September 1742. On 1 December 1742 the Court of Directors ordered an enquiry 'into the conduct of Captain Francis Steward of the *Godolphin* and Captain Charles Birkhead of the *Queen Caroline* relating to the cloth and lead clandestinely shipt on their respective ships and report.' On 11 March Captain Birkhead was dismissed the Company's service and from his career record it appears this may have been a second offence. Captain Steward was suspended but on 8 July 1743 this was lifted as, after an investigation, the Court was satisfied that he was not personally involved in the matter, either directly or indirectly. Francis Steward was the man who had captained the *Dawsonne* when Charles made his first voyage as purser. Having completed two voyages as first mate and four as a captain, he retired from the sea. He had been paid £3634 4s 1d in January and £3429 12s 6d in July 1743, so with his wages, in today's terms Steward received something like £1.45m from his final voyage. However, his brother Gabriel, having served on four voyages as first mate and two as captain of the *India* (an EIC yacht), died while on his first voyage as captain of an East Indiaman, the *Winchester*, on 26 July 1744. Like many new captains, he had taken out a loan in order to maximise his potential profit on the voyage but instead left his widow in debt. She appealed to the EIC Court who were aware of her plight and granted her a pension of £30 a year.[92]

On his last, longer voyage Charles was paid wages of £309 (less deductions). He received £2604 16s 9d from his deposits in India and approximately £2930 was recorded in the Court Books as payment from his private trade. This was well over £1m in today's terms. Charles's steward, Richard Darling, also made a profit on his own trade being paid £62 17s 9d while his wages were £59 6s 8d (less deductions).

It is significant that Charles Raymond only sailed to India, never China where private trade could bring a greater reward, but it usually had to be conducted through intermediaries (the supercargo and Chinese officials). Without any family papers to provide supporting information additional figures from the EIC Commercial Ledgers are difficult to interpret accurately. They show that after his last voyage Charles paid £780 duty (at 5 per cent) on his private trade which suggests his private trade income *could* have been £15,600 on his last voyage. This would equate to over £3m in today's terms.[93] The fact that Charles paid much more in customs fees on his private trade than most of his fellows also suggests that he had contacts in Calcutta who sourced luxury

Living by the Sea

items, with the best profit margins. It seems highly likely that Hugh Raymond had established trading links in Calcutta which were used by the Raymond family throughout the century.

When Charles retired from the sea and managed voyages for EIC, many of the men selected to captain his ships were related, or had an avuncular connection. They could be trusted to continue ensuring a good reward from the voyage for the family investments. This is illustrated by the career of Raymond Snow, the son of Charles's cousin Lydia and grandson of Baynham Raymond. He was nurtured by the Raymond circle and would have been ideally placed to continue working with the family contacts in Calcutta.

The Career of Raymond Snow (born 1745)				
PMO	**Ship**	**Date**		**To**
Charles Raymond	Duke of Richmond	1763/4	Snow, Raymond, 5th mate	China
Andrew Moffatt	Europa (1)	1766/7	Snow, Raymond, 3rd mate	Bengal
Richard Crabb	Royal Charlotte (1)	1768/9	Snow, Raymond, 2nd mate	Bengal
John Raymond	Talbot	1770/1	Snow, Raymond, 1st mate	China
John Raymond	Duke of Kingston (2)	1772/3	Snow, Raymond, Captain	China
John Raymond	Talbot	1774/5	Snow, Raymond, Captain	Bengal
John Raymond	Ceres (1)	1778/9	Snow, Raymond, Captain	Bengal
Thomas Newte	Winterton	1781/2	Snow, Raymond, Captain	Bengal
Thomas Newte	Winterton	1784/5	Snow, Raymond, Captain	Bengal

Andrew Moffatt and Richard Crabb were closely associated with Charles Raymond, John Raymond was Raymond Snow's uncle (he was the brother of Lydia Snow) and Thomas Newte became Charles's son-in-law. This also illustrates how the PMO did not work in isolation and was the representative of a wider group of investors. This will be explored in greater detail in part two.

Risk was a central feature of EIC trade, balancing the extraordinary profit which Company men could, in a good voyage, hope to achieve. Charles Raymond had proved his ability, taking command at a young age and bringing his ship home safely four times. Over the time he was able to spend ashore in India on each voyage his private trade made him an extremely wealthy man. After a total of six voyages to India, having travelled more than 180,000 miles, he prepared for his new life with his wife, planning his future in the footsteps of his uncle Hugh Raymond.

[1] White's Devon. A History, Gazetteer and Directory of Devonshire by William White (1850) p.252

[2] M.E.Williams *Memorials of Withycombe Raleigh* (1946) Vol.I p.128, 140 (unpublished typescript in the Westcountry Studies Library at Exeter)

[3] From the late Peter Foley, a local historian in Ilford with family in Devon, in a private letter but the source of this information has not been found.

[4] Tiverton museum

[5] Parish registers at Devon Record Office, Exeter

[6] NA Will of Amy Jones, Widow of Stepney, Middlesex, 08 November 1721, PROB 11/582

[7] Matthew Martin served as captain of the *Tavistock (1)* 1699/1700, 1702/3 & 1707/8, and *Marlborough (2)* 1711/2, 1715/6 for the EIC. James Osborne was captain of *New George* 1708/9 and *Hanover* 1712/3 & 1716/7, also sailing for EIC.

[8] Memorial to Amy Burrell at St.George's, Beckenham. She died 16 August 1789 aged 89.

[9] H. Davison Love *Vestiges of Old Madras 1640-1800* (1913) Vol.II p.133

[10] BL, IOR/L/MAR/B/671A Journal of *Dawsonne* 1718/9, April 1719; NA Will of John Raymond, Mariner of London, 25 October 1720, PROB 11/576

[11] John Carswell *The South Sea Bubble* (Sutton Publishing, Stroud, 2001, ISBN 0 7509 2799 2) pp.35, 44-45

[12] John Carswell *The South Sea Bubble* (op.cit.) pp.58, 61, 64 & 253; NA Will of Baynham Raymond, 16 February 1719, PROB 11/567

[13] Rev. Philip Morant *The History and Antiquities of the County of Essex* (1763-68) Vol.II p.411

[14] Derek Morris & Ken Cozens *Wapping 1600 – 1800*, (East of London History Society, 2009, ISBN 978 0 9506258 9 8)

[15] John Carswell *The South Sea Bubble* (op.cit.) p.115

[16] John Carswell *The South Sea Bubble* (op.cit.) p.203-4

[17] Guildhall Library, London A 9.5.2 *A True and Exact Particular and Inventory of all and singular the lands, tenements and hereditaments, goods, chattels, debts and personal estate whatsoever ...* relating to the South Sea Company in 1720. Hugh Raymond Esq, late one of the Directors of the South-Sea Company....

[18] John Carswell *The South Sea Bubble* (op.cit.) p.226, 253

[19] Parish Registers of Withycombe Raleigh

[20] For a detailed study of the ships of the East India Company, their crew and management see *Lords of the East: The East India Company and its Ships (1600 – 1874)* by Jean Sutton (Conway Maritime Press, 1981 new edition 2000, ISBN 0 85177 786 4)

[21] Essex Record Office D/DRU B19 Ships' books of Samuel Braund

[22] See also BL, IOR/G/17/3 Part 2: ff.294-301 : 30 May 1769. Charter-party agreement between the Company and the owners, Charles Raymond & Andrew Moffatt, and master, Captain Patrick Maitland, of the *Bute*

[23] BL, IOR/B/60 EIC Court Book p.384, 17 December 1729

[24] Charles Daggett with Christopher (Kris) Shaffer *Diving for the Griffin* (Weidenfeld and Nicholson, London, 1990, ISBN 0 297 81063 4) p.53; See also Jean Sutton *Lords of the East* (op.cit.) p.47-52 and Appendix 8

[25] Jean Sutton *Lords of the East* (op.cit.) p.108

[26] John Keay *The Honourable Company* (Harper Collins paperback, London, 1993, ISBN 0 00 638072 7) p.237-9

[27] William Burney, ed., *Falconer's New Universal Dictionary of the Marine* (London, 1815)

[28] NA Will of Francis Steward, Gentleman of Weymouth and Melcombe Regis, Dorset, 21 June 1751 PROB 11/788; BL, IOR/B/69 EIC Court Book p.153, 7 November 1746

[29] BL, IOR/L/MAR/B/671D Ledger of *Dawsonne*, 1729/30; BL, IOR/L/MAR/B/653G Journal of *Derby (2)*, 1729/30

[30] "Reminiscences of a Voyage to and from China" from Paxton's *Horticultural Register and General Magazine* Vol 5 (1836) p.66, pp.98-9

[31] John Keay *The Honourable Company* (op. cit.) p.167

[32] BL, IOR/L/MAR/B/671D Ledger of *Dawsonne*, 1729/30; BL, IOR/L/MAR/B/653G Journal of *Derby (2)*, 1729/30; BL, IOR/L/MAR/B/578K Ledger of *Drake (1)*, 1728/9

[33] BL, IOR/B/62 EIC Court Book p.251 2 February 1733 Jones Raymond second charterparty to *Heathcote* with his father, and p.477 24 October 1733 second charterparty to *Duke of Dorset* with his father

[34] Plymouth and West Devon Record Office, 69/M/2/689, Morley of Saltram 24th & 25th December 1750, quotes lands formerly belonging to Charles Raymond...

[35] BL, IOR/L/MAR/B/510B Journal of *Princess of Wales (1)* 1732/3 shows Charles Raymond as third mate, IOR/L/MAR/B/510L (1) Ledger lists him as fourth mate. [Anthony Farrington *A Biographical Index of East India Company Maritime Service Officers 1600-1834* (British Library, 1999) gives details of his career, though in this case the entry of Third Mate *Prince of Wales (1)* 1732/3 is a mistake]

[36] BL, IOR/B/61 EIC Court Book p.332, ongoing 349, 371-5, July & August 1731

[37] BL, IOR/B/61 EIC Court Book p.375-7 18 August 1731, Anthony Farrington *A Biographical Index of East India Company Maritime Service Officers 1600-1834* (London, 1999)

[38] BL, IOR/B/62 EIC Court Book p. 251, 2 February 1733

[39] John Keay *The Honourable Company* (op. cit.) p.252-4

[40] BL, IOR/L/MAR/B/510B Journal of *Princess of Wales (1)* 1732/3

[41] Jean Sutton *Lords of the East* (op.cit.) p.59

[42] J G Parker *The Directors of the East India Company 1754-90* PhD thesis Edinburgh University, 1977, pp.213-5

[43] BL, IOR/B/63 EIC Court Book p.129, p.132 (4 Sept 1734), p.136, 226 (18 Dec 1734), 237; BL EIC Letter Book E/1/25 ff. 141-142v (3 September 1734)

[44] BL, IOR/B/63 EIC Court Book p.148, 20 September 1734

[45] BL, IOR/L/MAR/B/592G (1) Ledger of *Wager* 1734/5; BL, IOR/L/MAR/B/592A Journal of *Wager* 1734/5

[46] BL, IOR/L/MAR/B/510L (1) Ledger of *Princess of Wales (1)* 1732/3

[47] BL, IOR/L/MAR/B/510C Journal of *Princess of Wales (1)* 1734/5

[48] BL, IOR/L/MAR/B/510B Journal of *Princess of Wales (1)* 1732/3

[49] Included with *Derby's* Impress Book BL, IOR/L/MAR/B/653-I (3) is an account of loss
See also Jean Sutton *The East India Company's Maritime Service 1746-1834: Masters of the Eastern Seas* (Boydell Press 2010, ISBN 978-1-84383-583-7) p.47

[50] BL, IOR/L/MAR/B/592G (1) Ledger of *Wager* 1734/5

51 BL, IOR/B/64 EIC Court Book p.487 19 October 1737

52 BL, IOR/L/MAR/B/592B Journal of *Wager* 1737/8

53 BL, IOR/L/MAR/B/482E Journal of *Latham (2)* 1769/70

54 As a postscript to this story: in February 2009 an American salvage ship, *Odyssey Explorer*, located the wreck of the *Victory* in the middle of the English Channel (forty miles to the west of the Caskets) and it is hoped she can be raised and preserved one day.

55 ODNB on line Sir John Balchen, Burney newspaper collection at BL

56 A few men usually 'ran' on each voyage. Three men on the fourth voyage of the *Wager* 'ran' to join the *Deptford* Man of War while others were 'discharged' by the captain and were thus entitled to payment when they eventually returned to England.

57 BL, IOR/L/MAR/B/592H (1) Ledger of *Wager* 1737/8

58 The baptism register for William and his siblings records only that they were the son or daughter of Francis Webber 'Vicar of this parish', no mother's name is given. It seems likely their father was the 'Mr Francis Webber' who married 'Mrs Julian Heron' on May 30 1706 at Clyst St.Mary, near Exeter. She could have been the widowed sister of Anna Maria Tanner, mother of Charles Raymond, but more research is needed.

59 BL, IOR/B/65 EIC Court Book p.516 21 November 1739

60 Glyn Williams *The Prize of all the Oceans: The Triumph and Tragedy of Anson's Voyage Round the World* (Harper Collins 1999, paperback ISBN 00 0 653178 4)

61 Article in *Diver*, August 2007, p.82-4, and private communications with Chris Holt at that time. See also Rear Admiral C H Layman *The Wager Disaster: Mayhem, Mutiny and Murder in the South Seas* (Uniform Press 2015, ISBN 978-1-910065-50-1) which was published after this book was completed.

62 BL, IOR/B/66 EIC Court Book p.221, 13 February 1741

63 BL, IOR/B/62 EIC Court Book p.251, 2 February 1733

64 BL, IOR/L/MAR/B/592C Journal of *Wager* 1740/1

65 BL, IOR/L/MAR/B/489B Journal of *Earl of Oxford*, 1782/3

66 Harleian Society Vol.49 Parish Records of St. Stephen and St.Benet Sherehog, London p.162

67 NA Will of John Webster, Gentleman of St Leonard Shoreditch, Middlesex, 09 December 1724, PROB 11/600

68 On 16 August 1726, at St Clement Danes church in the Strand, William Guy of Stepney, Batchelor, married Judith Cooke of Bromley in Kent, Widow. It seems likely her designation as a 'Widow' was a politeness as she had five children, although it is possible she had been married previously. (Parish Register at Westminster archive)

69 E L S Horsburgh *Bromley, Kent, from the Earliest times to the Present Century* (1929) p.221

70 Gentleman's Magazine Vol.25 p.187 (1755)

71 Guildhall Library. Land Tax Assessments: Tower Division: Well Close Liberty, MS 6004.

72 NA Will of William Guy, Salter of London, 15 May 1755, PROB 11/815; NA Will of Judith Guy of Saint George in the East , Middx 19 December 1759 PROB 11/851. They were buried at St. Leonard's Shoreditch with Sarah's father, John Webster, and other members of the Webster family.

73 London Borough of Bromley Archives, ref.1115/A/I/i/e/9 dated 1723

74 The on-going work by Derek Morris and Ken Cozens, which has resulted in several excellent publications, has proved that Stepney, Wapping, Whitechapel and other areas previously thought

Living by the Sea

of as impoverished were also home to many wealthy and influential people. See http://www.singsurf.org/stepney/

[75] Baptism and burial registers, Wapping and West Ham

[76] BL, IOR/B/67 EIC Court Book p.506, 25 January 1744

[77] BL, IOR/L/MAR/B/592D Journal of *Wager* 1743/4

[78] BL, IOR/L/MAR/B/592D Journal of *Wager* 1743/4

[79] This conversion (x 200) roughly corresponds with the Bank of England calculator http://www.bankofengland.co.uk/education/Pages/resources/inflationtools/calculator/index1.aspx

[80] BL, IOR/B/69 EIC Court Book p.404, 28 October 1747; p.417, 18 November 1747

[81] BL, IOR/B/69 EIC Court Book p.160, 14 November 1746

[82] Burial of Joseph Tolson of Well Close Square, (no age), 8 Dec 1752 at St Mary, Whitechapel

[83] BL, IOR/L/MAR/B/592H(1) Ledger of *Wager* 1737/8

[84] BL, IOR/L/MAR/B/592J(1) Ledger of *Wager* 1743/4

[85] H V Bowen *Privilege and Profit: Commanders of East Indiamen as Private Traders, Entrepreneurs and Smugglers, 1760-1813* in International Journal of Maritime History, XIX, No.2, December 2007, p.50-51

[86] BL, IOR/B/64 EIC Court Book p.487, 19 October 1737

[87] Hertfordshire Archives ref. D/ER B 311/2

[88] BL, IOR/B/67 EIC Court Book p.341, 6 July 1743

[89] BL, IOR/B/67 EIC Court Book p.251, 25 February 1743

[90] BL, IOR/B/65 EIC Court Book p.403, 11 July 1739; p. 473; 26 September 1739; p.467, 19 September 1739;   p. 543, 19 December 1739; p.607, 12 March 1740

[91] For more on smuggling see H V Bowen *Privilege and Profit: Commanders of East Indiamen as Private Traders, Entrepreneurs and Smugglers, 1760-1813* in International Journal of Maritime History, XIX, No.2, December 2007, p.43-88

[92] BL, IOR/B/69 EIC Court Book p.243, 11 March 1747; p.250, 25 March 1747

[93] BL, IOR/L/AG/1/6/11 EIC Commercial Ledger p. 85 April 1737; IOR/L/AG/1/6/12 EIC Commercial Ledger p.219 June 1747; p.224 August 1747; conversion using the Bank of England calculator http://www.bankofengland.co.uk/education/Pages/resources/inflationtools/calculator/index1.aspx

Map from *The Environs of London:*
being an historical account of the towns, villages and hamlets within twelve miles of that capital
by the Rev. DANIEL LYSONS   Vol.4 1796
showing the villages to the east of the River Lea and their proximity to the ships yards at Blackwall

1. Gilbert Slater Junior
2. Henry Hinde, the Pelly family
3. Richard Warner, Charles Foulis
   Robert Preston, Pitt Collett
4. John Raymond
5. Charles Raymond
   William Webber, Andrew Moffatt
6. Henry Fletcher, Donald Cameron
7. John Williams, Pinson Bonham

PART TWO – FAMILY, FRIENDS AND FELLOW CAPTAINS
Upton and Ilford

Soon after he retired from the sea and started to manage ships, Charles moved to a more prestigious residence at Upton.[1] This is located east of the City, near West Ham, and at that time was a small hamlet consisting of a few select houses with attractive gardens or larger parks. The house and extensive estate at the south-east corner of Upton Cross was owned by Henry Hinde, father of Elizabeth Pelly, so it seems likely Charles's wife, Sarah, and Elizabeth, as two captain's wives, continued their (assumed) friendship. The parish registers of All Saints church, West Ham, show baptisms for the Raymonds and Pellys around this time. As has already been mentioned, the registers also record the burials of Anna Maria Raymond (2) who died aged thirteen months in August 1748 and Anna Maria Raymond (3) who died in April 1749 just seventeen days after her baptism.[2] There is also a burial recorded at West Ham on 6 April 1751 for a Charles Raymond. There is no indication if this was a child or an old man, but it is quite likely it was the only son born to Charles and Sarah, and he had been baptised elsewhere. However, it was at West Ham church that their eldest surviving child, a daughter named Sophia, was baptised on 6 May 1753. Charles was now forty and he had inherited the family property in Devon. Some, if not all, of this had been sold by this time and he probably used the money to finance the house at Upton and some of his shipping investments.[3]

In part two the family life of Charles and Sarah will be considered and the EIC connections of some new members of the extended family explained. In the 1750s and 1760s Charles developed his role as a PMO so that, for example, in the 1758/9 season he was PMO for a third of the ships chartered to carry EIC cargo out to the east. However, the journey was fraught with danger and what were physical risks at sea became financial risks for Charles as an investor. Six and a half per cent of the ships which traded for the EIC between 1727/8 and 1789/90 did not return. Statistics will illustrate Charles's importance as a leading member of the EIC shipping lobby where he managed ships alongside these friends and neighbours as they, in turn, retired from the sea and invested their fortunes. One group clustered around Charles in Ilford while a second group was centred nearby in Woodford Green. Some of the adventures which befell his friends and neighbours will be explained and extracts from ships' journals will be used to illustrate the dangers they faced. But the financial rewards could be enormous for those who invested in these voyages.

Sir Charles Raymond of Valentines and the East India Company

Valentine House

On 31 January 1753 Charles Raymond took over as PMO of the *Sandwich*. She had been managed by Robert Surman and Simon Rogers for her previous two voyages. However, Rogers died some time between 8 November 1752 and 17 January 1753, and Charles signed the charterparty for the 1753/4 voyage with Edmund Godfrey, a London merchant and brother of EIC Director Peter Godfrey.[A] Perhaps Charles visited Robert Surman in the course of their business dealings. Surman had lived at Valentine House in Ilford since 1724 but on 10 October 1754 Charles Raymond became the owner of this property. The sale paperwork stated that Sarah Webster was entitled to one fifth of the personal estate and one quarter of the real estate of her late father, John Webster, deceased. This was to be sold and the money given to her husband but her step-father, William Guy, took care to safeguard her interests. John Raymond and William Webber are also mentioned in the document as trustees.[4]

In the eighteenth century Ilford was part of the much larger parish of Barking which extended from the banks of the Thames northwards to Hainault Forest. The small village was a mile to the north of Barking town, but there were many estates set in the farming countryside to the north and east. The Valentine estate and its farmland extended across the area we know today as Gants Hill. From his front windows Charles would have had a good view of the magnificent house built nearby at Wanstead by Sir Richard Child (later Earl Tylney), one of the first Palladian houses in the country. At that time Valentine House was not quite as large as the one we know today: it was little changed from the building constructed with red (or grey) bricks sixty years earlier. Although three storeys, it probably had a more steeply sloping roof with dormer-windows for the attic rooms. The main entrance was on the south side of the building, facing towards Cranbrook Road. On 7 March 1755 Charles insured his "dwelling house, offices and stables" with the Sun Fire Office for not exceeding £2,000, and separate outbuildings were insured up to £300. The household goods in the house were covered up to £500.[5]

Although the house had not been substantially changed since it was built, the gardens had been transformed in the Rococo style. In the mid-1720s Robert Surman had created a canal, or long water, possibly employing Adam Holt to supervise the project. There was a grotto at the north-west end (nearest to Cranbrook Road) which had been built when the canal was created, or soon after. The southern grotto may also have been built by Surman, or if not, it was Charles who built it soon after he purchased the estate. It was decorated with conch and other shells which could well have been brought home

---

[A] Both Edmund and Peter Godfrey are commemorated on the Godfrey column in St. Mary's churchyard at Woodford where they are buried. (see page 83)

Family, Friends and Fellow Captains

from the East Indies. The alcove seat beside the canal was also decorated with shells. Charles took a keen interest in his garden and extended the estate, but this will be explained in detail later.

Ilford's evolving network

See Appendix 8 for the careers of some of the men mentioned

© *London Metropolitan Archives*

On 15 February 1755 Charles's friend William Webber married Elizabeth Webster at the church of St Mary le Bowe in the City of London. He was described as 'of the parish of St.Dunstan in the West' while Elizabeth was being married in her own parish church. Charles was one of the witnesses who signed the register, but there is no doubt his wife was also there as the bride was her sister.[6] William continued his career with two more voyages as captain of the *Harcourt* before he retired in September 1761. He was elected a Director of the EIC in 1762, serving until 1765. He represented the Raymond circle interests when John Raymond stepped down as a Director to continue as a PMO.

By this time Webber was renting the Highlands estate near Valentine House but on the west side of Cranbrook Road. The property was owned by Charles and he had recently rebuilt the house.[7] No children have been traced for William and Elizabeth Webber, and none are mentioned in their wills. William Webber junior who became captain of the *Oxford* 1758/9 was mentored by William Webber senior and must have been related (probably a nephew). He served as third mate on the *Harcourt (1)* 1752/3, before William and Elizabeth were married.

41

Valentine House, 1799

Highlands, 1798
Both pictures inserted into a copy of Volume 4 of The Environs of London
by Rev. D. Lysons (1796) © London Metropolitan Archives

Family, Friends and Fellow Captains

By the time the Webbers were married Charles and Sarah had another daughter, Juliana, who must have been born in 1754, although her baptism has not been found. Their last child, Anna Maria, was baptised on 20 January 1756 at West Wycombe in Buckinghamshire. There does not seem to be any family connection with the area so perhaps the baby was born early while her mother was travelling in the area. Having lost so many little ones, it is understandable the christening would not have been delayed – particularly if the baby was premature. The ceremony would have taken place in the old church, or the fifteenth century 'Church Loft' in the High Street, as it was not until 1763 that the hilltop church of St Lawrence, with its design based on the Temple of the Sun at Palmyra, was reopened for worship.[8]

Sarah and Elizabeth had two surviving step-sisters and the eldest, Ann Guy, also married an East India captain, John Williams. He was born in Dorset around 1723, so was about eleven years older than his wife. He came from a family long established at Herringston, south of Dorchester, where the ancient family home is now listed Grade II*. John Williams's mother died while he was very young, but his father remarried and had a total of five sons. Robert (1734-1814) and Stephen (1739-1805) will also appear in this story later.

John Williams was about ten years younger than Charles and he started his career with the EIC as fifth mate on the *York (1)* 1743/4, when Charles was on his last voyage as a captain. His first voyage was to Madras and then on to China, two places which cannot have been like anything he had seen before. On the return voyage they stopped at St Helena, arriving on 24 May 1745, and the last part of his journey must also have been a memorable experience for the fifth mate. The *York* left St Helena on 10 July in convoy with thirteen other East Indiamen, under the command of Captain Richard Crabb of the *Durrington*, and it must have been an amazing sight to be among the fleet of ships under full sail in mid-Atlantic. Between 15-17 September the fourteen East Indiamen anchored in the safety of Galway Bay on the west coast of Ireland. Here they waited for an escort of four Royal Navy Men of War and finally arrived at the Downs on 19-20 December, where they were boarded by the Press Gang.[9] One of the ships in the convoy was *Prince William (2)* under Captain William Webber, who had taken over when Captain Thomas Langworth died.

Williams served as third mate, second mate and first mate before he married Ann Guy at St Paul's, Covent Garden, on 7 December 1754. He was then taken on to captain the *Hector (2)* by his brother-in-law, Charles Raymond, and served in that capacity for four voyages before retiring from the sea in April 1768, aged about 45.

John and Ann had a number of children, and those born after 1765 were baptised at Loughton which suggests they made their home there at that time. In the spring of 1772 the family moved to a prestigious home at Aldborough Hatch. The house was probably on the site of the present Aldborough Hall farmhouse and the property would have stretched down to include the listed gazebo on the south side of the present 'Dick Turpin' pub. Some of the old brick walls of the farm enclosure between the farmhouse and the pub may date back to that time.

Sadly, John did not live to enjoy bringing up his family in this rural retreat for long. He died in June 1774, aged 51, and was buried at St Leonard's, Shoreditch, with the Webster and Guy families. From his will it is clear he had already started to make himself known in a similar way to Charles who he describes as 'my brother-in-law and faithful friend'. He mentions his third part share in a 'Rope Ground at Blackwall Causeway' in which Charles was also part owner. Williams had become PMO of the *Nassau* and had shares in several other ships trading with the East Indies and he requested that his executors, Charles Raymond and Henry Fletcher, continue to manage his investments to the advantage of his children until the eldest son reached the age of twenty-one. His will also mentions his involvement in banking and investments in the 'Manchester Fire Office'. In these ventures he was also in partnership with Charles and Henry Fletcher, as will be explained later.[10]

Like Charles, William Webber and John Williams, Henry Fletcher had worked his way up through the ranks serving on East Indiamen until he became a captain. He was born around 1727, the seventh son of John Fletcher of Clea Hall, Cumberland, and served as fifth and then fourth mate before coming under the wing of PMO Charles Raymond as second mate on the *Salisbury (1)* 1752/3. He then sailed for Charles as first mate on the *Harcourt (1)* 1755/6, with William Webber as his captain, and finished with two voyages as captain himself.

Fletcher returned to the Downs at the end of his last voyage at the end of May 1766, when about 39, and presumably returned to his family seat as he was elected MP for Cumberland in 1768. He continued to represent Cumberland at Parliament until shortly before he died. On 20 October 1768 he married Catherine, daughter of John Lintot of Southwater in Sussex. The following year he was elected a Director of EIC and he served in that role until 1783.

By 1774 a Henry Fletcher Esq was paying rates on a property in Ilford which he had either purchased from, or rented from, Charles Raymond, to the south of Valentine House. It seems reasonable to assume this was the retired captain. He continued to pay the rates until 1781 when Donald Cameron took over this considerable estate.[11] During this time Fletcher was working in a banking partnership with Charles alongside his other commitments in parliament and at the Court of Directors of the EIC. Henry

Family, Friends and Fellow Captains

Fletcher was created a baronet on 20 May 1782 and he died on 29 March 1807, aged about eighty, at Ashley Park in Walton-on-Thames, Surrey.[12]

With retired captains William Webber and Henry Fletcher as such immediate neighbours and John Williams not far away, they must have enjoyed some happy evenings when they dined together. A new interest would have been added to their social gatherings when Crisp Molineaux (1730-1792) of Garboldisham Hall in Norfolk built a house on land owned by relatives at Ley Street (adjacent to Fletcher's property) in the early 1770s. He was elected as the Whig MP for the Castle Rising constituency in 1771 and then for King's Lynn in 1774 which he represented until 1790. He named his house after his Castle Rising Constituency, not because it in any way resembled a castle. Molineaux had been born in St.Kitts, West Indies, and was apparently quite a colourful character.[13]

Charles Raymond as a Principal Managing Owner

Signing the charterparty agreement for the *Wager* on 18 November 1747 with Joseph Tolson was the start of Charles Raymond's forty-year career as the Principal Managing Owner of ships sailing for the East India Company. Tolson also signed with him as PMO for the *Duke of Dorset (2)* 1747/8 a week later and the *Godolphin (3)* 1747/8 on 9 December 1747.[14] Charles did not manage any ships in the following season but for 1749/50 he signed as PMO for *Shaftesbury (2)* with Edward Bookey as the second signature and William Bookey as captain [15] At the end of 1750 Charles became PMO of four ships, three with Joseph Tolson as the second signature and the other was backed by Richard Crabb. He had recently retired as captain of the East Indiaman *Durrington* and may have known Charles while they were at sea on Raymond's last voyage. It was 1757 before Crabb signed as first signature but he had been back-up for ten other voyages by then, with different PMOs.

As the Principal Managing Owner Charles was responsible for liaising with the EIC Court of Directors, provisioning the ship, working with the captain to engage the crew etc.[16] He was not necessarily the major investor but would be their representative. In some cases the PMO would commission a ship for which he sought investors, alternatively he may have been approached by someone who had the finance and needed a PMO to take charge. Often the investors wanted to build a ship for their own family member to captain. However, investing in shipping was a classic example of not 'putting all your eggs in one basket'. It was much better financially to buy an eighth share of eight ships.

Sir Charles Raymond of Valentines and the East India Company

At times of war the government issued East Indiamen with 'letters of marque' which gave them legal protection should they engage in enemy action and, as government papers, many have survived and can be found today in the National Archives. They give a full list of the investors in the ship concerned and give greater insight into the workings of the Raymond circle. For example, Francis Salvador and Captain Joseph Tolson signed the charterparty agreement for the *Wager (2)* on her 1743/4 voyage, under Captain Charles Raymond. The full list of owners from the letter of marque [17] was 'Matthew Martin, Francis Salvador, Thomas Lockyer, Richard Binion, Samuel Clayton, Richard Mickelfield, Jonathan Micklethwaite, Nicholas and Thomas Crisps, Joseph Salvador, Timothy Motteux, Joseph Tolson and John Raymond of London, merchants.' Matthew Martin was related to Charles's uncle Hugh Raymond by marriage, Richard Mickelfield was a retired captain and fellow PMO who worked alongside Francis Salvador. Thomas Lockyer was a significant PMO in the 1740s and early 50s. Joseph Tolson was a retired captain and PMO and John Raymond was Charles's cousin.

Thirteen years later, Charles Raymond and Richard Crabb signed the charterparty agreement for the *Norfolk (1)* on her 1756/7 voyage,[18] under Captain Pinson Bonham. The full list of owners from the letter of marque [19] was 'Richard Crabb, Charles Raymond, Charles Savage, Richard Benion, John Legg and Edward Page of London.' An Edward Page had signed as second charterparty for voyages of the *Anson* 1746/7 and *Lord Anson* 1749/50, Captain Charles Foulis. He signed again for the next voyage of the *Lord Anson*, and as second charterparty to Charles (for the *Sandwich*) shortly before he died early in 1753, so this may have been his son. Richard Benion may have been the retired Governor of Madras, Richard Benyon, who had returned to England in 1744 and had purchased the Newbury estate in Ilford in 1747. This shared a boundary with Charles's Valentine property.

The following season Charles Raymond and Shearman Godfrey signed the charterparty agreement for the new ship *Osterley (1)* on her 1757/8 voyage, under Captain Frederick Vincent.[20] In this instance, it may not have been a case of the Raymond circle working together. The full list of owners from the letter of marque [21] was 'Sir Richard Lyttleton, Francis Child, Jonathan Ewer and Charles Raymond of London, merchants.' Francis Child (1735-63) MP was the owner of Osterley House at Isleworth at that time and Sir Richard Lyttleton was a soldier and an MP who lived nearby. Child was a partner in Child & Co. bank and owned nearly £33,000 worth of East India stock.[22] Perhaps he had arranged the finance and just required Raymond to manage the voyage. Shearman Godfrey signed at least ten times as second signature to Charles for EIC voyages. He was a wealthy distiller who lived at Limehouse but he was not related to Captain

Family, Friends and Fellow Captains

Benjamin Godfrey, nor to Peter, Edmund and Thomas Godfrey of Woodford. It is significant that although he signed as the second PMO he is not listed as an owner in the letter of marque.

Seasons 1747/8 – 1787/8		
PMO for 10 or more voyages	Total	%
Raymond, Sir Charles	113	12.36
Durand, John	61	6.67
Hallett, John	44	4.81
Foulis, Charles	38	4.16
Crabb / Boulton, Richard	32	3.50
Willson, George	26	2.84
Raymond, John	22	2.41
Moffatt, Andrew	20	2.19
Preston, Robert	20	2.19
Buggin, Barrington	19	2.08
Braund, Samuel	18	1.97
Williams, Robert	18	1.97
Hotham, Sir Richard	17	1.86
Hume, Alexander	16	1.75
Lane, Thomas	16	1.75
Boulton, Henry	15	1.64
Moffatt, William	14	1.53
Slater, Gilbert, Sen	14	1.53
Neave, Sir Richard	11	1.20
Black, William	10	1.09
Dent, William	10	1.09
Lockyer, Thomas	10	1.09
Newte, Thomas	10	1.09
Rogers, Simon	10	1.09

Charles Raymond was the PMO of 113 voyages of the 914 made by East Indiamen in the forty-one years between retiring as a captain in 1747 and his death in 1788.[23] (This excludes sixty-six voyages made by Company ships.) This is almost twice the number of any other PMO. Of these gentlemen, several were associated with Charles Raymond: retired captain Charles Foulis lived at Woodford; retired captain Richard Crabb (later Boulton) became related when his son Henry married Charles's daughter Juliana; John Raymond was a cousin; Andrew Moffatt was a close neighbour in Ilford; retired captain Robert Preston lived at Woodford. Of course some men, like Preston, managed more voyages after 1788, while others like Simon Rogers were similarly involved before 1747 while Charles was at sea.

Charles Raymond was the second signature on many occasions to people like his cousin John Raymond, his fellow captain Richard Crabb (Boulton), and Crabb's son Henry Boulton who became Charles's son-in-law. He clearly had a very close association with Andrew Moffatt, each signing first or second signature for different voyages of the same ships.

Two other men also managed large numbers of ships between 1747/8 and 1787/8. John Durand is not shown as having a career at sea on East Indiamen, but he is noted in Court Books as 'Captain John Durand of London, Mariner' because he had commanded ships trading in the Eastern Seas under licence from the EIC. He is shown as PMO for sixty-one voyages between 1760/1 – 1786/7. He died at his home in Carshalton in 1788 and his will listed several 'natural or reputed' children.[24] John Durand junior (born *c*.1748), Captain of the *Northington* 1776/7 (PMO John Durand), was his son, as was John Hodson Durand who served as second mate on the East Indiaman *Contractor* (PMO John Durand), and who took over as PMO of a number of ships when his father died.

John Hallett had served on four voyages for EIC between 1736 and 1743, two as captain, and he is shown as PMO for forty-four voyages between 1750/1 and 1764/5. It seems likely that he was the John Hallett who married Elizabeth Pinnell on 2 February 1742/3, shortly before he set out on his last voyage when he was captain of the *Harwicke* (1) 1742/3. The Pinnell family were also heavily involved with EIC. Richard Pinnell senior had been Captain of *Susanna (2)* 1709/10, 1712/3 & 1715/6 and became PMO while Richard and William Pinnell became captains alongside Elizabeth's husband. John Hallett died early in 1765 leaving children under the age of twenty-one.[25] His brother James Hallett, who was PMO for the *Clinton* 1752/3 – 1761/2, was approved to sign the charterparty for the ship *Hardwicke* in John's place on 6 March 1765.

It is likely that Durand and Hallett each had their own group of investors and colleagues. With regard to the Raymond circle, it is worth noting that in the 1758/9 season, of twenty-four ships which sailed for the EIC three were company ships and of the remaining twenty-one, seven were managed by Charles. By this time William Webber and John Williams were his brothers-in-law and established as captains. Henry Fletcher was employed as a captain for the first time but had served on his previous two voyages, as second and then first mate, on ships managed by Charles. Bernard Forrester had served under Charles on his last voyage as captain of the *Wager*.

It was in this season that Charles launched a new ship, named *Valentine* after his home.

PMO	Second signature	Ship	Sailing	Captain
(	Moffatt, Andrew	Ajax	1758/9	Lindsay, George
(	Crabb, Capt Richard	Duke of Dorset (2)	1758/9	Forrester, Bernard
Raymond, (	Godfrey, Shearman	Godolphin (3)	1758/9	Hutchinson, William
Charles (	Godfrey, Shearman	Harcourt (1)	1758/9	Webber, William
(	Crabb, Capt Richard	Hector (2)	1758/9	Williams, John
(	Crisp, Nicholas	Stormont (1)	1758/9	Fletcher, Henry
(	Godfrey, Shearman	Valentine (1)	1758/9	Fernell, William

See Appendix 10 for details of the owners for some voyages in the 1766/7 and later seasons.

In the table on page 48, all those signing as second signature were close members of the Raymond circle and had been the main signature for at least one voyage.

East Indiaman Dutton (1781) taking a pilot off Dover by Robert Dodd
© *National Maritime Museum, Greenwich, London*

Risk and Loss

As a captain Charles had faced physical dangers, but as a PMO it was his investment which was at risk. The charterparty agreement stated what financial penalties would be demanded for each delay to the agreed timescale. Although loss of the ship was the major risk taken by investors, damage could involve considerable expense in repairs and often occurred in English waters. A young gentleman passenger on board the *Boscawen* 1748/9, wrote that coming round in the ship from Gravesend to Deal 'often proved the worst part of the voyage, not only from the confused state things then are in, but the danger of running upon some of the sands and shoals.'[26] Having left the safety of the Thames, the ships would congregate off the coast near Deal to await their final instructions from East India House and a favourable wind. Indeed the Company employed its own agent at Deal to handle the business matters of its ships at anchor

Sir Charles Raymond of Valentines and the East India Company

there.[27] The sea between Deal and Ramsgate, known as The Downs, was a good anchorage, not too deep and not too shallow, protected by the Goodwin Sands from the easterly wind. An area of around fifty square miles could, if necessary, accommodate the entire British fleet and hundreds of vessels could lie anchored for weeks. However, it could be treacherous in an extreme storm, which might drive a ship so hard the anchor rope broke. When such a storm came, many ships might have taken shelter and were thus a danger to each other as they drifted out of control.[28]

At low tide exposed sandbanks are visible from the shore. If a ship should come aground on the sandbank, the waves wash the sand from beneath the hull and gradually it sinks, giving the Sands the name 'Ship Swallower'. By the same token the sifting nature of the sandbank means that a shipwreck can be uncovered after many years under the sand.

Returning home up the English Channel also had its dangers from the sheer volume of shipping. James Main, head gardener to Gilbert Slater of Knotts Green, later wrote about his expedition to China on *Tritan (3)* 1792/3 and it makes fascinating reading. Apparently, the final part of his voyage nearly ended in disaster, as he explains:

> When we left St.Helena on 1st of July... the fleet was increased by the *Sampson*, sixty-four, and the *Assistance* fifty, gun ships, besides several South Sea whalers...

> When the fleet arrived off the Western Isles, the Spanish and Portuguese frigates fired their salutes and left us, we standing on for the chops of the English Channel, which we made on the 5th of September, 1794.

> At sunset on the 4th, the greater part of the fleet were in sight, proceeding up the channel with a fine top-gallant-sail breeze, with thick cloudy weather and light drizzling rain. At the second hour of the middle watch (two o'clock in the morning), the officer and men who had the "look-out" on the forecastle cried, "A sail on the lar-board bow;" and in an instant afterward the same voice cried, "A sail on the starboard bow;" and in the next instant a dreadful shock was felt. All was consternation and dismay. Two-thirds of the crew and officers were asleep – all was darkness and uncertainty. The thundering noise of the best bower cable running out – the noise of the officers of both ships giving orders – the calls of our own officers to sound the well, and fire signals of distress – the rubbing and crashing of the two ships against each other's sides – was altogether a scene for half an hour which cannot be described. At last our ship was brought up in forty-seven fathoms water, which brought us head to wind; and after much destruction of the rigging of both ships, the stranger fell off, leaving part of her rigging on our deck. We then found that we had been run foul of by the *Latona* frigate belonging to the grand fleet, then beating down the channel on a cruize, after repairing the damage sustained in the glorious action of the previous 1st of June.

> When it was found that the ship made no water, orders were given that the fore-tackles be got to the *night-heads* to secure the fore-mast, now deprived of its fore-stays (as the *Latona*

Family, Friends and Fellow Captains

had carried away the bowsprit, figure-head, both cat-heads, and one anchor which brought us up). Before, however, the foremast could be secured, or the cable could be cut to get the ship again before the wind – the ship riding heavily – the foremast went by the board, falling directly back on the mainmast. The fall of the whole now appeared inevitable. The men on the main and mizzen tops were desired to come down, and every one on deck were loudly called upon to take care of themselves. At last the mainmast also went by the board, carrying with it the mizzen-mast and every particle of standing rigging abaft. The thundering noise of such a weight of masts, yards, rigging, and sails, (which were clewed up, but not furled,) all falling in-board, was most appalling. A deep silence of a few seconds only succeeded, but neither groans of the dying, nor cries of the wounded were heard; for although the deck was crowded with people not an instant before the fall of the masts, not a man was hurt, the greater number having rushed into the captain's apartments while the masts were falling.

Two or three men who lingered in the main-top came down there-with, but luckily falling between the hen-coops on the poop among the cordage, escaped with only very slight bruises. The corner of the main-top was forced through the poop-deck, and nearly killed an officer who was nearly under the place. The whole of this catastrophe happened in little more than half an hour, and from the state of a towering well-founded ship, was reduced to an unmanageable but still sound hulk, covered with wreck.

At daylight we found ourselves directly off Plymouth, and in the midst of the grand fleet under Lord Howe. Several other Indiamen, as well as King's ships, disabled like ourselves, were near; but the greater part of old companions had passed up the channel. Lord Howe, after hailing us and learning the particulars of our disaster, ordered us to be towed into Torbay by the *Venerable* seventy-four, Captain Sir John Ord, to which place the whole of the grand fleet and disabled Indiamen returned, and anchored on the evening of the same day...

During a fortnight's stay in Torbay, the ship was re-rigged under jury-masts, and prepared to proceed to the river Thames, but was towed the whole way by the *Assistance* fifty-gun ship...

On doubling the South Foreland, we were desired to lay aside our sailing dress, and resume our *go-a-shore* habiliments. The press-gangs were then on the alert, and the officers knew that the crew would be mustered and *thinned* on our arrival at Gravesend. No sooner had we cast anchor, and the towing hawser of the *Assistance* thrown off, than the first lieutenant of that ship (our old friendly acquaintance!) came with a boat's crew, and selected the *elite* of our company; the Lieutenant thinking he had the best right to those able seamen whose skill and fearless actions he had often witnessed. This scene was distressing; for we saw many worthy men – quarter-masters and others – torn from the outstretched arms of their wives and friends on shore.[29]

The loss of a ship could mean the ruin of an investor if insurance had not been taken out.

From the journal of the Suffolk 1755/6 © The British Library Board, L/MAR/B/397D

EIC Ships which did not return home in the seasons 1727/8 - 1789/90

Returned	1254	93.51%
Burnt or blown up	10	0.75%
Lost or abandoned	49	3.65%
Wrecked	11	0.82%
Captured	17	1.27%
TOTAL	1341	100.0%

1379 voyages were made by East Indiamen between 1727/8 and 1789/90 but thirty-eight of the ships were sent to remain abroad.[30] They could be sold for use in the coastal trade. Charles purchased the ship *Prince of Wales (3)* from Henry Hinde at Lloyd's Coffee House on 1 February 1764 and this was sent to remain in Bengal.[31]

Of the remaining 1341 voyages made only 93.5 per cent of the ships returned home with 5.2 per cent burnt, wrecked or lost. Much of the time the ships were in danger from enemy action and with long periods at sea the captains could not always be certain who was friend and who was foe when they reached land! It was common practice for East

Family, Friends and Fellow Captains

Indiamen to travel in small convoys for their mutual protection and the EIC's Secret Committee issued sealed orders to aid their protection. Seventeen (1.3 per cent) of the ships were captured due to European warfare.

On his last voyage Charles was lucky to leave Madras when he did, as in mid-October 1746 it was taken by the French and was under their control until 21 August 1749. Three East Indiamen were captured by the French around this time: *Princess Mary (1)* 1744/5 was captured at Madras on 10 September 1746, *Princess Amelia (2)* 1745/6 was decoyed and taken on 17 February 1747, the day after she arrived at Madras, and the *Anson (1)* 1746/7 was captured off Bombay on 2 September 1747. Much later, five ships were captured together on 9 August1780 by the Franco-Spanish fleet. The only ship owned by Charles which was captured was the *Ajax* 1758/9. She was returning after her first voyage when she was captured by the French warship *Proteus* off the Scilly Isles on 6 March 1761. She was purchased from her captors by the French East India Company, for whom she sailed until 1776.[32]

None of the ten ships shown as burnt or blown up was owned by Charles Raymond, although his cousin John Raymond was PMO of the *Duke of Kingston* which caught fire and eventually blew up in 1783. It is likely that Charles had a share in the ship and would have lost some money. In this case travelling in convoy did not prevent the financial disaster but it helped to limit the loss of life.

A great many ships are shown as 'Lost'. Some set off from a port, lost contact with any companions, and were just never seen again. Given the vast ocean and tropical storms and their lack of modern navigation equipment, this is not surprising. Almost every port had an element of danger in the approach whether from rocks, tidal currents or sand banks and mud. At least six ships were lost in mud of the Hugli River outside Calcutta in this period. John Raymond was PMO of the *Verelst* 1769/70 which was lost near Mauritius on 25 April 1771. His cousin Charles was the second charterparty signature for this ship so would also have suffered financially from the disaster.

Eleven ships are shown as 'wrecked' which implies they foundered on rocks, although this is not always the case. The *Duke of Cumberland* 1749/50 was washed onto a sandy beach on the coast of Senegal. Charles Raymond was PMO of the *Lord Clive* 1766/7 which was driven onto the shore south of Boulogne. The *Doddington* 1754/5, *Colebrooke* 1777/8 and *Grosvenor (2)* 1779/80 were all wrecked off the coast of South Africa, *Colebrooke* near Cape Town, the other two ships around on the eastern side of the southern tip of Africa. Charles's ship *Valentine (2)* 1776/7 was wrecked on rocks off the island of Sark when returning home up the English Channel.

A famous and tragic wreck in this period was the *Halsewell* 1785/6 which was broken up on the cliffs of the Dorset coast near St Albans Head, south-west of Swanage. It was

Sir Charles Raymond of Valentines and the East India Company

early in January 1786 and she was at the start of her voyage when she was hit by a bad storm causing damage to the ship. She tried to return to Portsmouth but foundered on the cliffs with great loss of life. At least 160 people died, including the captain and his two daughters, who were passengers on the ship. Mercifully some souls were saved, including about seventy-four people who were rescued by being hauled up the cliffs by a team from a local quarry, who worked tirelessly for many hours.[33]

Charles Raymond seems to have been a lucky owner as of the 113 ships he managed, just the three mentioned above (*Ajax* 1758/9, *Lord Clive* 1766/7 and *Valentine (2)* 1776/7) did not return home.[34] Retired Captain Richard Mickelfield was not so lucky as he had been charterparty signatory, along with Francis Salvador, for both the *Princess Mary (1)* 1744/5 which was captured at Madras on 10 September 1746 and *Princess Amelia (2)* 1745/6 which was decoyed and taken on 17 February 1747.

On the first voyage traced for Richard Mickelfield, as first mate of the *Marlborough (2)* 1711/2 under Captain Matthew Martin, they survived an attack by three French warships. After another voyage on the *Marlborough* under Matthew Martin, he took over as captain himself for the next four voyages of *Marlborough (2)* and *(3)*. It appears that Hugh Raymond was involved as PMO for at least some of these voyages and had helped Mickelfield financially in 1718.[35]

Mickelfield's last voyage ended with the ship being destroyed by fire in the Thames as she was being unloaded at the end of her voyage. The EIC Court of Directors agreed it was 'an unhappy accident' and did not make any financial penalty for the cargo lost. He then became a PMO, signing the charterparty for *Marlborough (4)* 1731/2 with Jones Raymond. The charterparty agreement for the first voyage of the *Wager* 1734/5, Captain Charles Raymond, was signed by Hugh Raymond with Captain Richard Mickelfield.[36]

The captain of the *Marlborough (4)* 1731/2 and 1734/5 was Thomas Hunt. He acted as a mentor to Richard Mickelfield junior who served as purser and then fourth mate on these two voyages of the *Marlborough* and then became captain of the *Colchester (2)*, following a similar career path to Charles Raymond. Sadly, he died at sea on his second voyage as a captain, on 8 October 1743, on a voyage to Borneo. Meanwhile, after two voyages as captain, Thomas Hunt retired from the sea and married Richard Mickelfield's daughter Catherine. He was the second charterparty signature with his father-in-law for the *Duke of Cumberland (2)* 1749/50 which was lost off Cape Verd. Richard Mickelfield died soon after this, leaving Thomas Hunt to manage his ships which he continued to do with Francis Salvador (who died in 1754) and then his son Joseph Salvador. Mickelfield left considerable property on his death, some of which went to the children of Thomas and Catherine Hunt, on the condition that they take the surname of their grandfather.[37]

Family, Friends and Fellow Captains

The Hunt Mickelfield Memorial in the churchyard at St Marys, Woodford, and the bell inscribed as the gift of 'Lady Elianor Rowe' anno 1668

Woodford's East India connections

As has been shown, several of Charles's relatives and friends lived near him at Ilford, but there was another cluster of men with connections to the East India Company nearby at Woodford. This was a more prestigious area than Ilford with more luxury mansions for the élite of the community.

William, son of Thomas and Catherine Hunt, was baptised 2 May 1743 at St Dunstan and All Saints, Stepney, and also had a swift rise to captain the *Tilbury* 1767/8 on his third voyage. A few months before he went to sea his uncle, William Hunt, who had been a governor of the Bank of England, died in April 1767. Young William inherited Woodford Hall from his uncle and while he was away at sea on his next (and last) voyage he had the Hall rebuilt. He is shown as paying the land tax on this considerable estate in 1782 but it appears he also owned property at Tilbury and he sold Woodford Hall in 1790. When he died in 1826 he was buried in his uncle's vault at St Mary's, Woodford under the name of William Hunt Mickelfield.

William had a younger sister Mary who was married at St. Mary's in 1771 while her brother was at sea. Her husband was Nicholas Caesar Corsellis of Gwynne House at Woodford Bridge (now the Prince Regent Hotel) who also had EIC connections. He was the great-grandson of Sir John Child of Surat who died on board ship near Bombay in 1690 leaving a fortune of £100,000. In his will he is described as 'Generall for the East India Company's affairs in India, Persia etc'. His son, Sir Caesar Child of

Sir Charles Raymond of Valentines and the East India Company

Claybury, (grandfather of Nicholas Corsellis) had lived in India and was only twelve when his father died, so was taken under the wing of Sir Josiah Child (1630-1699) of Wanstead until he was old enough to be married in 1698.

Sir Josiah Child was extremely influential with EIC towards the end of the seventeenth century, both as a major share holder and by serving as a Director and then as either Deputy Governor or Governor (Chairman) between 1681-1690.[38] He had argued in London that the future of the EIC depended on operating from secure bases with adequate firepower and efficient government. At the same time Sir John Child [B] had waged war in Bombay causing considerable damage to the EIC as a result. Much earlier, in 1614, King James I appointed Sir Thomas Roe Ambassador to Jehangir, Mogul Emperor of Hindustan, in north-west India. He was instructed to negotiate a commercial treaty for the East India Company and his skills in diplomacy laid the foundations for the expansion of British India. Unlike the Childs, he took the view that 'if you will profitt, seek it at sea and in a quiett trade; for without controversy it is an errour to effect garrisons and land warrs in India.' In 1640 Roe became a member of the Privy Council and in that year he acquired the manor of Woodford. He died four years later and was buried at St.Mary's Church on 8 November 1644. The bell donated by his widow is still used today.[39]

There were also EIC administrators living in the area in the eighteenth century. Sir John Salter, who lived near Whipps Cross (Leyton), served as a Director for at least twelve years until his death in 1744.[40] Harts House at Woodford Green was the home of Richard Warner (1713-1775), an exact contemporary of Charles. Warner was qualified as a barrister but his family wealth meant that he could enjoy life indulging his various interests. He had an extensive library with many rare books but his main passion was botany and he cultivated rare plants in his garden at Woodford. He was a Director of the East India Company 1760-63 serving on their legal and accounts committees.[41] William Hornby (1723-1803) had served as Governor of Bombay from 1771 until 1784 before he purchased Higham Hills (now Woodford High School) at Woodford in December 1785. Although Charles retired from the sea before Hornby was established in India, they may have met socially and chatted about their experiences when Charles was elderly.

Charles may also have enjoyed the company of retired captain Jeffrey Jackson (*c.*1730-1802) who lived at Woodford Bridge. He had a slower rise than Charles up the EIC ladder, serving as fifth, third, second and then twice as first mate before becoming a captain. He commanded the *Speke* on three voyages 1768/9, 1770/1 and 1773/4. His

---

[B] No relationship between Sir Josiah Child and Sir John Child has been traced, nor with the Child banking family.

Family, Friends and Fellow Captains

wife Dorothy mentions in her diary that she had a 'black boy' named Harry Speke who, presumably, had come from India with her husband. Jeffrey Jackson's first experience as a PMO ended in disaster as his ship *Fortitude (1)* 1780/1 was captured by the French on her maiden voyage. He was more successful with the *Manship (1)* which was launched in 1785 and made six voyages under his management.

Charles had an uneventful career at sea in comparison with some of his fellow captains. Three East India captains lived at Woodford Green very close to Richard Warner at Harts House. In the 1770s Captain Charles Foulis resided in a large house close to Harts, while Captain Pitt Collett lived in a more modest house nearby.[42] Captain Robert Preston later lived at the property which had been the home of Charles Foulis, his mentor, and later his business partner and friend. There must have been some fascinating conversations at Harts if Foulis, Preston, Collett and Warner met together for a meal, as the three captains all had some excitement in their careers. It is likely all of these men and their wives would have visited Charles at Valentine House occasionally, for business and for pleasure. Charles signed as second charterparty for Foulis on at least two occasions, while he was PMO for ships on which Preston and Collett served as captain. They were all part of the EIC network.

Picture of Harts House, Woodford, from the 'Gentleman's Magazine' 1789

Charles Foulis (*c*.1714 – 1783)

Charles Foulis was descended from an ancient Scottish family, and he too became wealthy from his career with the EIC, working alongside Charles as a PMO when he retired from the sea. Although just a year or so younger than Charles, Foulis did not have family connections to get him off to an early start. Charles was already serving on his second voyage as captain of the *Wager* before Foulis started on his first (recorded) voyage with EIC. This was as third mate on the *Lynn* in 1738/9, returning home from India in September 1740. He was then aged about 26 so probably wanted to put down roots in London. On 12 March 1741 he married Jennell Shiels at St Mary Aldermanbury and then six months later he returned to sea.

His next voyage was quite an adventure. On 11 December 1741 he left England as first mate on the *Harrington* 1741/2 bound for St Helena, Bombay and China under Captain Robert Jenkins. Within five weeks there was fever among the soldiers on board and it quickly proved fatal. By 27 January five men had died, fever was raging in the ship and there was also a touch of scurvy. Cleanliness on board was becoming a problem as some of the soldiers had only the clothes they were wearing. Soon the fever spread to the crew and there were more deaths. A total of twelve men died before they reached St Helena on 22 March. They stayed until 10 May so that they could thoroughly clean the ship.

They continued their journey, calling at Johanna (Comoro Islands, north of Madagascar) which was a regular 'refuelling' stop for East Indiamen. The king, royal family and their retinue dined on board *Harrington*, which must have been a memorable experience. They arrived at Bombay at the end of July, unloaded their cargo, and carried out the usual maintenance tasks on the ship. They then sailed down to Tellicherry, just as Charles had done nine years earlier as third mate on the *Princess of Wales*.

However, unlike Charles, they had an encounter with Angria on the return voyage, while in company with *Salisbury*. Foulis wrote in his journal on 17 November 1742 'At 2PM engaged the enemy being the pyrate Angria's fleet. The *Salisbury* and us fired pretty smartly for two or three hours but they kept at such a distance that not one in 20 [of our shot] did them any harm. Fired away twixt 150 and 200 shott. We sustained no damage, some time in the night our Antagonists left us.'

They returned to Bombay a week later, but on 18 December 1742 Foulis recorded the death of his captain. 'This evening abt 6 died Captain Robert Jenkins of a feaver and flux, the eleventh day of his illness.' He was buried with military honours in Bombay, and so Charles Foulis took over as captain of the *Harrington*.

Family, Friends and Fellow Captains

The next part of their voyage took them northward to Surat, then back southward and in February, near Goa, they saw a vessel in shore in a damaged condition. She proved to be an English country ship taken some years previously by Angria, with 15 hands on board but no cargo. Now regarded as belonging to the enemy, she was towed to Bombay by *Harrington*, as a 'prize'.

Foulis had visited the west coast of India on the *Lynn* but when they left India bound for China early in May, this was a new experience for the inexperienced captain. After three weeks they reached 'Pul Verua' (Poolo Varella, a small island just north of Sumatra) where they landed some of the crew on three evenings to catch 'tortoises' (turtles) as they started to lay their eggs, which proved 'excellent food'.

They arrived in the Canton River (Pearl River) on Sunday 17 July 1743 and 'found lying here the *Centurion* man of war, Commodore George Anson, a sixty gun ship the remaining ship of the Squadron sent to the South Seas. Saluted her with 21 guns, they returned 19. In her last cruise off Manila she fell in with one of Aquapolcha's [Acapulco's] ships mounting 60 guns and having on board 600 men and after a fully smart engagement of about 3 hours the *Centurion* carried her, and is at present at anchor by her. She proves a very rich prize.'

The *Centurion*, a towering armed warship, had caused considerable alarm when she first called at Macao, seventy miles downstream from Canton, in November 1742. European trade with the Chinese was conducted under very fragile agreements, requiring the utmost delicacy. It was not the responsibility of the captain or his crew but was undertaken by skilled negotiators, referred to as supercargoes, who represented the interests of the Company with Chinese officials. No EIC personnel were permitted to live permanently at Canton but they could use buildings by the waterfront during their stay. Neither the English and other Europeans, nor the Chinese, wanted the threatening ship to approach Canton. However, she was badly in need of repair, water and stores, and assistance was reluctantly given. Everyone breathed a sigh of relief when she departed on 19 April 1743, supposedly returning to England. There was huge consternation when she returned nearly three months later, towing the Spanish treasure galleon *Covadonga* as her 'prize'. In modern day terms she carried something like £100 million,[43] and the loss of this treasure would affect trade between Canton and Manila.

Commodore George Anson had some understanding of the situation, but felt he should receive the respect due to a representative of the king of England. He unloaded some of the Spanish prisoners at Macao and then made his way up river towards Canton, threatening violence to the Chinese officials who tried to stop him. The huge warship navigating among the junks and sampans, with paddy fields at the waterside, must have

Sir Charles Raymond of Valentines and the East India Company

been a terrifying sight. When the *Harrington* arrived she gave Anson a new ploy for negotiation.

Captain Charles Foulis was now caught up as a pawn in the affair. He obviously respected the English Admiral and wanted to assist, but at the same time had his responsibility to the East India Company. His journal records 'I went on board the Commodore [*Centurion*] and in the evening returned again. The occasion of our stay here is the Mandreens [Mandarins] are unwilling to grant the *Centurion* liberty to go to Wampoe [Whampoa] to clean unless she pay the Duties customarie to merchant ships which the Commadore will by no means agree too and for fear of hurting our trade resolves to try all easie methods.' Eventually on 28-29 July the *Centurion* was allowed upriver and *Harrington*, with a local pilot aboard, guided her through the channels.

The *Centurion* moored by the English factory, or trading station, at Whampoa but there were still many delicate negotiations before Anson was permitted to visit Canton for an official meeting with the chuntuck, the representative of the Emperor of China. However, on 14 October Foulis records 'At 3PM past by us at Wampoe and bound for Canton Commadore Anson in his barge, attended by the Swedes, Danes, Country ships and our pinnace. When past here was saluted by all the ships, French excepted, some 17 some 21 guns.'

By this time Foulis had another problem to deal with. The East Indiaman *Haeslingfield* was in distress at an island some distance away, so Foulis sent the longboat with twelve hands and a months' provisions to the *Haeslingfield*'s assistance. This unfortunately met with an accident beside the *Haeslingfield* and was lost, so he sent four men and a quartermaster in another longboat in a further attempt to assist them. No doubt they were as pleased to see *Haeslingfield* arrive at Whampoa early in November, as the Chinese officials were to see *Centurion* depart a month later. Before he left Foulis records 'Dined on board Commadore George Anson in his way on board his own ship. When on board fired 21 guns.'

The rest of their time in China was a matter of routine in loading the cargo, stores and water and preparing for the voyage home. The *Harrington* and *Haeslingfield* left at the end of January, called at St Helena in May, and arrived at the Downs at the end of August 1744, too late to see Anson's magnificent procession of thirty-two wagons of treasure pass through the streets of London. Their own joint cargo from Canton was worth £75,000.[44]

Charles Foulis returned home to find his wife had died while he was away. A few months later, on 27 April 1745, he married Elizabeth Crichton at St.George, Botolph Lane. His next voyage was as captain of the *Anson (1)* 1746/7, for PMO David Crichton,[45] a relative of his wife. This was a new ship which must have been named to

60

commemorate Foulis's association with Anson in the Canton River. Sadly, this voyage ended in the ship being captured by the French. As the *Whitehall Evening Post* reported on 14 April 1748:

> This Day came Advice over Land, that the *Anson*, Capt. Charles Foulis, bound to Persia and Bombay, was attacked, in sight of Bombay, by the *Apollo* and *Anglesea*, French Men of War, and after a brave Resistance of two hours, was taken. The Captain had before the Engagement sent the Company's Treasure and Packets to Bombay.

Foulis managed to return to England and on 5 October 1748 he appeared before the EIC Court seeking permission to explain how his ship had been captured. After an internal enquiry, on 2 November 1748 it was agreed that Captain Foulis had 'done his Duty and behaved like a Gallant and Discreet Officer and is Justly entitled to the Courts Favour.'

He went on to captain the ship *Lord Anson* for two more uneventful voyages before retiring to manage voyages for the EIC himself. Between 1759 and his death he managed thirty-eight voyages made by twelve ships and was a significant figure in the shipping lobby. He had an avuncular relationship with Robert Preston, managing the three voyages which he made as captain and then working with him in the City. Foulis had other connections with the EIC: his sister Margaret married William George Freeman, a Director 1769, 1774-76 and 1778-81. His wife had a sister who married Andrew Moffatt of Cranbrook House in Ilford, another PMO who was involved in shipping insurance.

The only child traced for Charles and Elizabeth Foulis was Charles, baptised on 29 November 1749 at St Andrew Undershaft, in the City of London. A man with this name is shown as purser on the *Anson (3)* 1768/9, PMO Charles Foulis. If this was his son, then he must have caused his parents great distress because he 'ran' at Madras, thirteen months after leaving home. Two other members of the crew are worth noting: a Henry Foulis, Midshipman, on his only voyage for EIC and Wm Dick Gamage third mate, both returned home. Gamage, who was the nephew of Charles Foulis, worked his way up on ships managed by his uncle to become a captain.[46]

What happened to the purser who 'ran' is not known, but Charles Foulis does not mention any children in his will. He appointed Captain Robert Preston as his 'residuary legatee and executor'. Preston erected a beautiful memorial to Foulis in St.Mary's church, Woodford, as a testimony of his gratitude.

Sir Charles Raymond of Valentines and the East India Company

Robert Preston (1740 – 1834)

Although a lot younger, Robert Preston also became well known to Charles Raymond who nurtured his early career. Like Foulis, he was born in Scotland, the fifth son of Sir George Preston of Valleyfield. He started his career with the EIC at the age of eighteen by serving as fifth mate on the *Streatham (3)* 1757/8, which left Portsmouth on 24 July 1758, bound for Bombay, Madras and Bengal, but the voyage ended in disaster. Having sailed around the coast of India, calling at various ports, the *Streatham* ran aground in the Hugli River downstream from Calcutta.

The journal of the first mate, Abraham Shippey, tells how on 11 October 1759 at 3pm, with little wind, the tide (a strong flood) set the ship directly on the shore. The men set about throwing out anchors and pulling on cables and rope to get her off. A sloop came up to help pull them from the mud but she was fast aground. They moved all the canons to one side and tried to ensure she did not get damaged. The journal tells that the local pilot advised Abraham there was no danger and they would get the ship off at the next tide, which would flow two feet higher. Another pilot came to their aid and agreed he should not be uneasy and that there was not the least danger of the ship coming to any harm. However, they were wrong. With the ebb and flow the ship sank deeper in the mud until she fell to one side and the upper decks filled with water. The first mate despatched the longboat to Calcutta to tell the captain that his ship was in danger (it was common practice for the captain to leave the ship under the command of the chief officer when in port). In the night they heard beams starting to break and she took in more water.

The journal goes on to describe the strenuous efforts made to save the ship, but later the mast broke. Some of the men refused to work knowing the loss of the ship meant the loss of their wages. The captain promised three months pay to those who stayed, but later several men became ill due to the heat and when one died, others asked to leave the ship. Native divers were called from Calcutta to salvage the cargo from the hold for the 'Honourable Company'. On 27 October seamen were sent to help from *the Duke of Dorset (2)*, another East Indiaman which had arrived in the Hugli River, but to no avail. Everything movable was salvaged from the hulk and on 10 November the *Streatham* was finally abandoned in the mud.[47]

Meanwhile, Europe was at war and other ships were not having an easy time. The Council of the EIC was concerned by the Dutch ships which were effectively blockading Calcutta and they issued an order for the *Duke of Dorset (2)*, the *Calcutta (1)* and the *Hardwicke (2)* to make a stand. As encouragement the Honourable Company promised £2,000 to the people of each ship for defending their property and saving their ships. At this time the first mate was paid £5 per month while a seaman

Family, Friends and Fellow Captains

earned just 23s (£1.15) per month, so this was a major incentive. After considerable negotiation with the commodore of the seven Dutch ships, conducted under Flags of Truce, it was clear that battle was inevitable.

Charles Raymond of London Esq and Shearman Godfrey of London Merchant had signed as charterparties for the ship *Duke of Dorset* on 30 August 1758. They had appointed Bernard Forrester as the captain. Charles knew Forrester well as he had joined the *Wager* as second mate on 26 August 1745 in Calcutta, serving under Charles on his last voyage.

The journal of the *Duke of Dorset* (edited here and made easier to follow) continues the story;

> Accordingly every ship was prepared for engaging. The *Duke of Dorset* to lead the vanguard, the *Calcutta* in the centre and *Hardwicke* in the rear. Captain Charles Mason of the late Honourable Company's ship *Streatham* came on board and with him 10 of his people [including Robert Preston]. Anchored at night about 3 miles above the Dutch fleet...
>
> In the morning... Instantly on the signal fired, a general engagement ensued between our ships and the Dutch fleet... .but we more closely engaged with the Dutch Commander. The ship next him, and from which ship were not distant a third of a cable the whole Dutch fleet, by help of springs on their cables got their ships athwart the tide. Thus they brought their broadsides to bear on us, we being end on, they marked us fore and aft. Those forward from the two aft guns plyed their small arms, and with the second broadside they gave us Captain Forrester was wounded. Mr.Scott, Master Attendant, cut the Best Bower cable and dropped the small bower anchor by which lucky circumstance we brought our broadsides to bear. Being now in the middle of their fleet we played on them as fast as we were able to load and fire, as did the Dutch on us, which was pretty galling on both sides but with the most success on ours. For, after a smart firing of two hours with double round & grape shot, the Dutch Commander struck his broad penant and hoisted a Flag of Truce, when we ceased firing at him. We continued engaging the other ships which, on ten minutes close fire, all surrendered. Our officers were sent on board to secure their magazines, spike their cannons and divide their prisoners on board our three ships. The killed and wounded on board our ships is very inconsiderable to that of the enemy. Captain Forrester was wounded in the knee by a grape shot in the second broadside, when bravely animating his people to load briskly and take good aim. Eight more men received wounds but not dangerous. Our ship appears like a wreck ... The crew behaved with great bravery and resolution. Little or no damage was received by the other English ships, they being barely in gun shot.

The surgeons of the two other ships were sent for to assist in dressing Captain Forrester's wound and they were optimistic about his condition. Later he was taken ashore and continued his authority from his house at Calcutta. However, on 2 February

1760 the most eminent surgeons and physicians of Calcutta assembled at Captain Forrester's house and reluctantly agreed that it was necessary to amputate his leg, an operation during which he 'bore the pain with surprising resolution. In the evening he was as well as a person in his melancholy situation could be.' Sadly, he died about a month later 'much lamented on board and likewise at Calcutta.'[48]

John Allen was the first mate on the *Duke of Dorset* and the National Maritime Museum at Greenwich has on display a cup awarded to him by the East India Company in recognition of his valour in taking command of the British Fleet after his captain was fatally wounded.

The cup presented to John Allen © National Maritime Museum, Greenwich

Robert Preston was not put off by his first, rather eventful, experience of the East Indies. His next voyage was as third mate on the *Clive* 1761/2, captained by John Allen, which sailed under the management of Charles Raymond.[49] On the next voyage of the *Clive*, again under Captain John Allen with Charles as PMO, Robert Preston was second mate. Then between 1767 and 1776 Robert Preston made three voyages as a captain, twice on the *Asia* and then on the *Hillsborough*, each voyage under the management of Charles Foulis of Woodford.

By this time he had accumulated enough wealth to invest in shipping himself and he took over the management of several ships for the EIC. It was common practice to name a new ship in honour of someone respected so perhaps it is not surprising that the first new ship he commissioned was called the *Foulis*. Another ship owned by Preston was named *Woodford* after the village where he lived. He became a significant force in the EIC and for a time served as chairman of the Committee of Managing Owners of Shipping.

Charles Foulis and Robert Preston set up in business in London as insurance brokers and both became managers of the Sun Fire Office. Preston was elected MP for Dover 1784 – 1790 and then for Cirencester 1792 – 1806, and he was an Elder Brother of Trinity House from 1781 – 1803 and a Deputy Master from 1796 – 1803.[50] By the 1780s Robert Preston was living in a substantial house which had been the home of his colleague and close friend, Charles Foulis, who left the house and other property to him when he died. However, on the death of his brother in 1800, Robert succeeded to the baronetcy and inherited Valleyfield, the family estate seven miles west of Dunfermline, in Scotland.

Family, Friends and Fellow Captains

Pitt Collett (*c*.1729 – 1780)

Captain Pitt Collett lived near Richard Warner and Charles Foulis in Woodford and he also had an adventurous career. He served on ten ships, five of which were managed by Charles Raymond, but he had a slow progress through the ranks of the EIC. Possibly, without family contacts, he struggled to accumulate the capital needed to purchase an existing command. Eventually after one voyage on the new ship *Hillsborough* Captain Robert Preston retired from the sea and Charles Foulis put forward Collett as the new commander. He was forty-eight when the Court approved him as captain of the *Hillsborough* on 1 October 1777 so must have been born around 1729.[51]

It is likely he was a grandson of Thomas Collett Esq of the Inner Temple who married Anne Pett [Pitt?] of St Botolph, Bishopsgate, on 2 July 1697. There is no evidence to link him with either of the brothers, later buried at Barking, who sailed for EIC around this time: Jonathan Collett (died 1746) was captain of the *Wentworth* and Thomas Collett (died 1743) was captain of the *Grantham*. Grisel, daughter of Thomas Collett, married Captain John Pelly junior as his second wife.

Pitt Collett's first voyage was as fifth mate on the *Wager (2)* 1750/1 under Captain Josiah Hindman, with PMO Charles Raymond and Joseph Tolson, when he was about twenty-one years of age. He then served as third mate on the *Onslow (2)* 1753/4 under Captain Thomas Hinde, managed by John Pelly, junior, with John Pelly, senior, as second signature. It was his third voyage, as second mate of the *Caernarvon (2)* 1755/6, which was Collett's real experience of danger.

The *Caernarvon* sailed under Captain Norton Hutchinson, with PMO John Hallett and William Wells, and this was her first voyage. The captain's journal has not survived: the journal which the British Library holds to record the voyage was kept by William Smith, fourth mate. Junior officers kept a journal as practice for promotion, and that written by Smith is very neat but also includes much more information than is usual in a captain's journal. This was his first voyage and perhaps he was writing explanations (or justification) of what occurred for his own information, for future use.

The *Caernarvon* left the Downs in January 1756 and joined a fleet of over eighty merchant ships and twenty Royal Navy battle ships with a vice admiral and two rear admirals for the start of her voyage. She called at Madras in August, Malacca (north of Kuala Lumpur in Malaysia) in September and stopped at Batavia (Jakarta in Indonesia) in December. On 16 January 1757 the crew heard the 'agreeable news of Admiral Watson's having retaken the English factory at Calcutta in Bengall from the Nabob of Muxadebath [Nawab of Murshidabad] and that Watson had taken and burnt Hughley which is a large town belonging to the said Nabob...' This news reached them six months after the terrible event known as 'The Black Hole of Calcutta' when it was said

Sir Charles Raymond of Valentines and the East India Company

that 146 prisoners were held by the Nawab in a small dungeon over night on 20 June 1756, and that only twenty-three of them survived.[52]

According to William Smith's journal, almost as soon as they arrived at Batavia, on 13 December 1756 they 'got the Longboat ready to sail. At 5PM gave the Longboat her dispatches for our Supracargoes. She is to go down the Streights of Sunda and wait for them at Princes Island.' Smith goes on to explain, in some detail, how the longboat had been fitted for the expedition. She was re-enforced, well ballasted and had stores and provisions for two months. Pitt Collet, second mate, was in command and he had with him Humphrey Davies, midshipman, Anthony Grace, quartermaster, and six seamen as well as a 'Malay Boy for a Linguist'. The following day, Tuesday 14 December, the journal records 'At 9AM the Longboat sailed for our homeward bound China ships at Princes Island with the packet. ... in order to give the Europe and Coast News to the homeward bound from China.' Given his junior rank, there may have been other reasons and secret information which the Longboat carried, which William Smith, fourth mate, was not aware of.

Towards the end of January the journal records 'In this month we have had a great deal of rain and squally weather but few of the squalls have been hard and for the generality land and sea breezes. In this month ships may sail for any part from hence. Daily expecting the return of our Longboat.' On 6 February 1757 there was bad news:

> At 4PM the *Grampus* tender (that sailed from hence the 21 January) returned into the road. Captain Jackson who commands her says he was chaced by a French Man of War of 74 guns off Thwart the Way Island; she fired several shot at him, and two whole broadsides, but by bearing away, and sailing between the Stroom Rock and Thwart the Way Island he happily got clear. In this chace Capt Jackson saw a Longboat, in the possession of the French, which he judges is our Longboat, that was dispatched with Advices to our homeward bound China ships, to Princes Island Dec 14th 1756.

This is confirmed by the entry for Pitt Collett in the Ledger where his pay is shown for thirty-three months twenty-four days, from 24 December 1755 until 18 October 1758, but it also records 'Taken with the Long Boat by the French in the Strait of Sunda, 1 February 1757'.

Although the longboat was lost, the *Caernarvon* continued her voyage finally arriving at Whampoa in July 1757. She left after six months and arrived at St Helena on 3 June 1758. From here she picked up the trade winds which took her across towards Brazil and on 2 August she called in at the Fernando de Noronha Archipelago. After resuming her voyage, the ship was captured by the French on 18 October 1758 as she was heading for the west coast of Ireland, probably to await a naval escort up the English Channel.

Family, Friends and Fellow Captains

However, Admiral Edward Boscawen, returning to England about ten days later, encountered the French squadron with the captured East Indiamen. He pursued the French and managed to rescue the *Caernarvon*, which was taken into Milford Haven on 30 October 1758. She eventually returned to the Downs on 27 March 1759. However, the Ledger shows that the crew were taken by the French.[53]

The Court Books of the East India Company record many details of the aftermath of this eventful voyage. On 10 May 1758 they noted a letter from Mr Pitt Collett, late second mate of the ship *Caernarvon*, who had been 'taken by the French in the Streights of Sunda and exchanged'. Then on 11 October 1758 the Court considered a translation of a letter from Samuel Rouge of the French East India Company in Paris, accompanied with an 'Account of Expenses incurred by Mr Pitt Collett, late Second Mate of the *Caernarvon* while Prisoner at the Isle of France [Mauritius] which he engages shall be discharged by the Company.' It wasn't until 27 June 1759 they agreed this should be paid. The amount of £66 12 10 was for expenses incurred 'during his stay at the Isle of France and from his Arrival in France till his Departure for London, his allowance as a Prisoner of War.'

Meanwhile on 8 November 1758 there was a series of entries and letters despatched to the Admiralty concerning the recapture of *Caernarvon* by Admiral Boscawen. Eventually, on 8 June 1759 an enquiry was held into the conduct of Captain Norton Hutchinson in allowing his ship to be captured by 'two of the Enemy's Ships of War in the Latitude of 53° 40 North on the 17th October last'. He had steered to the eastward of the course given him by the Secret Committee so that he was not in company with the other ships sailing home. Captain Hutchinson and the Commadore of the small fleet were reprimanded that neither had recorded their consultation on the course to be followed in their journals, but neither Hutchinson nor any of his officers was found to be at fault for the capture of the ship. However, Hutchinson was reprimanded for his error of judgement 'to hazard the Secret Committee's instructions falling into the Enemy's hands by the capture of his Long Boat by a French Ship of War in the Streights of Sundy.'[54]

That wasn't the end of Collett's adventures. His next voyage was as first mate on the *Calcutta* which fought alongside the *Duke of Dorset* and the *Hardwicke* against the Dutch in the Hugli River on 24 November 1759. Whether or not he made the acquaintance of Robert Preston at that time, they were soon to become ship mates. Collett was first mate and Preston was third mate on the *Clive* 1761/2, and then Collett was first mate and Preston was second mate on the *Clive* 1764/5, both voyages captained by John Allen, sailing under the management of Charles Raymond.[55] Pitt Collett served on a further voyage as first mate of the *Clive* and then Charles took him

67

Sir Charles Raymond of Valentines and the East India Company

on as first mate of the *Duke of Richmond* 1770/1. He returned from this voyage in August 1772 but did not return to the sea for over five years. He had married Mary Kibbel on 26 June 1761 at St.George Hanover Square, Westminster and no doubt he enjoyed spending time with his young family. His son, Pitt Collett junior, also went on to have a career with the EIC. By this time they were living near Richard Warner at Woodford. Charles Foulis is shown as responsible for paying his rates in 1776/7, so it seems reasonable to assume Collett rented his house from Foulis.

Eventually Charles Foulis employed him as captain of the *Hillsborough (1)* 1777/8. The previous voyage had been captained by Robert Preston and he was the second charterparty signature to Foulis for this voyage. All captains were obliged to swear an oath to trade under the rules of the EIC before the Court of Directors before leaving for each voyage. Pitt Collett seems to have taken advantage of at last becoming a captain by going in sight of Madeira (close enough, perhaps, for some cargo to be taken on board) and then parting from his companion ships near the Cape, and calling in at False Bay. The Directors would have been well aware that Madeira, apart from providing a profitable trade in wine, was a centre for trade with America and the West Indies. Worse, Collett appeared to have made a false entry in his journal that this was agreed in consultation with his officers, when no such consultation took place. On 26 April 1780 he appeared before the Court of Directors and was reprimanded for parting with the *Osterley* and *Grosvenor* off the Cape of Good Hope outward bound on his previous voyage, contrary to the orders of the Secret Committee, and not keeping an accurate record of decisions in the Log Book. Even so, he was then sworn as captain of *Hillsborough (1)* for her 1779/80 voyage.

At the end of May the Court gave Collett permission to remain in London due to his ill health, and the *Hillsborough* was taken round to Portsmouth by the chief mate. She eventually left with Collett at the helm on 27 July in convoy with several other East Indiaman, *Gatton*, *Godfrey*, *Mountstuart* and *Royal George*. On 9 August all five ships were captured by a combined Franco-Spanish fleet to the north of Madeira. A letter from Captain Collett at Cadiz, reporting the loss of his ship, was received by the Court of Directors on 20 September 1780 and on 25 October 1780 they considered 'Letters from Captains Collett [*Hillsborough*], Grueber [*Godfrey*] and Haldane [*Mountstuart*] dated at the Island of Leon the 20th Ultimo being read requesting the Court would apply to Government to obtain at least their return to England on Parole.' However, their decision was irrelevant in the case of Pitt Collett as he died soon after the letter was written.[56]

It is worth noting that the 1779/80 season was catastrophic for the East India Company as of the twenty-six ships which left London, only eighteen returned. Apart from the

68

Family, Friends and Fellow Captains

capture of the five East Indiamen mentioned above, the *Earl of Dartmouth* was lost on the Carnicobar (Indian Ocean) towards the end of her voyage, the *Grosvenor* was wrecked on the eastern side of the southern tip of Africa on her way home and the Company's packet ship *Eagle* was also captured by the French.

Pinson Bonham (1724 – 1791)

Pinson Bonham was another close associate of Charles Raymond who had an eventful career at sea. He was the son of Samuel and Jane Bonham and was baptised at St.Dunstan's in Stepney on 25 January 1724. (Pinson was his mother's maiden name.) He first appears in the records of the EIC when he sailed to Benkulen (Sumatra) as fourth mate on the *Duke of Lorraine*, leaving England in the Spring 1742 and returning two years later. This appears to have been a fairly routine voyage. [57]

This cannot be said of his next voyage when he served as second mate on the *Princess Mary (1)* 1744/5, leaving English waters in March 1745 to visit Madras and Bengal. After completing the usual trade, the ship was captured by the French at Madras on 10 September 1746 and the journal was either taken by the French or, more likely, destroyed before she was captured. It has not been possible to discover exactly what happened, but on 14 April 1748 a newspaper reported 'that the *Princess Mary*, which was taken by the French at Madras, was lost at Gogo.'[58] The majority of the crew appear to have survived and made their way back to England on various passing ships. In February 1749 Pinson Bonham was in London to petition the Court of the East India Company 'setting forth he was employed in the Defence of Madras, and the Hardships he underwent as therein mentioned after the surrender of that Settlement therefore praying such relief as the Court shall judge fit.'[59] It is possible that he and a few chosen seamen left the ship and went ashore to assist in the defence of the Company's headquarters at Fort St. George which surrendered to the French.[60] Unfortunately no response to this appeal has been found, though it seems likely he was given some compensation.

This did not put Bonham off the sea and he soon set sail again, this time as second mate on the *Duke of Cumberland (2)* 1749/50 bound for Cuddalore (India) and China. As with his previous voyage the captain was Robert Osborne, and once again they were not to complete the journey. In fact they had been at sea less than four weeks when the ship was wrecked in the sandy Bay of Ayoff, (Yoff) a little to the northward of Cape Verd and Dakar, on the coast of Senegal. Again the journal of the voyage did not survive but it has been possible to piece together what happened from the journal of the *Grantham*,[61] another East Indiaman which had been travelling in company with the *Duke of Cumberland*, and other records held at the British Library.

69

Sir Charles Raymond of Valentines and the East India Company

When the Court of the EIC ordered an enquiry, their Committee of Shipping found that 'the ship *Duke of Cumberland*, Captain Robert Osborne, was lost in the Bay of Ayoff on the coast of Africa in 17th January last [1750] by their being out in their reckoning.'[62] (This was before Harrison's clock made it possible to accurately calculate longitude.) It appears that the *Grantham* nearly suffered a similar fate but managed to anchor in slightly deeper water. She heard her sister ship fire several guns to signal distress in the night and at daylight her officers were dismayed to see the *Duke of Cumberland* 'among the Breakers with all her Masts and Bowsprit gone and the Sea making a Break over her.' Another smaller ship, a Guinea man of war, was also wrecked nearby.

The *Grantham* lost no time in sending their yawl (a boat rowed with 4 - 6 oars, or sailed) under the command of Mr Lewin, the second mate, and Mr Horner, supercargo, to see how they could assist, but when they 'went within hale of the ship, they called to them from the ship and begged for God's Sake they would desist coming any nearer without they had a mind to loose their lives.' The yawl returned to the *Grantham*, and was then sent to try and get through the breakers to see if there were any survivors on the shore. Meanwhile at about noon 'came on Board the *Cumberland's* Longboat whom we found had made their miraculous escapes. Abt 4AM with Mr Harrison Supercargo and 25 men in her and got on board the Guinea Man who then lay about 1 mile without them.'

The following day (Thursday) 'Abt 4PM dispatched the *Cumberland's* Long boat with their own people in her with our kedge anchor and 7 inch hawser to go to the wreck and try and assist if possible. Abt 5 PM the Yawle returned after having tryed along shore but without success. They chased 3 canoes in shore but could not get to them.' Meanwhile 'Mr Palmer held a consultation of the Officers and twas thought possible to make a large Catamaran in order to send ashore with one of our Boats to try if we could by that means be of any assistance to them.'

Messrs Horner and Palmer were supercargoes of the *Grantham*, the officials appointed by the EIC to act as their agents in Canton. Negotiations with the Chinese were extremely delicate and none of the crew was allowed beyond the English factory compound. Supercargoes ranked alongside the captain and would have the final say on any discussion about the cargo, while the captain was responsible for the ship and the voyage. The supercargoes of the *Duke of Cumberland* were Messrs Torriano, Misenor and Harrison. Ships to India did not carry a supercargo as the EIC had their own administrative headquarters in each of the major cities. Apart from the normal cargo, the *Duke of Cumberland* carried seventy-three chests of Company silver [63] so it was important that every effort should be made to safeguard this until it was possible to attempt recovery.

Family, Friends and Fellow Captains

On the Friday 19 January they again sent the yawl to try to land but found the surf so high they were obliged to return. However, they could see that the 'wreck had drove Nigher the shore and had broke her back. Saw several people on board her.' Later in the day, 'the surf being something abated, I went again with the yawle and tryed as before and about a league to the southward of the wreck put the boat through the surf and with much difficulty got ashore. Having fill'd the boat as soon as landed was taken prisoners by the natives and strypt of our clothes and drove to a hut where we found Capt.Osborne, Mr Mesiner and Mr Toriano and the rest of the *Cumberland* ship's crew [presumably including Pinson Bonham] all prisoners under the Natives in a deplorable condition. They took from me the casket which contained the letters from Messrs Palmer & Horner as likewise Capt. Wilson's, as likewise took everything out of the yawle and hawl'd her up.'

Journal of the Grantham, 19 January 1750 © The British Library Board, L/MAR/B/617K

The next day they managed to persuade the natives to let them return to their ship and, under orders from Mr Misenor, they sailed on to the island of Gorée (Gora, just south of Dakar, a settlement belonging to the French East India Company) and then on to James

Sir Charles Raymond of Valentines and the East India Company

Fort, in the River Gambia, which belonged to the Royal Africa Company. Considering the proximity of these centres of the slave trade it is hardly surprising that the natives took the English sailors captive when they were shipwrecked. The *Grantham* reached Gorée within a day, but it wasn't until the 1 February they could anchor near James Fort, having had some difficulty in finding their way up the River Gambia.

On Monday 12 February at about noon the Captain of the *Grantham* welcomed on board Mr Misenor and Mr Toriano, the supercargoes of the *Duke of Cumberland*, along with the chief, second (Bonham), third and fourth mates from on board a French sloop. Fifty hours later they 'despatched the Gentlemen of the *Cumberland* in the French and English sloops, with proper stores for to go on the wreck.'

It appears that Mr Toriano stayed on board the *Grantham* when she continued her voyage. On Sunday 4 March the *Durrington* East Indiaman was sighted returning home and the *Grantham* made a signal to her so that the two ships could come together. The *Durrington*, Captain Richard Crabb, sent their boat to the *Grantham* and transferred Mr Toriano to their ship, and so he went with them back to London. He reported on the loss of the *Duke of Cumberland* to the officials of the EIC at the end of May [64] and on 1 June several letters were despatched to get a rescue effort under way. The Lords of the Admiralty were 'pleased to send His Majesty's ship the *Blandford*, Captain Edward Pratten Commander, purposely to protect and assist the Company's Agents in fishing upon the wreck, which will be immediately followed by two vessels belonging to the Company with proper persons and furnished with everything necessary for such an undertaking.' The Court also sent instructions to the officers of the *Duke of Cumberland* to ensure they did all they could to protect the wreck and assist in the salvage operation (quaintly termed 'fishing' by a diver) while ensuring they were sent a good supply of Madeira wine to keep their spirits up. However, by this time many of the crew were well on their way home.[65]

Back at James Fort in January, the *Expedition* sloop (packet ship) had immediately been sent out to help collect survivors. Her journal [66] survives at the British Library in carefully conserved fragments, but it helps in continuing the story, as does the receipt book of the *Duke of Cumberland*.[67] It appears that only four men were drowned, but the captain, Robert Osborne died at Gorée. At least twelve of the crew, including the first and third mates, came home in the longboat. Although this would have had a mast and sails, it must have been a challenging journey. They left on 8 May and reported back to the Directors in London on 11 July. Six men went on a ship to Liverpool (probably a slave ship), another six entered into the service of the Africa Company at Fort James, five continued on to the East Indies in other ships and three went on a sloop to America.

Family, Friends and Fellow Captains

What exactly happened to Pinson Bonham is unclear, but he was almost certainly held captive by the natives for a time before being rescued by the French sloop and taken with the others to the *Grantham* early in February. It is likely he stayed at Fort James when the other officers left for England on 8 May, to assist in ensuring the remaining sailors were able to find a passage to whatever new destination they chose. None of them would have been paid for the voyage which ended in such disaster. It is interesting to note that among the crew listed was a 'Black' called 'London' who was servant to Pinson Bonham, second mate.[68] Somehow Bonham did get a passage back to London as by the end of the year he was signed up as second mate on the *Scarborough (2)* 1750/1, PMO Charles Raymond (with Joseph Tolson).

The two men can't have met before, as Charles returned from his third voyage as captain in 1742 while Bonham was on his way out to Sumatra on his first voyage. He returned to England just after Charles left on his final voyage, and he left Bengal a few months before Bonham was caught up in the defence of Madras.

Scarborough (2) 1750/1 left England in February 1751 for Madras and Bengal. Within a month the chief mate, William Foreman, died of a fever and was buried at sea so presumably Bonham took over as chief mate. They arrived in India in July and, as was the custom, it seems the captain went ashore leaving the routine of unloading and repairing the ship to his chief mate. Then, on Saturday 10 August 1751, they received 'the melancholy news of the death of Capt. Dauverge who dyed suddenly. Hoisted the colours half mast up as did every ship at Culpee.'[69] So Pinson Bonham became the captain.

Their departure from India was delayed by the EIC officials, which may have caused her to get caught up with the monsoon. *Scarborough* had to call into Mauritius in June 1752 for repairs to a leak so instead of arriving back home in the summer, she did not reach England until February 1753. Some time later Charles Raymond and his co-owner, Joseph Tolson, were involved in a court case with the East India Company over who was responsible for the late arrival of the ship back home, and the financial implications of this.[70]

Pinson Bonham made three more voyages for the EIC, all as captain of the *Norfolk*, managed by Charles with Richard Crabb.[71] He returned home safely from each voyage and when he retired he became the PMO of the *Duke of Portland* for four voyages for the EIC between 1769 and 1780. Charles was the second charterparty signature for the third voyage [72] and it is probable that this was the case for each of the four voyages, Charles giving financial and practical support to Bonham.

By 1779 the Rate Books for Ilford [73] show that Captain Bonham was living in the house at Aldborough Hatch which had previously been the home of Captain John Williams.

Sir Charles Raymond of Valentines and the East India Company

He would have been welcomed into the circle of retired Company men and must surely have visited Charles on many occasions, for business and pleasure. Three years after Charles died, on Friday 18 March 1791 a newspaper reported 'Died on Wednesday last, at his seat, Aldborough-Hatch, in the County of Essex, Pinson Bonham, Esq. formerly a Commander in the service of the Honourable East India Company.'[74]

The East Indiaman York and other vessels by Thomas Luny, 1788
© *National Maritime Museum, Greenwich, London*

Alongside Charles, retired captains William Hunt Mickelfield, Jeffrey Jackson, Charles Foulis and Robert Preston at Woodford, as well as William Webber, John Williams, Henry Fletcher and Pinson Bonham at Ilford, all illustrate the wealth which was made through trade with Asia. Each of them took a villa where their families could enjoy the country air in that part of Essex which is now the London Borough of Redbridge. Their houses were not grand mansions but comfortable 'weekend' homes where they could relax and enjoy the luxury they had earned while staying close to their business activities at the docks and in the City of London. They had proved their capability at sea, had qualities of leadership and were used to commanding respect. They were all men with money to invest and were able to make important decisions quickly. For most of them their lives were further linked in the City, as will be shown in part three.

Valentines is the sole survivor of these eighteenth century houses as Harts was rebuilt soon after it was purchased by William Mellish in 1815 and the others were demolished long ago.

Family, Friends and Fellow Captains

1 BL, Add. MS 36200, Hardwicke Papers ff. 247-264

2 Baptism and burial registers, Wapping and West Ham

3 Plymouth and West Devon Record Office, 69/M/2/689, Morley of Saltram 24th & 25th December 1750, quotes lands formerly belonging to Charles Raymond...

4 Essex Record Office D/DU 539/1 p.27

5 Guildhall Library, Sun Fire Office policy registers, MS 11936 Vol.109 policy no. 145324 p.614, 7 March 1755

6 Harleian Society Vol.45 Parish records of St. Mary le Bowe, p.365

7 Victoria County History of Essex Vol.V p.205; Barking Rate Books held at Valence House Local Studies and Archives, Dagenham (Ref. 2/3/1, etc)

8 Correspondence with Revd Nigel Lacey at West Wycombe, 31 August 2006

9 BL, IOR/L/MAR/B/237B Journal of *York (1)* 1743/4

10 NA Will of John Williams of Barking, Essex, 09 August 1774, PROB 11/1001

11 Barking Rate Books held at Valence House Local Studies and Archives, Dagenham (Ref. 2/3/1, etc)

12 Sir Lewis Namier and John Brooke *The House of Commons 1754 – 1790* (London, 1964)

13 Letter from a relative of Crisp Molineux, Thomas James, dated 28 January 1965, at Redbridge Local Studies and Archives, Ilford; Sir Lewis Namier and John Brooke *The House of Commons 1754 – 1790* (London, 1964)

14 BL, IOR/B/69 EIC Court Book p.421, 25 November 1747; p.437, 9 December 1747

15 BL, IOR/B/70 EIC Court Book p.578, 10 January 1750

16 For more information on the role of the PMO of East India Company ships see *Lords of the East: The East India Company and its Ships (1600 – 1874)* by Jean Sutton (Conway Maritime Press, 1981 new edition 2000, ISBN 0 85177 786 4)

17 NA HCA 26/4/23

18 BL, IOR/B/74 EIC Court Book p170, 3 November 1756

19 NA HCA 26/6/97

20 BL, IOR/B/74 EIC Court Book p.465, 24 August 1757

21 NA HCA 26/8/107

22 Osterley case study on the East India Company at Home 1757-1857 website, http://blogs.ucl.ac.uk/eicah/osterley-park-middlesex/

23 Data from a spreadsheet compiled by the author from Anthony Farrington *A Catalogue of East India Company Ships' Journals and Logs 1660-1834* (British Library 1999) and from Court Books.

24 NA Will of John Durand of Carshalton, Surrey, 31 July 1788, PROB 11/1168

25 NA Will of John Hallett of Red Lyon Square, Middx, 28 February 1765, PROB 11/906

26 BL, Tr.133 Journal or narrative of the Boscawen's voyage to Bombay in the East Indies... 1749. By a Young Gentleman, communicated to his father in London, August 1750.

27 Gregory Holyoake *Deal, all in the Downs* (2008) p.33; BL, IOR/B/69 EIC Court Book reports regular letters from Mr John Bell at Deal, August 1746 etc

28 William Hickey *Memoirs of a Georgian Rake* Edited by Roger Hudson (Folio Society 1995) pp.158-163

29 "Reminiscences of a Voyage to and from China" from Paxton's *Horticultural Register and General Magazine* Vol 5 (1836) pp.295-7 and pp.335-6

30 Data from a spreadsheet compiled by the author from Anthony Farrington *A Catalogue of East India Company Ships' Journals and Logs 1660-1834* (British Library 1999) and from Court Books.

31 Rowan Hackman *Ships of the East India Company* (World Ship Society, Gravesend, 2001) p.175

32 Rowan Hackman *Ships of the East India Company* (World Ship Society, Gravesend, 2001) p.57

33 Website *dorsetsea.swgfl.org.uk*

34 Charles's ship *Prince of Wales (3)* 1763/4, sent to remain in Bengal, was in addition to the 113 quoted.

35 Guildhall Library, London A 9.5.2 *A True and Exact Particular and Inventory of all and singular the lands, tenements and hereditaments, goods, chattels, debts and personal estate whatsoever ... relating to the South Sea Company in 1720. Hugh Raymond Esq, late one of the Directors of the South-Sea Company....* p.3 Bottommree bonds

36 BL, IOR/B/61 EIC Court Book p.300, 12 May 1731; p.322; p.510, 9 February 1732; BL, IOR/B/63 EIC Court Book p.226, 18 December 1734

37 Jewish Historical Society of England Transactions Vol.XXI (1968) p.104; NA Will of Richard Mickelfield of Saint Matthew Bethnal Green, Middx, 8 January 1750 PROB 11/776

38 Dictionary of National Biography

39 John Keay *The Honourable Company* Harper Collins paperback (London, 1993) p.100-1, 141-7, DNB

40 BL, IOR/B/63 EIC Court Book p.3 10 April 1734; BL, IOR/B/69 EIC Court Book p.45 18 June 1746

41 Private research, J G Parker *The Directors of the East India Company, 1754-1790* (PhD thesis, Univ. of Edinburgh, 1977) see also Sharon Eames *Harts and Flowers* (published privately 1989)

42 ERO D/P 167/8/2 Woodford, St Mary the Virgin, Vestry Minutes 1761 – 1787 (Poor Rate 1768, 1776)

43 Glyn Williams *The Prize of all the Oceans* (Harper Collins 1999) p.216 gives various values for the treasure captured but suggest £400,000 in 1743/4 as realistic, *The Greatest Treasure, Philip Saumarez and the voyage of the Centurion* (Guernsey Museum, 1994) p.44 suggests the treasure captured was worth twice this amount. (Converted to 2013 value as £500,000 x 200)

44 BL, IOR/L/MAR/B/654D Journal of *Harrington* 1741/2; Glyn Williams *The Prize of all the Oceans* (Harper Collins 1999) pp.149 – 206; p.216.

45 BL, IOR/B/69 EIC Court Book p.148, 31 October 1746

46 BL, IOR/L/MAR/B/549X (1) Ledger of *Anson (3) 1768/9*; NA Will of Charles Foulis, Gentleman of Woodford, Essex, 14 July 1783, PROB 11/1106

47 BL, OIR/L/MAR/B/605J Journal of *Streatham (3)* 1757/8

48 BL, OIR/L/MAR/B/612H Journal of *Duke of Dorset (2)* 1758/9

49 John Raymond in Farringdon; BL, IOR/B/77 EIC Court Book p.134 2 Sept 1761 shows Charles Raymond and Samuel Hough signing charterparty

50 Sir Lewis Namier and John Brooke *The House of Commons 1754 – 1790* (London, 1964) Vol.III p.326; P G M Dickson *The Sun Insurance Office 1710 – 1960* (OUP 1960) p.278

51 BL, IOR/B/93 EIC Court Book p.321 1 October 1777; Anthony Farrington *A Biographical Index of East India Company Maritime Service Officers 1600-1834* (London, 1999) gives his age as 48.

52 John Keay *The Honourable Company* Harper Collins paperback (London, 1993) p.304

53 BL, OIR/L/MAR/B/589E Journal of *Caernarvon (2)* 1755/6; BL, OIR/L/MAR/B/589L(1) Ledger of *Caernarvon (2)* 1755/6

54 BL, IOR/B/75 EIC Court Book p.30, 10 May 1758; p.141, 11 October 1758; p.388, 27 June 1759; p.163, 8 November 1758; p.368, 8 June 1759

Family, Friends and Fellow Captains

[55] John Raymond in Farringdon, BL, IOR/B/77 EIC Court Book p.134 2 Sept 1761 shows Charles Raymond and Samuel Hough signing charterparty for *Clive* 1761/2; BL, IOR/B/80 EIC Court Book p.362-3, 23 January 1765 Charles Raymond and Andrew Moffatt signed for *Clive* 1764/5

[56] BL, IOR/B/96 EIC Court Book p.22-3, 26 April 1780; p.121, 31 May 1780; p.297, 20 September 1780; p.346, 25 October 1780; NA Will of Pitt Collett PROB 11/1069

[57] Details of all voyages taken from Anthony Farrington *A Catalogue of East India Company Ships' Journals and Logs 1660-1834* (British Library 1999)

[58] *Whitehall Evening Post or London Intelligencer*, Thursday April 14, 1748

[59] BL, IOR/B/70 EIC Court Book p.246 17 February 1748/9

[60] BL, OIR/L/MAR/B/410B Journal of *Earl Talbot (1)* 1781/2 reports an incident when several men went ashore to assist with the capture of Mangalore Fort from the French, 9 March 1783

[61] BL, OIR/L/MAR/B/617K Journal of *Grantham (2)* 1749/50

[62] BL, IOR/B/71 EIC Court Book p.121 1 August 1750

[63] BL, IOR/B/70 EIC Court Book p.540 6 December 1749

[64] BL, IOR/B/71 EIC Court Book p.59 23 May 1750

[65] BL, IOR/E/3/110 EIC Letter Book p.533-42

[66] BL, IOR/L/MAR/B/621A Journal of the *Expedition(4)* Packet ship

[67] BL, IOR/L/MAR/B/562M (2) Receipt Book of *Duke of Cumberland (2)* 1749/50

[68] BL, IOR/L/MAR/B/562M (1) Imprest Book of *Duke of Cumberland (2)* 1749/50

[69] BL, IOR/L/MAR/B/355F Journal of *Scarborough (2)* 1750/1

[70] BL, Add. MS 36200, Hardwicke Papers ff. 247-264

[71] Anthony Farrington *A Biographical Index of East India Company Maritime Service Officers 1600-1834* (London, 1999)

[72] BL, IOR/B/92 EIC Court Book p.374 23 October 1776

[73] Barking Rate Books held at Valence House Local Studies and Archives, Dagenham (Ref. 2/3/1, etc)

[74] *World (1787)* (London, England) Friday March 18, 1791

PART THREE – CITY GENTLEMAN
BUSINESS MAN, BANKER AND BARONET

Part three is divided into four sections which will look at different aspects of the last forty years of Charles's life. Having recently retired from the sea, the City of London had several exciting prospects to offer an intelligent, confident and hard-working man of means in early middle age, so the first years of his business life will be considered. Meanwhile, new sources of wealth enabled Charles and Sarah to establish themselves in their newly acquired home at Ilford. As little documentation is available the second section is largely conjectural, but it attempts to paint a picture of their home life at Valentine House. The third section returns to Charles's later business life. As his colleagues retired from the sea Charles had involved them in the Raymond shipping circle, confident they had proved their ability. After 1770, when he embraced new challenges as a banker, some of them joined him in this enterprise. Royal recognition came in 1774 when he was created a baronet. Finally, the last ten years (after his wife died) will be considered.

Early City interests

London in the 1750s was an exciting and vibrant place, the largest city in the world with a population of 679,000. The City which Charles Raymond knew must have been quite a stunning sight with most of the buildings being brick-built following the Great Fire which had destroyed so much of the City in 1666.[1] For the wealthy, town houses usually had five storeys with two rooms on each floor. Charles is shown at a number of addresses throughout his career, for example in 1755 'Captain Charles Raymond' is listed at 'St Paul's Churchyard'.[2] This would have been a house with business premises at ground level and living accommodation above. In the 1770s Charles lived in Birchin Lane, close to the Bank of England. Valentine House would have been a weekend and summer residence for the family.

East India House, at the corner of Leadenhall Street and Lime Street (the site of Lloyd's today) must have been a very familiar place to Charles, who would have been a frequent visitor in the autumn and winter when new voyages were planned. It had been rebuilt in 1726 and was described by Sir John Fielding in 1776 as follows:

> **East-India House**, (Leadenhall Street) is a plain Doric Structure, on a Rustic Base, in which there is not much to praise or much to censure, though deemed by Persons of perhaps over-nice Taste inadequate to the Wealth, Consequence and Power of the Proprietors. It must be confessed that the House is too small in Front, when we consider the Importance of the

multiplied Business carried on there. However it stretches far backwards, and is thereby rendered very spacious, having large Rooms appropriated for the Directors, and their respective Offices appointed for the several Clerks. There is also a spacious Hall and Court Yard for their Reception who have any Affairs to transact, and who are to pay Attendance to the Company on their Court Days; every Wednesday is appointed for that Purpose. On the back Part of it, towards Lime-Street, there is a Garden with Warehouses, to which there is a Back Gate for the bringing in of Goods in Carts, &c. They have some besides in other Parts of the Town, as the Royal Exchange, Steel Yard, &c.[3]

Throughout the century there was regular work for builders in the City, just as today, with new structures replacing old ones throughout the course of Charles's life. The Mansion House was erected between 1739-52 as a residence for the Lord Mayor during his year in office. The architect was George Dance and the building was first inhabited in the Mayorality of Sir Crisp Gascoigne, 1752-3. After 1778 Charles is recorded as having premises at George Street, beside the Mansion House.[4]

The Mansion House, 1754 © London Metropolitan Archives

The Bank of England building opposite the Mansion House would also have been very familiar to Charles. It was designed by George Sampson and opened in 1734 but between 1767-70 Sir Robert Taylor extended the building. At this time the main facade of the Royal Exchange was that now seen on the opposite side of the building, in the pedestrianised Royal Exchange Buildings. Behind the Royal Exchange (to the west), in the space now occupied by a statue of the Duke of Wellington and the entrance to the underground station, there were more buildings and small alleys. However, in 1765 the Bank of England was granted the right to construct a new road from Cornhill to their headquarters and the site was cleared and rebuilt. Bank Buildings were erected here at the junction of Cornhill, Poultry and Threadneedle Street.

Apart from the Bank of England, there were five leading financial institutions in the City of London in the eighteenth century: the East India Company, the South Sea Company, Royal Exchange Assurance, London Assurance and the Sun Fire Office. Charles must have decided against standing for election as a Director of the East India Company, relying on the support of his business associates to promote family interests among the Court of Directors. As has been shown, he soon made a name for himself managing ships for the Company and EIC policy prevented a PMO from being a Director at the same time. Once he became established in the City network he started to spread his interests further. His experience in financial dealings in Calcutta and the wealth he had earned from his voyages must have given Charles considerable assurance. He would have been accepted on equal terms with many of the Directors who he soon came to know in other business fields.

Free British Fishery

In September 1750 Charles was elected to serve on a committee set up as a result of an Act of Parliament to encourage the British White Herring Fishery.[5] The General Court of the Free British Fishery had a President and a Vice President, with thirty members including his fellow EIC PMO, Simon Rogers. This was a national initiative to encourage herring fishing by giving a bounty (or grant) and initially the Governor was HRH Frederick, Prince of Wales.

Ships, called busses,[6] with two masts and two small cabins were used to catch the fish in nets. They were then cured and packed in barrels with salt. In the first year (1751) the nine ships commissioned by the Society caught 3,600 barrels of herrings and as their skills improved and their fleet increased, eighteen ships caught 9,000 barrels the following year. The Society went to some lengths to find new markets for Yarmouth herrings and by 1754 the demand far out-stripped supply in the West Indies, where they fetched 25s. (£1.25p) per barrel, as opposed to 16s. (80p) in Europe.[7]

The first meeting, following the Act, was held in the King's Arms tavern in Exchange Alley on 19 September 1750 but in July 1752 they took rooms in the Royal Exchange.[8] No records of the organisation have been traced, but it seems likely the Court met once

Sir Charles Raymond of Valentines and the East India Company

a quarter so this would not have been an onerous position. Charles appears to have served on the General Court of the Free British Fishery for its first five years.

Sun Fire Office

A man with Charles's experience and ability was an asset in the commercial world, and on 8 April 1756 he became one of the twenty-four managers of the Sun Fire Office, an insurance company founded in 1710. This position involved a considerable commitment of time as each manager served on at least one sub-committee, which met every week. It was also a position which the newly appointed manager could expect to hold for the rest of his life. Many positions were passed through generations of a family, so it was very much a closed shop and quite how Charles gained entry is not known. He was elected by the other managers 'in the room of Mr Lewis Combrune disqualified' which suggests that by this time his ability had been noticed in City circles beyond the EIC.[9]

Charles's colleagues were men who had power and influence in the City and the commitment was a very shrewd career move. Several of them were also known to him in other ways. As well as being a manager of the Sun Fire Office 1751 - 1774, marine underwriter William Braund was a Director of the EIC in the early 1750s. His brother Samuel was a PMO of East Indiamen, while his nephew Benjamin was an EIC captain. In fact Charles's was the second charterparty signature to Richard Crabb for the voyage of the *Boscawen* 1760/1 on which Captain Benjamin Braund died while in the vicinity of Calcutta. William Braund and his siblings lived in the Romford, Hornchurch and Upminster area to the east of Ilford. Another Braund relative, John Harrison of Chigwell Row, served as a manager of the Sun Fire Office (1761 – 1794), as a Director the EIC (for periods between 1758 -1782) and a Director of the Bank of England from 1788 until he died in 1794.[10]

Charles now had regular contact with men like Sir Crisp Gascoigne (who had been Lord Mayor of London in 1752) and Peter Godfrey, who was at that time the Chairman of the Court of the EIC (in the seventeenth century he would have been referred to as Governor). His brother, Joseph Godfrey, was also on the Sun Fire Office committee, serving as secretary in 1756. Straight away Charles was asked to serve on the Management Committee which met every Thursday. Others on the committee were Joseph and Peter Godfrey, Calverley Bewicke and Brice Fisher.

The Godfrey family also had Essex connections from their grandfather, Michael Godfrey (1625-1689), a very successful mercer who purchased a house called The Rookery, in George Lane, Woodford, as his out-of-town house. His eldest son, Michael, was also a member of the Mercers' Company and was one of the founders of the Bank of England, but he died quite young. The Rookery passed to Peter Godfrey (1662-1724), Michael's only surviving brother. He was also a prosperous City merchant, a Director of the Bank of England and Director of the EIC (1698-99 and 1710-18), and he served two terms as a Member of Parliament for the City. He married twice and had eight children, but although five of them reached middle age, all died unmarried, although not necessarily childless!

The Godfrey Memorial in the churchyard at St Mary's, Woodford

Peter Godfrey's third son, Peter Godfrey (1695-1769), joined the EIC's service as a supercargo in 1712 (aged seventeen) and became Chief of the Council at Canton in 1728. He was admitted to the Mercers' Company in 1723 and became a Director of the EIC, serving for about sixteen years in several sessions between 1734 and 1760. He was buried at Woodford on 21 July 1769. After his death a tall Corinthian column of Siena marble was erected over the family vault. It was designed by Sir Robert Taylor and is a replica of those he designed for the Bank of England, none of which have survived. It is Listed as Grade II*.[11]

Apart from Joseph, Peter Godfrey had two other brothers, Edmund (1696 – 1765) and Thomas (1693 – 1772), who were also involved with the EIC. Edmund had sailed to China as a supercargo around 1729-31, and had been on the fringe of the Naish affair.[12] Edmund and Thomas both signed charterparty for voyages during the 1750s, sometimes working together. On 9 April 1746 Thomas and Joseph Godfrey were two of seven scrutineers who presided over the election of the Directors, with Thomas as the Chairman. In the 1770s the illegitimate sons of Peter and Thomas, William and David Godfrey, signed the charterparty for the ship *Godfrey*.[13]

Charles continued as a manager of the Sun Fire Office for seventeen years and must have learned a great deal about finance and how the City worked. As time went by he was joined by his friend, William Webber of Highlands (elected 5 January 1764). Charles Foulis of Woodford was also elected as a manager from 11 October 1764. By mid-1768 the Sun Fire Office committee also included John Moffatt, brother of Andrew

Sir Charles Raymond of Valentines and the East India Company

Moffatt of Cranbrook House in Ilford. The Sun Fire Office took over first one, and then more, of the new Bank Buildings erected in Cornhill, in front of the Royal Exchange and the Bank of England.[14]

Scotch Mines

The *London Evening Post* of 7 April 1757 reported that 'The following Gentlemen are chosen Governors and Directors for the Scotch Mines, viz Governor, Peter Godfrey, Esq; Dept Gov. Brice Fisher ...' and fifteen Directors were named including Charles Raymond Esq. Of the seventeen names, eleven were also managers of the Sun Fire Office.

The Company had been incorporated by royal charter in October 1729 and was initially known as the 'Governor and Company for working mines, minerals and metals in that part of Great Britain called Scotland'. It appears to have been very closely linked to the Sun Fire Office, providing loans on occasion and later used their offices at Bank Buildings, Cornhill. All the men with whom Charles first served on the Sun Fire Office Management Committee in 1756 were also Directors of the Scotch Mines and Joseph Godfrey was the treasurer. Few records of the company have survived and those which relate to the workings of the company in the eighteenth century are purely financial. It has not been possible to discover how long Charles served on the Scotch Mines Court but it is unlikely to have been a heavy commitment. The company had a working capital of £100,000 and in the 1750-60s had three mines producing lead and ore. Much of the lead was shipped to Rotterdam, although later some was sent to London for the EIC (which sent it on to India). Andrew Moffatt's name crops up as insuring some of their voyages.[15]

It is worth noting that both companies banked with Surman, Dinely & Cliffe and that Thomas Dinely was also a Director of the Scotch Mines. The bank had been started by Robert Surman, the man from whom Charles had purchased Valentine House in 1754. He had the honour of being elected the Prime Warden of the Goldsmith's Company for 1756/7, but at the end of January 1757 his bank failed. By this time Thomas Dinely had resigned from the bank, which must have saved him great embarrassment. The managers of the Sun Fire Office held a special meeting on 10 February 1757 to approve a decision to borrow from Joseph Hankey and Co. in response to the fact that 'Messrs Surman & Cliffe Bankers where the cash of this office was kept having stopped payment the 1st instant...'

Charles attended that meeting and must have been saddened by the news. In December 1748 Robert Surman's eldest daughter, Thomasina, had married Colonel John

City Gentleman

Boscawen, son of Hugh Boscawen, 1st Viscount Falmouth, with the celebrations held at Valentine House - and now he was ruined, for the second time. As a much younger man, before he lived at Ilford, Surman had been the deputy cashier of the South Sea Company, assisting his uncle Robert Knight, who was the chief cashier and who had to flee abroad when the 'Bubble' burst in 1720. Charles's uncle Hugh Raymond had been caught up in the scandal as he was a Director of the South Sea Company at that time.[16]

South Sea Company

Once the shock waves of the 'South Sea Bubble' had subsided, the company continued to function as one of the leading financial institutions of the City until 1856. Charles followed in his uncle, Hugh Raymond's, footsteps by being elected a Director of the South Sea Company in January 1766. Again this made sound business sense as it enabled him to meet with another group of City businessmen and financiers on equal terms. Unlike the EIC, which had a strongly contested election for Directors every year, the South Sea Company Directors were elected for a three-year term and, as the newspapers were able to publish a list of who would be elected in advance, this seems to have been agreed behind closed doors. The EIC elections were much more open, with the names of those put up by different factions listed and the votes cast for each candidate published after the election.

The Court Books for the South Sea Company still survive and show that this was simply a financial institution with no shipping interests by the 1760s. The Court usually met on a Thursday and the frequency varied across the months, but in total thirty to thirty-five times each year in the mid-1760s. Directors were divided between three committees: Accounts, Treasury, and Law suits & Trusts, but this was not as heavy a commitment as the Sun Fire Office and nothing like as arduous as being a Director of the EIC, which met very frequently.[17]

Hugh Raymond's grandson, Dr William Burrell (son of Amy, who had married Peter Burrell), was already a Director (he served 1763 – 1775). He was about twenty years younger than Charles and the extent to which the family had kept in touch is not known. He had studied at Cambridge, became a doctor of law, and achieved the distinction of being elected to the Doctors' Commons.[18] Charles joined him as a member of the law suits & trusts committee.

Charles may also have been on friendly terms with Richard Salway who was the Chairman of the South Sea Company accounts committee for many years. He lived at Woodford, where he was buried in July 1775 and gave his name to Salway Hill. William Black, another prominent EIC PMO who worked in partnership with

Sir Charles Raymond of Valentines and the East India Company

Alexander Hume, was also elected a Director in 1766 and served until 1781. Charles served for just one three-year term, but his cousin John Raymond was elected to the Court of the South Sea Company in 1772 and continued until 1784. He later served a further term, 1788-1790.

All of these business interests earned Charles an attendance allowance, but more importantly taught him how the City systems and networks operated and he became an established and respected figure. Interestingly, in June 1777 there was a newspaper report [19] suggesting that the government wanted to 'dispossess' the two leaders of South Sea Company Court and were hoping that Charles and William Burrell would replace them, but this obviously came to nothing. As already mentioned, their elections were held in private. On 8 January 1778, the *Morning Post* reported that:

> There will be the strongest contest, the latter end of this month at the South Sea House, that ever was known, on the election of Directors for the present year. Sir Charles Raymond opposes the house list, in favour of his son-in-law Dr Burrel; stocks have rose astonishingly, in consequence of this long declared opposition.

One incident, which Charles may have witnessed, was to be significant later in his life. Dr Archibald Cameron, a Scottish physician whose family was heavily involved with the 1745 Jacobite Rebellion, met a gruesome death. On 7 June 1753 he was carried on a sledge from the Tower of London to Tyburn (now the site of Marble Arch) where he was hanged. The presiding Sheriff, Sir Richard Glynn, showed compassion and let his body hang until all signs of life ceased. He was then cut down and stripped, his head was cut off and his bowels taken out and burned. The body was not quartered as it should have been, but was given to an undertaker in order to be given a decent burial. The event would have drawn a great crowd.

Unlike his father and brother, Dr Cameron had never fought with the Jacobites but had gone with them to give medical aid. Previously he had lived quietly assisting his community as their doctor and mentor, while he raised his own large family. When the rebellion failed he settled with his family in France as a doctor to others in the Scottish refugee community. In 1746 he was attainted for taking part in the Jacobite Uprising, although he had not fought himself and may actually have tended to the English wounded as well as the Jacobites. On 26 March 1753 he returned from exile in France to see to family matters and, despite the Act of Indemnity of 1747, was imprisoned in Edinburgh Castle. He was brought down to London, to the Tower, and was condemned to a terrible death, receiving the sentence with dignity, but asked to send for his wife and seven children at Lisle in Flanders. His wife visited him in the Tower and during the interval between the sentence and execution she used all possible means to obtain a pardon, but to no avail. When the sentence was carried out his behaviour was firm and intrepid and he said he died in charity with all men. He was the last Jacobite to be executed.[20]

One of his children, Donald, was aged thirteen in 1753 and presumably returned to France with his mother who was granted a pension by King Louis XV of France. When he again returned to England is not known, but on 12 July 1763 Donald Cameron married Mary Guy, the youngest of the sisters of Mrs Sarah Raymond. At the time both were said to be 'of Woodford' where they married at St Mary's. The witnesses were John Cameron and Mary's sister Ann Williams.[21]

Governor of the Hospitals of Bridewell and Bethlem

Many of the wealthier businessmen were involved in some charity work and several of Charles's relatives and friends became governors of the Foundling Hospital. This was created by Royal Charter on 17 October 1739 when there were approximately 375 governors named, including eighty-eight lords, earls and aristocrats and some of Charles's relatives. Charles was away at sea until the end of August 1739 and did not actively support the Foundling Hospital then or later.[22]

However, having retired from the sea at the end of 1747 he took an interest in another, perhaps less fashionable, charity as reported in the *London Evening Post* on 13 April 1749:

> On Thursday was held a General Court at Bridewell, when Edward Popham, Charles Raymond, and John Chilwell, Esq, received their Charges as Governors of the Hospitals of Bridewell and Bethlem.

Bridewell was the City of London's 'House of Correction' situated near Blackfriars Bridge. A plaque on No.14 New Bridge Street marks the site and the original gatehouse (which includes a relief portrait of Edward VI) has been incorporated into the building. It served as a prison for a wide range of petty felons, vagrants, and prostitutes who had appeared before magistrates, such as Henry and John Fielding at Bow Street (Westminster). The chief magistrate for the City was the Lord Mayor of London who held his own court at the Guildhall. Although the Court of Common Council was involved in the management of Bridewell it was important that most of the governors were not associated with the Guildhall and remained independent.

Bethlem (Bedlam), or the Bethlem Royal Hospital, had been rebuilt at Moorfields in the 1670s and its design was based on the Tuileries in Paris. It had an impressive facade and a gateway crowned with statues of two large figures depicting 'melancholy and raving madness'. The main building housed 175 'lunatics' of whom about two thirds were 'restored to understanding'. Two wings were added in 1734 to accommodate an additional 100 inmates who were considered incurable. It seems inhumane to us today, but it was common practice to allow the public admittance by paying 2d. A letter published in *The World* in 1753 describes how at the Easter weekend at least 100 people had been admitted so that they could see the lunatics, gawp and, sadly, make fun of them.[23]

By 1750 the two institutions had been administered together for about 200 years. There were around 300 governors who were entitled to meet at the General Court. Day-to-day business was carried out by committees which met weekly or fortnightly. Charles seems to have continued as a governor throughout his life, although he did not appear to have taken an active role.[24] What sparked his interest is a mystery. Bridewell was well off his normal stamping ground. Bethlem was between the present-day London Wall and Finsbury Circus and so, in 1749, it was nearer his home at Wellclose Square, but he would not pass by on a regular basis. Was it just a matter of Christian duty to help others? It would have given him a degree of status, social privilege and contact with others in the City, who had influence. It is just possible there was a family connection for his wife, although no evidence has been found to support the suggestion. Could it be that John Webster had not married Judith Cooke because he already had a wife living, or rather existing, at Bethlem?

That William Hogarth became a governor of the Foundling Hospital is well known. The present-day museum at Brunswick Square (Bloomsbury) displays a number of his paintings. Less known is that he became a governor of Bridewell and Bethlem in 1752. Hogarth's depiction of Bridewell in scene four of *The Harlot's Progress* (1732) and of Bethlem as the final painting in his *Rake's Progress* series (1734) illustrate his personal knowledge of both establishments.

In 1733 Hogarth was also working on *Southwark Fair* which served as an extension of the *Rake's Progress* pictures, putting the series into perspective. Like so many of Hogarth's works it is a complex picture, full of topical references, and with a wider meaning. It shows a crowd of the lowest classes at the Fair, wearing shoddy clothes. In the centre, a drummeress advertises a show booth for travelling actors. Their play will offer the crowd a brief moment of escape, creating an illusion and allowing them to live out their dreams. The open countryside and blue sky glimpsed through the buildings indicate loftier ideals and a better way of life.

The painting and printed engraving were unveiled together in December 1733 and sometime around 1762 the painting was purchased by Charles Raymond. The Cincinnati Art Museum, which now owns the picture, has provided the text of a letter dated London, Nov 11th 1797 which explains that the painting had just come up for sale and could be had for 600 guineas (£630). The letter goes on to say that 'about 30 or 40 years ago Sir Charles Raymond gave 200 guineas for the picture, when Hogarth's *Marriage a la Mode* sold for only £120'. Although the picture is now in America, Valentines Mansion has an original engraving of *Southwark Fair* on display today.[25] Charles's purchase of this expensive painting, by one of London's most fashionable artists, indicates both the wealth acquired through his EIC trade and his secure place within the wider London business and philanthropic networks.

Southwark Fair by William Hogarth

Valentine House and park

In 1769 Charles substantially rebuilt his house, and three rain-water hoppers still bear that date with the Raymond motif today. It was extended with an additional bay on the west side bringing the building closer to the separate orangery, which had six large glass windows and a central doorway. Much later this was converted into the dairy wing by the then owner, Charles Welstead. Charles (Raymond) raised the walls of the house to meet a new roof (which sloped less steeply) at a parapet. The whole building was refaced with new brickwork and a porch was added to the entrance, which may have been moved to make the extended building symmetrical and in keeping with Palladian ideals.[26] The whole effect was a much more fashionable Georgian residence, the type of home described by Sylas Neville in 1785 as 'the small but neat box of the retired East India captain'.[27]

Valentine's the Seat of Charles Raymond Esq.

The line drawing (*above*) frequently used as an illustration of the Georgian house dates from 1771, not long after the work was completed. It appeared in *A New and Complete History of Essex by a Gentleman*, Vol.IV, and accompanied the following text:

> VALENTINES, about four miles north from the church, is the seat of Charles Raymond, esq, High Sheriff of this county for the present year 1771; and it may, with great propriety, be called a Cabinet of Curiosities. This building is one of the neatest, and best adapted of its size, of any modern one in the county; its ornaments are well chosen, and the grounds belonging to it laid out with great judgement and taste. The elevation of it, upon the well executed plate hereto prefixed, is the gift of the present worthy and liberal owner; to whom we present our sincere thanks.[28]

Some forty years later, after Charles Welstead became the owner in 1808, the entrance was moved to the opposite side of the house and the porte cochère was added. The balcony was added on the south side when the porch was removed.

The description of the house as 'neat' suggests it was in fashionable good taste, elegant but without ostentation, which fits with what little we know about Charles Raymond. The reference to it being a 'Cabinet of Curiosities' indicates that Charles had accumulated a variety of souvenirs from his eastern travels as well as gifts from his captains. There is nothing now to indicate what these might have been, but we do know that he gave a neighbour, the antiquarian Smart Lethieullier of Aldersbrook, a piece of

City Gentleman

sculpture of a hard dark marble which had been brought back from the Island of Elephanta.[29]

As has been mentioned already, on 7 March 1755 Charles insured his 'dwelling house, offices and stables' with the Sun Fire Office for not exceeding £2,000 and separate outbuildings were insured up to £300. The household goods in the house were covered up to £500. A new policy dated 21 April 1769, after the restoration of the house, shows the buildings insured for the same amount (total £2,300) but the contents insurance was quadrupled: household goods for up to £1,500 and china and glass for £500 (total £2,000). Put in plain terms, this means that the value of the contents of the house were nearly equal to the value of the house itself.[30]

When Charles died Valentine House was sold by his daughters to their uncle, Donald Cameron, so there is no surviving record of the contents. When Cameron died in 1797 some of the contents of the house were sold at auction and an advertisement for the sale shows a number of items which had possibly been obtained by Charles and sold on with the house. For example, there were 'pictures by eminent masters, amongst which is the *Southwark Fair*, by Hogarth, in his best stile' which Charles had purchased in the 1760s. The house contained 'Oriental articles, china, library of books' It is frustrating that as no family papers survive, none of these items can be fully identified. The auction also included a good deal of Madeira, claret and port. The Madeira was a 'perk' of being a captain and the port could well have come from Burrell family connections who were wine merchants in Lisbon. There was also a coach, a chariot and a number of horses, as well as items relating to farming on the wider estate. [31]

By the mid-eighteenth century the craze for Chinese porcelain was at its height. This translucent white material was far superior to the coarse earthenware and finer stoneware mass-produced in England. It seemed so delicate but was resistant to heat and when knocked with a spoon it rang like a bell but did not chip or break. The fact that it was produced in a remote part of China near the Kaoling Hills and travelled 600 miles over mountains and down the Yangtse River just to reach the coast before the long voyage to England on an East Indiaman, added to both its desirability and its price. The blue and white designs aimed at the European market were imported from early in the seventeenth century, with quantities increasing dramatically to satisfy the wide demand. The shards of porcelain located at the *Valentine* wreck site illustrate this with some very fine and other, coarser, fragments intended for those less affluent.[A]

Services of armorial porcelain are sometimes displayed in the country houses of the aristocracy today, but often they are illustrated simply with a large family coat of arms.

[A] See illustration page 144

Sir Charles Raymond of Valentines and the East India Company

It is certain that Charles and Sarah Raymond had their own dinner and tea services, with their own family arms, as pieces have come up at auction in the past. Obtaining a set of individualised chinaware was no easy matter as it was necessary for a supercargo to negotiate the commission with the Hong merchants who had the right to trade with westerners at Canton. Charles was ideally placed to commission his own service and he chose a coloured Chinese design with his arms and that of his wife, much smaller at the top. Blue and white designs were more common as they only needed one firing, but what Charles chose was the very best that money could buy.[32]

One plate from the service made for Charles was purchased by the author and is displayed at Valentines Mansion. (*see right*) A wider range of items from a service made at a similar date for Sir Francis Sykes is on display at Basildon House (National Trust). It isn't hard to imagine Sarah inviting her sisters round to spend time drinking tea, and they would have had the best of that too!

Another item from China which Charles owned was a book showing a series of 814 watercolour illustrations of plants and insects in China, with captions detailing medical use. The text is in both Chinese characters and clear English handwriting, although the punctuation might suggest that it was copied out by someone who did not really understand the meaning of the words. The book was a present to Charles from Captain Josiah Hindman and is now in the library of the Royal College of Physicians of London. Josiah had been an officer on all four voyages made by the *Wager* when Charles was the captain and he took over as the captain when Charles retired from the sea and became PMO of the ship – so he had every reason to be grateful to his friend.[33]

Without any family archives we can only speculate on how the house was furnished by the Raymonds. Did they obtain hand-painted wallpaper from China for any of the rooms? As Charles never visited China himself perhaps he favoured an Indian influence in his decor. Did they import ivory chairs from India, or commission English furniture from Thomas Chippendale?

In her own way, Sarah Raymond was as much an administrator as her husband, running the household, managing the servants, and arranging dinner parties. Perhaps her menu was something like that provided by Frances, The Honourable Mrs Boscawen,[B] whose husband (later Admiral Boscawen) was away at sea when she gave a dinner party for herself and six guests in 1748. She wrote to tell him about it. 'Our company made 7 - just the number I choose at table. I won't trouble you with my bill of fare in the exact order it was. Let it suffice that I had soup, fine dish of fish, salmon and smelts, turkey, brawn, oysters, etc., partridge ragout, fricassee, asparagus, mushrooms, mince pies, blanc manges, jellies, fruit, etc., etc. Everything extremely good of its kind, well dressed and well served. Everybody praising it, and, what pleased me better, eating very heartily. In the evening some company, and I had two tables at cards.'[34] Sarah would have been able to please her guests with grapes, melons, peaches and pineapples from her own garden.

It would be wonderful to know more of the social life enjoyed by Charles and Sarah. When the Surmans lived at Valentine House a dance tune called 'Miss Sally Surman's

---

[B] Frances (née Glanville), The Honourable Mrs Boscawen, was a step-daughter of Charles's cousin Bridget (daughter of Hugh Raymond). The guests included Robert Surman, the previous owner of Valentines, and his daughters, as the eldest, Thomasina, was soon to be married to Colonel John Boscawen, brother of Frances's husband.

Sir Charles Raymond of Valentines and the East India Company

Delight' was written by Thomas Collett who appears to have visited several houses in the locality offering his services. It was set in the Key of Bb for violin and German flute and was published in *A Choice Collection of Two Hundred Favourite Country Dances* by John Johnson in 1750. There were two other tunes which may also have been written for the Surmans: 'Vallentines Maggot' could be associated with 14 February, but they must surely have commissioned 'Valintine House' written in 1748. Did the Raymond girls enjoy dances like this, performed by three couples in a longways set? Did they play a harpsichord or harp, and sing together?

It is likely Charles and Sarah attended concerts in London. They might have heard music by Handel (who died in London in 1759, aged seventy-four) or by the young Mozart who performed at Buckingham House for the King and Queen in 1764, at the age of nine. Did they enjoy the symphonies of William Boyce, for which he is best known today? He also wrote the patriotic anthem 'Heart of Oak' with its rousing chorus:

> 'Heart of oak are our ships, jolly tars are our men,
> We always are ready; steady, boys, steady!
> We'll fight and we'll conquer again and again.'

The words refer to battles against the French in 1759 and were probably just as popular with the sailors on East Indiamen as they were on ships of the Royal Navy.

Did Charles and Sarah enjoy the London theatre? A play called 'The Foundling', written by Edward Moore, included a Colonel Raymond and Sir Charles Raymond among the leading characters. This was first performed at Drury Lane on 13 February 1748, more than ten years after Col. Hugh Raymond had died and long before Charles became a baronet. Did it cross his mind that he might, one day, become Sir Charles Raymond himself?

As her daughters Sophia, Juliana and Anna Maria grew up, managing them was the responsibility of their mother. It seems likely they were given some education at home before learning the refinements of a fashionable young lady. Among the archives of the Conyers family of Copped Hall, near Epping, there is a collection of bills and receipts for the daughters of that household, including for writing and dancing masters, for dress materials and dress making, and an advertisement for a warehouse selling, among other things, the newest fashioned riding habits, quilted and hooped petticoats, a great choice of masquerade habits etc.,[35] which give some idea of what the three Raymond girls might have demanded of their parents.

John Conyers (1717 – 1775) had aristocratic connections and lived at Copped Hall in some style as a country gentleman, becoming an MP. However, Charles seems to have preferred the City buzz and making the smaller Valentine House a comfortable home rather than a show place, although he possessed greater wealth than Conyers. His eldest daughter Matilda Conyers (1753 – 1803) was a talented artist and a number of her watercolour paintings of plants survive. Many are native flowers but some are exotics from abroad, including China.[36] Matilda was an exact contemporary of Sophia Raymond, Charles's eldest daughter, who was also a talented artist, so perhaps the girls became acquainted. Maybe they painted together in the heated conservatory at Valentines which probably contained many exotic plants from the East. There is no evidence to link the Conyers family to the EIC, but they did follow the fashion among the élite of hanging hand-made wallpaper from China. The design in the drawing room at Copped Hall depicted the pleasures of life in China, and it was similar to wallpaper displayed at Blickling Hall in Norfolk. It is thought the Copped Hall paper dated from around 1775.[37]

The previous owner of Valentine House, Robert Surman, had been on friendly terms with the Child family of nearby Wanstead House and his younger daughter was included in some of their family outings.[38] It is likely Charles and his family were also invited to Wanstead on occasions. John, second Earl Tylney, built an ornate grotto beside one of his lakes in the 1760s. This was the setting for an elaborate and bizarre masquerade in 1768 which was described by an Italian noble-woman who was staying at Wanstead at the time. This involved the guests fishing near the grotto for 'treasure' when 'King Arthur' asked Earl Tylney to take his sword and 'smite' the water in front of the grotto. When he did so:

> a rumble sucking noise comes in front of the opening of the grotto the water as if boiling and to the horror of all the company both on the water and on the shore scream with fright, appearing as though from the depth of hell arose a ghastly coffin covered with slime and other things. Silence as though relief, when suddenly with a creaking and ghostly groaning the lid slid as if off and up sat a terrible apparition with outstretched hand screeching in a hollow voice, give me my gift with such violence, that some of the company fell into the water and had to be saved, and those on the shore scrambled in allways confusion was everywhere. We allmost fainted with fright and was only stayed from the same fate by the hand of his Lordship, who handed the keeper the dove (fake) the keeper shut its hand and with a gurgling noise vanished with a clang of its lid, and all went pitch. Then the roof of the grotto glowed two times lighting the water and the company a little, nothing was to be seen of the keeper or his coffin, as though it did not happen.[39]

Perhaps Charles and Sarah were among the guests at this extravagant entertainment.

Sir Charles Raymond of Valentines and the East India Company

The gardens, plants and birds

Charles took a keen interest in his garden with the canals and grottoes created by Robert Surman in the 1720s, which reflected the magnificent gardens at Wanstead. In *c.*1770 Earl Tylney built a garden feature disguised as a small temple which was used as a poultry house (by 1815 it was a pheasantry and keeper's lodge). Until the 1970s there was a garden seat which looked like a small temple in the garden at Valentines.[40] This was close to the Cedar of Lebanon tree which is such a magnificent specimen today. It is likely that Charles planted the tree and had the seat built beside it.

We do know that by the end of the century there were large glasshouses on the Valentine estate which were almost certainly erected by Charles. In the autumn of 1797 the gardens were visited by William Robertson, an architect, who was preparing a book about glasshouses.[41] He mentions in his notebook the considerable quantity of glass for forcing, three extensive uniform tiers rising one above another, each 70 foot in length. There were melon pits, pineapple pits and a glasshouse 13 feet wide which housed a remarkable Black Hamburg vine, planted by Charles.

On 26 July 1783 the *Morning Chronicle & London Advertiser* reported:

> Those who are fond of vegetable curiosities, cannot easily be told of one that is more extraordinary, than a vine in Essex. It is of that kind, which the gardeners call the Brown Hamburgh Grape. The branches of it are so wide spread, and so extremely fruitful, and so exquisite in the flavour of the fruit, that its produce is literally farmed at one hundred and fifty pounds a year! The settled price is half a guinea a pound before June – then for a short time six shillings – afterwards four shillings. The vine is the property of Sir Charles Raymond, and grows in the garden of the house, occupied by the late Lord Talbot.[C] It should be added, that the vine was so long sterile, that the gardener had more than once proposed to cut it down.

A cutting of this vine was taken to Hampton Court around 1768-74 and it is still flourishing there now. The head gardener at that time was a certain Lancelot (Capability) Brown and it would be nice to think he may have travelled across to Valentines to take the cutting in person.[42] There was also a peach house at Valentines, which was 70 foot long and 12 feet wide, against the wall in a separate garden. Robertson said that in 1797 the gardener picked ninety-eight peaches.

[C] See page 121 for Lord Talbot

City Gentleman

Having travelled to the East Charles, like many other captains turned PMOs, took an interest in plants from Asia and he was credited with introducing a new species of camellia *Camellia japonica, variegata* into this country. It was described in 1819: 'This was one of the first varieties of the Double Camellias seen in this country. It was brought over from China sometime about the year 1792. We remember to have seen the first plant, soon after this period, at Sir Charles Raymond's, Valentine House, Essex.'[43] However, Charles had died in 1788. The last ship of which he was PMO was *Earl Talbot*. This made four voyages under his management, the last leaving England in April 1788, visiting China and returning in April 1789 after Charles had died. Donald Cameron managed the next voyage between March 1790 – Sept 1791, when the *Earl Talbot* visited China again. It seems likely that this variety of Camellia did bloom first at Valentine House, but while it was the home of Donald Cameron, Charles's brother-in-law and business associate.

Charles's fellow captain and PMO Robert Preston was also interested in botany and he is credited with introducing the double red camellia *C. japonica 'Pleno Rubro'* into this country while he was living at Woodford.[44] When he inherited the Valleyfield estate in 1800 he wasted no time in inviting renowned landscape gardener Humphry Repton up to Scotland to suggest improvements. Repton lived at Romford in Essex and had worked on several properties in or near Woodford. In 1818 Preston employed the young David Douglas as under-gardener on his Valleyfield estate. Valleyfield was later taken over by the East Fife Coal Co. and much of the landscape was destroyed, but what remains is now managed by Fife Council as a public amenity.[45]

Another company man known to Charles was Gilbert Slater (1712 – 1785) who had served as fifth (1734/5) and third (1737/8) mate on the *Wager* under Captain Charles Raymond. He also went on to become a captain and later a PMO, following a similar path to Charles. He became a Director of the London Assurance Company and was Deputy Master of the Trinity House for the last two years of his life. His son Gilbert Slater (*c.*1753 – 1793) did not serve on board ship but he followed in his father's footsteps as PMO for a few voyages, as a Director of the London Assurance Co. and an Elder Brother of the Trinity House.[46] He married Elizabeth, daughter of Philip Jackson of Durham and seems to have been a pleasant and very corpulent gentleman of 'opulence and honour'.

Gilbert Slater junior was passionately fond of plants and, being in contact with the supercargoes at Canton, was able to use his influence to import new plant species into this country. He wrote and printed a small tract of lists of plants and instructions for collecting them and packing them for the voyage home. He lived at Knotts Green, Leyton, where he had an extensive garden with stoves, greenhouses and conservatories.

Sir Charles Raymond of Valentines and the East India Company

In addition he made sure that Joseph Banks received some of every specimen he obtained for Kew, to better preserve new species.

In 1792 he sent out a young man, James Main (later to become the Chelsea gardener and editor of Paxton's *Horticultural Register and General Magazine*) on the *Triton* under Captain Burnyeat, to collect specimens for him. Sadly Slater died before the ship returned to Gravesend in September 1794 and little is known of the plants Main had collected. Gilbert Slater is credited with introducing at least seventeen new species of plant into this country, mainly from China. They include camellias, magnolias and hydrangeas.[47]

But it was not just plants which interested Charles; he introduced the first live secretary bird into England. A letter from George Edwards FRS was read to the Royal Society on 17 January 1771 in which he described seeing 'some curious birds and other animals, from the East Indies' when he visited Valentine House 'last August'. Edwards said ... 'among these, I discovered a rare bird, not known to me before. ... It is about the bigness of a heron...' He went on to describe the bird and provided a drawing. He added 'This bird was called a snake-eater, by those who brought it from India.' ... 'Another bird was brought with this, supposed to be the male of this species, which died soon after it was landed. Mr. Raymond's servant told me that it was something larger...' which suggests that Charles had sent a servant to collect the birds from the docks. A footnote to the letter says 'This bird was described, under the name of *Sagittarius* from the Cape of Good Hope, by Mr. Vosmaer, keeper of the Statholder's Museum at the Hague.... in 1769.'[48]

'Snake-eater' Reproduced by kind permission of the Royal Society from their Philosophical Transactions Volume 61 (1771)

City Gentleman

The bird must have come on a ship with Charles as PMO, which called into Cape Town on the homeward journey in 1770, and the most likely ship is the *Granby* which arrived at the Downs on 16 June. *Granby* had stopped at False Bay on the way out. This is on the other side of a promontory from Cape Town and today it appears to have great holiday beaches and a sanctuary for the African penguin. Presumably this is the 'Pengwin Island' referred to by the captain in his journal. It is possible that Charles sent out an agent who was landed at False Bay to collect 'some curious birds and other animals' and who was picked up, with them, at Cape Town on the return journey. The journal makes no reference to this but there is no reason why it should – the birds were private trade to all intents and purposes.[49]

Even a small menagerie requires a proper enclosure and it is frustrating that no map indicates the site of this. In 1794 the artist William Hayes published a book of *Portraits of Rare and Curious Birds, with their descriptions, from the Menagery of Osterly Park*, home of the Child banking family. This included a coloured illustration of the secretary bird which was kept there in a large menagerie described as a small wooded and walled 'park within a park' around 1780. Surprisingly it sounds as though it was a good pet as Hayes described the bird as social, gentle and inoffensive, soon expressing a grateful attachment and attention to the person who fed it.

At the Audley End menagerie exotic pheasants strutted across open lawns enclosed by high walls, while a Gothic style building (completed in 1774) housed eagles, parrots, canaries and goldfinches, amongst others. A large octagonal aviary was built at Knole in Kent *c*.1761, also in a Gothic style, to house exotic pheasants from China. The octagonal dovecote at Valentines, set into the wall of what was later referred to as the kitchen garden, is thought to date from the mid-eighteenth century.[50] It is possible that in Charles's time the garden was a walled enclosure for these 'curious birds and other animals' with the octagonal building as a viewing tower. It does have high quality brickwork and elaborate windows which may have been partly bricked in when the building was converted into a dovecote. We can only speculate!

William Hayes's book also includes an illustration of an elegant and valuable 'Chinese duck' which 'the English in China called the Mandarine'. He reported they were frequently for sale at Canton in China, at the rate of from six to ten dollars a couple. There are Mandarin ducks on the canal at Valentines today, but they were acquired in 2008/9 by the Valentines Park Manager. However, it seems very likely that others of the species lived at the same place 250 years ago.[51]

Sir Charles Raymond of Valentines and the East India Company

Cranbrook House, 1798

The Mausoleum at Highlands (undated)

Both pictures inserted into a copy of Volume 4 of The Environs of London by Rev. D. Lysons (1796) © London Metropolitan Archives

City Gentleman

Other property in Ilford

Although Charles invested heavily in shipping he also used his wealth to purchase property which brought him an income from rents. When he purchased Valentine House and estate from Robert Surman in October 1754 Charles also purchased Valentine Farm, later known as Middlefield Farm, to the north of Valentine House. This was rented by William Harvey for many years, certainly from 1765 until after Charles died in 1788. Quite who this man was remains a mystery, but no EIC connections have been traced.[52]

The Valentine estate owned by Charles Raymond covered a substantial amount of land but he soon added other properties in the Ilford district so that it extended from the River Roding to Ley Street. This included the estates of Cranbrook, Wyfields and Highlands between Cranbrook Road and the Roding. Some of the fields he retained, others he sold on.[53]

In 1763 the Cranbrook estate was purchased by Andrew Moffatt (*c*.1730 - 1780),[54] who was an insurance broker and was married to Katherine Crichton, whose sister Elizabeth Crichton was the wife of Charles Foulis. Although London-based, the Moffatts had several links to Scottish families and Andrew's sister Martha married his friend Charles Bruce, the Earl of Elgin. Another great friend was William, Earl of Mansfield, an eminent lawyer. Andrew's brother James Moffatt, of Charlton in Kent, served as captain of *Latham* for Charles in 1759/60, 1762/3 and 1766/7. He was a Director of EIC from 1774 for several periods until he died in 1790. Another brother, John, joined Andrew in his insurance company in Lombard Street around 1762 and became a Director of the Sun Fire Office alongside Charles in 1767.[55]

Andrew Moffatt not only lived very close to Charles but also worked very closely with him in managing voyages for EIC. For a number of new ships the first charterparty signature was Charles and the second was Andrew Moffatt, but for some later voyages the responsibility was reversed. Andrew was the second signature on the charterparty agreement for the voyages of the *Latham* when his brother James was the captain. Nothing has been found so far to link Andrew, or James, to a William Moffatt who was a PMO in the 1780s.

In around 1765 Charles built a new house at Highlands which became the home of his friend William Webber and his wife Elizabeth, Sarah Raymond's sister. Charles also built a three-sided crenellated tower on the Highlands estate in 1765, which he intended for use as a family mausoleum. Apparently it had catacombs with fourteen compartments in the underground vault. Above this was a chapel and above that a room where refreshments could be served. However, no-one was ever buried there as Charles

Sir Charles Raymond of Valentines and the East India Company

and the Bishop could not agree over certain points connected with the consecration, so the ceremony was not performed.[56] At this time Ilford did not exist as a separate parish, so Charles and Sarah were buried at St. Margaret's at Barking when the time came.

After Charles died in 1788 his daughters sold Highlands to Sir James Tylney-Long and it was merged into the Wanstead House estate. Highlands was demolished early in the nineteenth century but the mausoleum survived to living memory and was known as Raymond's Folly, Ilford Castle or Cranbrook Castle. During the Great War the tower was used as an observation point but it was demolished by the Port of London Authority in 1923. They built a pavilion on the site which remains there today, Listed Grade II. It has been converted into the administrative block of the primary school which has been built beside it.[57]

The Rate Books for Barking parish, which included Ilford, show Captain Raymond acquiring other property soon after he purchased Valentine House. In September 1763 Charles purchased a sizeable house with yards, gardens, orchards and fields to the south of the Valentine estate, stretching from Cranbrook Road, for £2,500. This had been the home of Richard Stone and later came to be known as Ilford Lodge. In 1765 this was rented out to a Mrs Shoemaker, but late in 1772 'Fletcher, Esq' was paying the rates. Soon 'Henry Fletcher' was shown paying for additional land, which probably extended the holding across to Ley Street. In 1781 this became the home of Donald Cameron and his wife Mary, the step-sister of Sarah Raymond.[58]

Although Charles was lucky that he lost just three out of the 113 ships he managed, he may well have lost funds invested in ships managed by others in the Raymond circle. Investing in land, and in the valuable works of art, porcelain and other treasures in his home, was a shrewd move to ensure that his investments were spread over more than just shipping. In managing these property deals Charles was using some of the wealth he acquired to enhance the environment around his own home. He also obtained additional income from rents both from the estates mentioned above and also from a number of smaller cottages he had purchased in the area.

When Charles was away at sea he would undoubtedly have met Richard Benyon while he was Governor of Fort St George, Madras. He returned to England in 1744 and purchased the Newbury estate in Ilford in 1747. This shared a Ley Street boundary with Charles's Valentine property. However, the Newbury estate was leased out when Benyon married his third wife (a wealthy widow) soon after he returned from Madras. They lived much of the time at a property left to her by her husband, the beautiful Englefield House in Berkshire. Their son Richard, who married Hannah Hulse in 1767, was made heir to Newbury and Gidea Hall at Romford. Benyon owned other property in Essex at Ockendon.[59]

City Gentleman

In November 1769 and again in 1770 Charles was short listed as one of three men who might serve as the Sheriff for the County of Essex for the following year. Every county still has a High Sheriff who is selected by the Crown literally by the prick of a pin from three men who are considered suitable. The main requirement in the eighteenth century was that he owned property in the county and would be able to perform the ceremonial duties required of a representative of the King. This was a great honour and would have incurred considerable expense, but great prestige. Sarah must have been very proud when they attended at the Court of St James's on the 6 February 1771, to be presented to 'The King's Most Excellent Majesty in Council' and her husband became High Sheriff. She was ideally placed to obtain the latest oriental silk for a new gown.[60]

They were now moving in exalted circles and would have been involved in events at Chelmsford and other places out in Essex, as well as in the City. For example, it was Charles's duty as High Sheriff to call a public meeting in January 1772 to nominate a 'Proper Person' to represent the county in Parliament when Sir William Maynard died. Charles was appointed to another dignified office as a Master Keeper of Epping Forest. He served from 1771 until 1785 for both the Lamborne & Chigwell Walk and the West Hainault Walk, while Andrew Moffatt filled the same role for the East Hainault Walk and Charles Foulis for the Woodford Walk.[61] With so many friends and fellow captains living in the area, relaxed dinner party conversation at Valentine House must have ranged from far flung places and adventures at sea, to mundane business matters, politics, and then to prestigious soirées. As their children got older, no doubt they were also a topic of conversation.

Family weddings

On 13 April 1773, a few days before his sixtieth birthday, Charles's eldest daughter, Sophia, married her second cousin William Burrell, son of Hugh Raymond's daughter Amy. William was twice Sophia's age and a very learned man, a doctor of law and MP for Haslemere. He and Charles had become colleagues when Charles was elected to the Court of the South Sea Company in January 1766. At that time Sophia was barely a teenager, but as the marriage took place a couple of days after her twentieth birthday, they would have known each other for a long time by then. Although comfortably off, William did not have an income which could provide for Sophia in the manner to which she had been accustomed. The marriage settlement allowed him to buy a house in Harley Street and he soon resigned from his legal work and from Parliament, to take up a more lucrative position as an Excise Commissioner.

Sir Charles Raymond of Valentines and the East India Company

William was a Fellow of both the Royal Society and Society of Antiquaries and spent much of his spare time travelling around Sussex, collecting information about its history. His entire collection was left to the British Museum Library and formed the basis of a history of the county published in 1815-35. Sophia probably accompanied her husband on some of his journeys around Sussex, although the couple had five sons and two daughters, which may have restricted her somewhat. Her husband had a stroke in 1787 but recovered and in 1790 the couple moved to a house at Deepdene, near Dorking in Surrey. Sadly William died on 20 January 1796 and Sophia later married again, the Revd. William Clay. She herself died on 20 June 1802.

Sophia spent much of her time at home in writing and it is for this that she was given an entry in the *Dictionary of National Biography*. Her work included poetry, two volumes of which were published in 1793, and two tragedies.[62] Sophia's poetry is mostly satirical and amusing. She was of the same generation as Georgiana, Duchess of Devonshire, and the following is an illustration of her witty observations:

Portrait of Lady Sophia Burrell (Private Collection)

City Gentleman

An extract from *Verses to a Lady, on her saying she preferred Commonalty to an Irish Peerage*.
May 20th, 1776 (published 1793)

'Behold that macaroni Lord!

So gay in clothes – profuse in board,

His fine apparel marks the fool,

And points him out for ridicule;

Proud as a peacock he appears,

Though to his tradesmen he arrears;

I know that his estate is dipped,

His name disgraced, his woodlands stripped,

To dress that carcase, and support

An idle puppy of the court,

A useless bawler in the House,

Whose brains would hardly serve a louse.

His pocket and his skull are brothers,

They thrive by borrowing from others;

I thank my stars, with heart sincere,

I was not born to be a Peer;

Make *me* an Alderman, kind fate!

And let these glory in their state.'

(see Appendix 11 for additional poems)

The early 1770s must have been a very happy time for Charles. He had proved his leadership qualities at sea and his business brain in commerce. His City interests were doing well and he founded a bank, as will be seen later. The greatest accolade was royal recognition when in May 1774 he was created a Baronet.[D] On 3 May 1774 the *London Chronicle* reported:

> St.James's, May 3. The King has been pleased to grant the dignity of a Baronet of Great Britain, unto the following Gentlemen, viz: including ...
>
> Charles Raymond, of Valentine House in Essex, Esq; and in default of male issue, to Wm. Burrell, of Beckenham in Kent, Esq; and his heirs male by Sophia his wife, daughter of the said Charles Raymond.

[D] There is some confusion as to the date. G E Cokayne *Complete Baronetage* p.177 gives the date as 31 May 1774 and the National Archives say that Grants of baronetcies are recorded on the Patent Rolls in TNA series C 66. The indexes for 1774 (14 George III) give the date as 31 May 1774.
However, contemporary newspapers published the information as for 3 May 1774.

Sir Charles Raymond of Valentines and the East India Company

The *Gazetteer & New Daily Advertiser* reported in its issue dated 5 May 1774 that the previous day a number of gentlemen, including Charles, 'had the honour of kissing his Majesty's hand at St.James's on being honoured with the dignity of Baronets of Great Britain.' If his wife and his three daughters accompanied him, they must have caused quite a stir in their magnificent silk gowns. Charles was now a man to whom others showed deference by his rank, not just his professional skills.

Later that year there was another happy event when Charles's middle daughter, Juliana, married Henry Boulton of Leatherhead, Surrey, on 3 November 1774 in the City church of St.Helen's.[63] Two days earlier her friend Elizabeth Moffatt had married Sir Thomas Mills, nephew of the Earl of Mansfield, at St Margaret's, Barking. There must have been considerable excitement at Cranbrook House and Valentines at the end of October!

Henry Boulton was the son of Richard Crabb who had worked his way through the East India Company at the same time as Charles, serving as a captain for four voyages and then becoming a PMO. The two men must have been very well acquainted, if not firm friends. Richard Crabb had a brother, Henry Crabb, who was a senior official for the EIC for many years and later became a Director. In 1745 Henry inherited considerable property from a cousin with the surname Boulton, and so he changed his name to include this. When he died in 1773 his brother was his heir and he also changed his name from Richard Crabb to Richard Boulton. His son was aged 21 but also made the change so that when he married Juliana Raymond the following year he was styled Henry Boulton.

After the death of his father in 1777 Henry Boulton inherited the estate of Thorncroft at Leatherhead and in 1783 he was High Sheriff of Surrey. He became a very successful manager of shipping for the EIC: taking over from his father in 1777 he was responsible for ten ships (which made forty-one voyages) until 1806.[64] In 1778 he is shown in partnership with his father-in-law in property at Blackwall Ship Yard. He, too, became a Manager of the Sun Fire Office.[65]

Later City interests

Apart from Valentine House, Charles had a London home and for much of the 1770s this was in Birchin Lane, which runs between Lombard Street and Cornhill. For business he could always be contacted via the Jerusalem Coffee House at Cowper's Court, just a stone's throw away.[66] Birchin Lane is quite modern today, but slipping down the side passages into Exchange Alley and its courts, one could be back in eighteenth century London. The George and Vulture tavern appears little changed from September 1768 when Charles gave a Turtle Feast there for the East India Company,

106

City Gentleman

using a creature that weighed 501 lb, brought from St Helena in the *Earl of Elgin*.[67] The Jerusalem Coffee House was a regular haunt for people involved with the EIC, whether as merchants, insurance agents or mariners. This was the place for a respectable father hoping to persuade a captain to give his son a start as a midshipman, or for a wife hoping to get a passage to India to join her husband. It seems likely that Charles would have had an agent present who would attend to any business which might be of interest to the Raymond family circle. Meanwhile he turned his skills in other directions within the City.

Charles continued as a Manager of the Sun Fire Office but eventually 'disqualified himself' so that his place could be filled by his new son-in-law, William Burrell, on 8 July 1773. Charles had been continually absent from the Management Committee for the past year and on 22 April, nine days after Sophia had married, Charles transferred his holding of fifty-six shares to William Burrell. Shortly before this he purchased a considerable parcel of land in Woodham Ferrers (including the manor of Champions) and Cold Norton which had been acquired by the Sun Fire Office in default of a loan. He added the manor of Edwin's Hall and in all the holding covered approximately 1,900 acres. Some of this is now covered by South Woodham Ferrers. There is nothing to suggest that Charles viewed this as anything other than an investment and a source of rent revenue and much of this property was sold at auction in July 1787.[68]

In his will Charles states that he was also entitled to 'a perpetual yearly rent charge or fee farm rent of four hundred pounds per annum issuing and payable out of an estate at Shiplake in the County of Oxford granted to me by Henry Constantine Jennings Esq.' He appears never to have owned Shiplake, nor to have lived there. The estate, known as Shiplake Court, belonged to Henry Constantine Jennings and when Jennings found himself in financial difficulties in 1769 he consolidated his debts and they were taken on by Sir Charles Raymond in exchange for an annual fee farm rent on the Shiplake estate.[69]

Banking

By building up his EIC shipping enterprise and sheer hard work Charles must have become extremely wealthy and looked around for new ways to maximise his assets. Apart from his wealth, he had become a respected figure within the business community so he had the other important asset needed in banking – trust. He was well known to many of those who had funds to invest in shipping and he understood the principles of accountancy. Success in private trade abroad had been dependent on having money to invest and those involved with the EIC were familiar with the concept of a loan covered

Sir Charles Raymond of Valentines and the East India Company

by a bill of exchange issued to pay a stated sum at a future date, providing credit to purchase goods and allowing time for their sale before the draft was presented.

By 1677 London was home to over 40 persons or partnerships offering banking services, and in 1694 the Bank of England was formed. From 1708 this new bank had certain exclusive rights concerning note issue which effectively prevented the formation of other joint stock banks in England and Wales for over a century, thereby capping the size of any potential competitors. However there were a growing number of smaller banking concerns, from informal arrangements in the country where a shopkeeper might offer credit or means of payment to his customers, to more formal partnerships, initially confined to London, set up specifically to act as bankers. London's banks fell broadly into one of two categories: 'City' banks which primarily existed to provide services to commercial and trading firms and institutions, and 'West End' banks such as Drummonds, Childs, Hoares and Coutts which were established by what became leading families to offer more personal banking services to the gentry and aristocracy, for instance in securing mortgages on property or investing customers' funds in government stocks.[70]

In January 1771 Charles along with John Williams were two of the five founder members of a new 'City' bank known as **Raymond, Williams, Vere, Lowe and Fletcher,** with each partner investing £5,000. (At the end of the nineteenth century, this firm merged to become part of the bank later known as Williams Deacon's Bank, whose modern successor is The Royal Bank of Scotland.) In 1778 Charles retired from this bank and established another as **Raymond, Harley, Webber & Co**. The Webber was almost certainly William Webber of Highlands, although he died the following year. By 1781 Charles had involved Donald Cameron and the bank was called **Raymond, Harley, Lloyd & Cameron**. This bank ceased trading with the death of Cameron in 1797.[71]

These bald facts conceal the family network as John Williams, Webber and Cameron were each married to sisters of Sarah Raymond. When John Williams died in 1774 his place at the bank was taken by his brother Robert Williams (1734 - 1814). He had been apprenticed at the age of fourteen to a Covent Garden cabinet-maker. Forty years later Robert had bought his master's business and had a thriving and fashionable trade, also probably supplying furniture and fittings to EIC ships. He invested in East Indiamen and became PMO of many voyages between 1778-1810. He was elected MP for Caernarvonshire in 1790 and served for over twenty years. Robert and his wife (Jane Chassereau, daughter of a Huguenot refugee) lived at Wallwood, Leytonstone, until he purchased the magnificent Moor Park in Hertfordshire in 1801. When died in 1814 he

City Gentleman

left the vast sum of £500,000, including landed estates in Hertfordshire and Dorset and a substantial interest in the bank.[72]

Like John Williams, their brother Stephen (1739 – 1805) went to sea for the EIC and served as captain on three voyages of the *Hector* (PMO Andrew Moffatt) and then three more voyages as captain on ships managed by his brother Robert Williams. When he retired Stephen became a Director of the EIC throughout the 1790s.[73] He does not appear to have been involved in banking but his role as a Director of EIC may have helped the family in their investments.

But banking was not all about making money. When new charities were started, with subscriptions invited, 'Sir Charles Raymond and Co. of No. 20 Birchin-lane' was frequently listed, just as today when many banks offer their services to the Disasters Emergency Committee. We are asked to assist the victims of earthquakes and tsunamis, and in 1781 a fund was set up to assist the victims of a hurricane disaster in St Vincent's and Dominica. More commonly in the 1770s the charities were for the 'Soldiers who are, or may be employed in his Majesty's Service in America, and for succouring the distressed Widows and Orphans of those brave Men, who have fallen' or for 'the distresses of the Poor, in this severe and inclement season' for new hospitals, etc.[74]

Charles's neighbour and retired EIC captain Henry Fletcher was also a founder member of **Raymond, Williams, Vere, Lowe and Fletcher**. Another, later, partner was Samuel Peach who was a Director of the EIC and a silk merchant who probably imported raw silk from Bengal. Among other property Peach purchased the estate of Luxborough at Chigwell in 1775.[75] Fletcher and Peach inadvertently involved the bank in a major scandal which resulted in the hanging of the Rev. Dr. William Dodd.

William Dodd studied at Cambridge University, was ordained, and in the early 1750s he was curate at West Ham. Although he did not christen Charles's daughter Sophia in 1753, Charles may well have been acquainted with the young man. He did well and in 1764 he became chaplain to the King. He was tutor to the son of the Earl of Chesterfield and also took the sons of other wealthy patrons as his pupils. By the 1770s Dodd was a fashionable London preacher whose sermons were well attended. He ascended the pulpit in great style, with a bouquet and a diamond ring glittering on his finger, but he delivered his sermons from the heart with energy and dramatic effect. This enthralled his congregation, which was more used to sermons being read by a less eloquent preacher. However, he was living well above his means and became seriously in debt. He tried to obtain financial help by dubious means and when his actions were realised he was ridiculed in the press.

In February 1777 he forged a bond for £4,000 supposedly signed by his former pupil, who was now himself the Earl of Chesterfield and to whom Dodd was now chaplain.

Sir Charles Raymond of Valentines and the East India Company

This was presented, along with a forged letter from the Earl, to an agent who did not have the means to fulfil it, so he presented it to Henry Fletcher and Samuel Peach at the bank. The crime was soon discovered and officials from the City Court at the Guildhall visited Dodd, who confessed the crime and returned most of the money. Fletcher was not eager to prosecute, but Dodd was taken to the Guildhall and charged with intent to defraud **Sir Charles Raymond and Co. Bankers**. His rhetorical skills were put to good use when he explained, in his own defence, that he had not intended any malignancy and that restitution had been made. The jury retired for about ten minutes and then returned with a guilty verdict, but at the same time presented a petition, humbly recommending the doctor to the royal mercy. This was to no avail and Dr Dodd was hanged at Tyburn on 27 June 1777. Charles had no personal involvement in the affair, but it reflected on him and caused him some distress.[76]

Another crime against Charles was reported three months later. In September 1777 six men were taken before the Justices at Ilford for stealing a vast quantity of lead from his house (Valentines) where they had been working as plumbers. One gave evidence against the other five and two more men were charged with receiving. This still rings very true today![77]

The 1770s was a time of massive expansion in the Midlands and the North and new local banks were set up to meet their financial needs. In November 1771, towards the end of their first year trading as bankers in London, **Raymond, Williams, Vere, Lowe and Fletcher** together became founding partners in the first bank to be established in Manchester.[78] Their bank paid £4,000 for a fifth share, with three men of local standing: Edward Byrom, William Allen and Roger Sedgwick, none of whom had previous experience of banking. The fifth partner was Samuel Peach, who used William Allen as an agent to pass imported raw silk to throwsters in Macclesfield and then send the silk thread to Spitalfields for weaving. Gradually most of the partners died or dropped out and Peach was declared bankrupt in 1781. William Allen managed the bank's affairs in Manchester, but sadly his brother-in-law, John Livesey, took advantage of his position and Allen loaned him far more than was prudent. By 1782 Richard Lowe and Charles Vere wrote from London to Allan, questioning the amounts being loaned to Livesey, Hargreave & Co. They were not satisfied by his reply, but decided to do nothing until they could consult with their senior partner, Sir Charles Raymond, who was at Bath.[E] Allen managed to continue with evasive tactics until it was discovered that Livesey had been involved in more serious fraud and in the spring of 1788 Livesey, Hargreave & Co. and William Allen were declared bankrupt. Charles lost an enormous sum of money

---

[E] See page 120 for his visits to Bath.

with the collapse of the Manchester Bank, something in the region of £50,000 which would be over £6.5m in 2013.[79]

Politics

Charles Raymond had earned his position by hard work and shrewd business sense and he now tried to extend his influence into politics. He may have become acquainted with Charles Watson-Wentworth, second Marquess of Rockingham (1730-1782) who served as Whig Prime Minster 1765-6. At that time Rockingham had asked to lease Wanstead House, empty while Earl Tylney was abroad, and it seems his request was granted, at least 'for the season', so he would have been a close neighbour of Charles.[80] Rockingham favoured a more conciliatory policy towards America and defended the rights of the East India Company.

In February 1773 Rockingham must have written to Charles, apparently about taxes on tea and the EIC, as Charles's reply has survived in the Wentworth Woodhouse Muniments in the Sheffield Archives.[81] It was in May that the Act of Parliament was passed which led to the 'Boston Tea Party' in December 1773.

In October 1774 Charles put himself forward to stand against John Wilkes in the Middlesex Parliamentary elections. However, after Wilkes was elected Lord Mayor of the City of London and it was clear he had a major body of support, Charles stepped down.[82] Nearly a year later there were rumours of him taking part in another election, as reported in the *Morning Post & Daily Advertiser* on 20 September 1775:

> Lord Waltham is very active in his canvass for the County of Essex.... He had a meeting of his friends at the coffee-house in Chelmsford ... – how the matter will end, the poll only can determine, as there are several other gentlemen who seem as anxious, if not as *capable* as his Lordship to represent the county: - Sir Charles Raymond, Bart. is now talked of pretty strongly; a man universally beloved: - Young Harvey will likewise put in a nomination...

However, this came to nothing. On 8 August 1774 Charles had been given the Freedom of the City of Exeter and in 1776 he wrote offering himself as a prospective MP for Exeter, but he was not supported as a candidate.[83]

East India Company

Charles continued managing ships for the EIC throughout the remainder of his life. In the 1750s he was responsible for over a fifth of the voyages and in the 1760s he was PMO for 18 per cent. On 11 August 1762 Charles signed charterparty agreements for five new ships to sail in the 1762/3 season [84] and was PMO for three other ships as well.

Sir Charles Raymond of Valentines and the East India Company

The number tailed off to 7 per cent in the 1770s when his other business interests took over. However, with his status and leadership qualities he remained an important figure within the EIC until he died and his various shipping interests must have been managed by a team of men providing legal, clerical and secretarial support.

As the century progressed larger ships were required and as new innovations became available this became increasingly possible. When Charles first sailed on the *Dawsonne* in 1730 this, and most other East Indiamen, were rated at 499 tons. The first nine ships Charles commissioned from 1747/8 until 1756/7 were also rated at the standard 499 tons. His new ship for the 1757/8 season *Osterley (1)* was 642 tons. The *Duke of Richmond* launched for the 1759/60 season was rated at 767 tons but the *Granby* 1767/8 rated at 786 tons was the largest of the ships Charles commissioned. To cope with the demand for oriental goods the Court soon required larger ships for the trade with China, like the *Earl of Abergavenny (1)* launched in 1789 and rated at 1182 tons and the *Royal George (4)* launched in 1802 at 1260 tons. These ships needed to be built with strength to survive an encounter with the warships of the French at this time.[85]

Another 'new' ship for which Charles signed as charterparty for the 1757/8 season was in fact a French East Indiaman, the *Pondicherry*, which had been captured on her maiden voyage in January 1757 by HMS *Dover*. After a refit she was renamed *Pitt (1)*, was rated at 600 tons, had thirty guns (canon) and was expected to have a crew of 120. She left Portsmouth on 6 March 1758 but her voyage was far from routine. This larger, more heavily armed ship was intended to protect the convoy of East Indiamen should they be challenged by the French. However, when they reached India her sheer size meant that the Madras Road was not a safe anchorage with the hurricane season approaching.

It had been intended that the *Pitt* would escort the East Indiamen going to China but she had been delayed and the convoy had already left. Her own passage to Canton was threatened by the approaching north-east monsoon but Captain William Wilson hatched a cunning plan.[F] He journeyed to Batavia and from there explored a route known to the Dutch but, since 1623, closed to the English. He took a smaller ship (a snow) to help him sound out a safe passage and by luck, skill and diplomacy he reached Canton. He spoke to the crew of boats they passed, and when obtaining food from the islands en route the captain presented gifts to the tribal leaders and in return obtained useful information about the course to follow. On one occasion he managed to pass the *Pitt* off as a Dutch ship, and it appears he obtained some Dutch charts somewhere along his way. On his journey Captain Wilson surveyed many of the important features and

---

[F] It has been suggested that Captain Wilson was ordered by the EIC to treat the voyage as one of discovery.

City Gentleman

hazards he encountered, making careful notes, and when he reached Canton he had two new sets of charts prepared. One he gave to the supercargoes at Canton and the other he took back to Madras. The new route he had charted meant that English ships could sail to Canton at any time of year and by a faster route. To avoid conflict with the Dutch his achievement was kept quiet but when he returned to London the Court honoured him by striking a commemorative medal. Within a few years other English East Indiamen were using this route to establish new trading links.

On the one occasion when *Pitt* did encounter and engage a French ship it was discovered that her weight meant the ship was too low in the water, which flowed in when the lower gun ports were opened, so these guns could not be used. Modifications were made to the ship when she returned to London and she carried out routine duty as a merchant ship.[86]

Insuring his ships was a major concern of a PMO who had a responsibility to the other investors. This was particularly important at times of war. It is likely much of this was handled for Charles by Andrew & John Moffatt & Co. in Lombard Street, but there was a wide choice of people who could be involved. Many agents gathered at the coffee house set up in Lombard Street by Edward Lloyd (who had died in 1713) where preliminary discussions could take place, although the actual underwriting was conducted on the floor of the Royal Exchange. In 1769 a rival 'Lloyds' coffee house was set up which was run on more efficient lines and eventually the original closed in 1785. However, this move towards greater efficiency led seventy-nine brokers to subscribe £100 each to form the Society of Lloyd's in 1771 and in 1774 they rented premises in the Royal Exchange building where they stayed until it was destroyed by fire in 1838.[87]

After 1778 Charles is recorded as having business premises at George Street, beside the Mansion House. He would have been familiar with the Royal Exchange from his early days on the committee of the Free British Fishery. Apart from conducting insurance business there, Charles, like the EIC, may have rented some of their storage facilities in the cellars for his more valuable goods.[88]

A trial at the Old Bailey on 19 October 1774 throws an interesting light on other management issues. Two men were accused of stealing 640 lb. wt. of cordage, value 32s. the property of Robert Roddam, John Cheshire, Robert Gregory, William Phillips, John Pope, Sir Charles Raymond, Bt., John Perry, Elizabeth Roddam, John Mill, Joseph Bird, Richard Benyon, John Raymond and Shearman Godfrey. They were acquitted, but this illustrates how the group must have had a joint investment in the rope.[89]

Half these men have not been researched, but John Perry was a ship builder at Blackwall and Richard Benyon of Englefield House has already been mentioned as the

Sir Charles Raymond of Valentines and the East India Company

retired Governor of Madras who owned property in Essex. Shearman Godfrey was a PMO partner with Charles and Joseph Bird of Upton House was his son-in-law. John Raymond was Charles's cousin who had an out-of-town residence at Chigwell.

Charles had a share in a ropeworks at Blackwall with his brother-in-law John Williams until he died in 1774.[90] Charles, John's brother Robert Williams, and Henry Fletcher were his executors and they were asked to manage his business affairs to the advantage of his family until his children came of age. The three men were friends, all involved in banking together and it is likely Charles took over the management of the ropeworks and other allied business interests. He probably mentored Williams's eldest son who was in his late teens when his father died.

Charles must have employed a number of people to keep his ships in the best condition after their routine refit and to provide physical labour at the dockside. He also had his own warehouses for storage. On 19 June 1778 a Sun Fire Office insurance policy was issued to Sir Charles Raymond Bt., Henry Boulton, John Perry & Joseph Hankey of Blackwall Ship Builders, on their stock in warehouses in one brick and timber building adjoining the Foreman's House in Blackwall Yard, for not exceeding £800.[91] It was not until early in the nineteenth century that the EIC constructed its own docks. Before this, EIC ship building was carried out beside the Thames, often at Blackwall, and this makes it easier to understand why so many of those involved as PMO lived in Ilford, Woodford, Chigwell and the neighbouring parishes.

As a senior figure in EIC shipping circles Charles had considerable influence and was able to offer patronage to many youngsters trying to climb the EIC ladder. One young man he was able to help when he became PMO was Gabriel Steward, son of the man of the same name who had helped Charles in his early career at sea. When Charles made his first voyage (as purser on the *Dawsonne*) the captain was Francis Steward and his brother Gabriel was second mate. On Charles's next voyage as third mate on the *Princess of Wales* Gabriel Steward was the first mate and he had gone on to become a captain. Sadly he died at Madras on 26 July 1744 while captain of the *Winchester*. They had had a very eventful voyage out with his son Gabriel making his first voyage as sixth mate. Robert Clive was a passenger, making his first trip to the country which was to make him famous as Lord Clive of India. Gabriel Steward junior worked his way up the EIC ladder to captain and his last four voyages, from 1756, were on ships managed by Charles.

Another youngster helped by Charles was Benjamin Godfrey who served as a midshipman on the *Wager* 1737/8 and then as fifth mate on the *Wager* 1740/1, both under Captain Charles Raymond with William Webber as third mate, and John Raymond as PMO. Benjamin was seven years younger than Charles but was born in

Exeter so there may have been a family connection or friendship when they were children.[92] It is clear Benjamin Godfrey was assisted by the Raymond circle. After his first two voyages on the *Wager* under Captain Charles Raymond, Godfrey worked his way up the ladder so that by the time Charles became a PMO he employed Godfrey as first mate on the *Sandwich* 1752/3 and then for three voyages as captain. Sadly Benjamin Godfrey died in Batavia on 1 February 1765.

Another young man mentored by the Raymond circle was Henry Hinde Pelly, son of Charles's friend and neighbour at Upton, Captain John Pelly. Henry's grandfather, John Pelly, died just before he left on his first voyage in 1762 and his father died later in that year. His first voyage was as fourth mate on a ship managed by his maternal grandfather, Henry Hinde. He then served as second mate for PMO Charles Foulis, captain of the *Europa* for Andrew Moffatt and then as captain of the *Europa* for his last two voyages under PMO Charles Raymond. When he retired from the sea he became the PMO of *Europa* and other ships himself. He married Sally Hitchen, daughter and co-heir of John Blake, and they had four sons. The eldest was John Henry Pelly (1777 – 1852), who became a governor of the Bank of England and of the Hudson Bay Company, Elder Brother of the Trinity House and was created a baronet. He married Emma, sixth daughter of Henry Boulton of Thorncroft, Surrey and his wife Juliana, the granddaughter of Charles Raymond.[93]

Captain Henry Hinde Pelly
© *Trinity House, with thanks*

As has been stated already, Charles seems to have been a lucky owner as of the 113 ships he managed, just three were lost. The *Ajax* 1758/9 was captured by the French off the Scilly Isles on 6 March 1761 but two others were wrecked even closer to home.

Sir Charles Raymond of Valentines and the East India Company

On 11 August 1762 Charles signed charterparty agreements for five new ships. One of them was the *Lord Clive* which he managed in partnership with his cousin John Raymond, but sadly she foundered at the start of her second voyage. She passed Dover and rounded the Dungeness headland on Wednesday 25 February 1767. The weather was squally with bad visibility, the wind coming from the west. They tacked to and fro trying to make headway down the English Channel but were instead blown towards the French coast, pushed along with the current of the Spring tide. Early in the afternoon of Saturday 28 February they saw land close by. Dropping two anchors in an effort to save the *Lord Clive* was to no avail and they felt the ship thumping hard on the sandy bottom in the heavy swell. They cut away the main and mizzen masts to minimise the effect of the wind, but soon there was seven feet of water in the hold. They got out the yawl (a smaller boat) to save the men and some attempted to get ashore on a raft. Sadly two men were drowned. By 4pm everyone else was safely on shore and they were amazed to find they were about nine miles south of Boulogne.

News of the loss reached the Court of Directors within a few days and they made arrangements for Messrs Gallet & Marteau at Boulogne to act as their agents for the salvage operation, with supercargo Mr Thomas Thomas staying to take charge. The two other supercargoes travelled out to China on another ship, but Mr Thomas was assured that although he did not visit Canton he would still be entitled to his commission on the voyage. The Court referred the whole matter to their Committee of Shipping to investigate the cause of the 'misfortune' but no record of their conclusions has been found. The owners did not suffer any financial penalty but the captain did not sail for the EIC again.[94]

It was over twelve years later that the *Valentine (2)* 1776/7 was wrecked when returning home up the English Channel on 16 November 1779.

Sir Charles Raymond's ship *Valentine*

Charles owned two ships called the *Valentine*. The first was built by Perry and had three decks, with 3 inch bottom, registered as 655 tons, and was launched in 1758. Her first voyage was to India and China and on her way home she witnessed the sinking of the *Griffin* with whom she was in convoy. This was in January 1761 when the *Griffin* struck a reef off the 'island of Zelo' to the east of the northern tip of Borneo.[95] The PMO was Thomas Hunt who had been the second signature to his father-in-law, Richard Mickelfield, for the disastrous voyage of the *Duke of Cuberland (2)* 1749/50. After her second voyage *Valentine* was rebuilt.

City Gentleman

Valentine (2) made four voyages and would have been rebuilt on returning to England, but she never made it home. On her last voyage, under Captain James Ogilvie, she left Portsmouth early in January 1777, called at Madeira and Cape Town, and arrived at Madras on 25 June. She then continued to Calcutta where she stayed until the end of December, loading redwood, salt petre and bales of raw silk, along with their private trade goods. On 29 December the ship was nearly lost when strong winds drove them onto a sand bank but help was summoned, the pumps were constantly at work and much of the cargo was taken off. *Valentine* sprang a leak but with 30 men from another East Indiaman, *Houghton*, to assist them, she was eventually freed and made it to Madras. Here she was patched up so that she could sail round to Bombay to be properly repaired and made safe for her journey home. She arrived back at Madras on 22 June 1778 to reload her cargo.

However, in July and August *Valentine* was shown as 'on a cruise' without cargo, off the coast of India. This was because hostilities had broken out with the French and Captain James Ogilvie had been summoned to the Select Committee of the EIC in Madras. After swearing him to secrecy he was informed of the Company's orders to besiege Pondicherry, that Sir Edward Vernon was to attack the French Squadron with HM ships and had requested the assistance of the *Valentine*. The captain's journal for Monday, 10 August 1778 tells the story:

> At 5PM the Commodore made the signal for all Commanders upon which I went on board the *Rippon* and at a Consultation respecting the eligibility of engaging the French fleet it was the unanimous opinion to fight them. Captain Panton in the *Seahorse* was appointed to lead upon both Tacks, with the *Valentine* second. I received orders to keep my ship prepared for action.

> At day light the French fleet to windward in sight from the Main Top, bearing down and showing their colours when immediately the Squadron haul'd up for them & having near'd them within two leagues the Commodore made the signal to form into a close line of Battle, one ship ahead of another. The *Seahorse* in the vanguard, the *Valentine* second, *Rippon* third & *Coventry* in the rear, the *Cormorant* sloop outside of the line upon the Commodore's off beam. In this order we went under our Topsails & Top Gallant Sails. The French squadron form'd themselves into a line of Battle ahead their flag on board the *Brilliant* leading the van, *Le Pourvcouse* second, *Le Sortain* third, *L'Orison* fourth, and *Le Brisson* in the rear; and in this order under their topsails they waited for us to attack them but with so light a wind that the two Fleets closed very slowly.

> At one o'clock, on the wind shifting in our favour, Sir Edward Vernon threw out the signal to make sail ahead in order to near the enemy & sent an officer with orders to Captain Panton of the *Seahorse* to keep at a farther distance ahead and with directions to me that when I should observe the *Seahorse* make sail to go ahead, to make sail in the *Valentine* to keep up with her, which orders were immediately obeyed by both ships.

Sir Charles Raymond of Valentines and the East India Company

Captain Ogilvie goes into considerable detail to explain that his orders, as specified by the signals and the Articles of the Fighting Instructions, could not properly be executed as the two fleets were sailing on different tacks, and it seems he wanted to justify his actions in case anything went wrong. However, the two ships *Seahorse* and *Valentine* complied as best they could and bore towards the French under their topsails. The story seems to unfold in slow motion...

> At two o'clock Sir Edward Vernon made the signal to engage, but I judged the distance too great and Captain Panton seem'd to be of the same opinion as he reserved his fire likewise. ~ ~ ~ At half past two the Vans of the two Fleets were very near when the *Brilliant & Le Pourvcouse* began the action by firing on the *Seahorse* and *Valentine,* which we returned soon after, and having a very light air of wind we were alongside of them very closely engaged for a considerable time. But the two Squadrons being, as I have before observed, upon different tacks and the *Rippon* coming into the action, we pass'd the *Brilliant* and *Pourvcouse* and with the *Seahorse* came up and engaged the three ships of the enemies rear.

> The *Valentine* having come the length in the enemies line of the *Sortain* I immediately bore down upon her & wore the ship round upon the same tack with her in order to lay her fairly alongside, which as the *Sortain* declined a closer action, obliged her to bear up. This broke the enemies line and occasioned the rear ships of their Fleet to fall to leeward, and entirely disjoin them from their leading ships, the *Brilliant & Pourvcouse*. They, upon coming along side of the *Rippon,* had set their foresails and soon passed ahead, to all appearance running off and leaving their rear to their fate. Sir Edward Vernon, when he had passed the *Brilliant* and *Pourvcouse* likewise wore ship and the whole Squadron got upon the same tack with the enemy.

> But now only the rear of their Fleet was engaged with the *Seahorse & Valentine.* As both ships had run the gauntlet and were almost wrecks in their sails and rigging and having got considerably to leeward of the *Rippon* and *Coventry* by endeavouring to bring the enemy into closer action, the French rear taking the advantage of our shattered condition; made sail in order to push ahead of us and to endeavour to close with their van. I set the foresail and what sail we could make in order to keep up with them but all we could make being very little, they drew ahead of us fast.

The English rearguard were in good condition, with no signs of having suffered in any material manner, and tried to engage the enemies rear. The French Commodore came to their assistance and with the *Pourvcouse* came back alongside, engaging the *Rippon & Coventry*. As they were again upon different tacks they soon passed each other, after which the two French ships both bore down upon the *Valentine* which obliged her to abandon any further pursuit of the enemy's rear. The log continues...

> Here I cannot omit without great unjustice to all my officers and men to make particular mention of the gallantry with which they received and sustained the very unequal fire of

118

those two heavy ships and the manliness with which they stood their quarters and plied their guns. For a considerable time we were unsupported against them, but in justice to Captain Panton of the *Seahorse* who was astern of the *Valentine*, it is my duty to observe that he did every thing in his power to get to our assistance as soon as possible, and very gallantly turning upon the *Valentines* weather quarter, betwixt the *Brilliant* and us, took off their fire from us, soon after which the *Brilliant* and *Pourvcouse* hauld their wind and crowded sail towards Pondicherry Road.

The three remaining French ships continued the battle but...

… I could only edge down a little to have a flying knock with the enemies rear ships as they pass'd us and we exchanged several broad sides with each of them as they came up, but they were in a great hurry to join their Van, who were flying with every sail out they could set. At this time the *Seahorse* had past ahead of the *Valentine* and during our last encounter with the three ships of the enemies rear was upon our off bow and we were left to bring up the rear, but in so shattered a condition that having very little sail to set the Commodore hove too in order to let us come up and thus at the close of the day ended our engagement. The French Squadron with all sail set standing, or more properly flying to Pondicherry Road and the English too much damaged to be able to pursue them. I say so at least of the *Valentine* ~

The *Valentine* lost two dead and fifteen injured, and limped back to Madras for yet further repairs. She was on her fourth voyage and would have been showing the signs of age even without the need for repairs. Consequently she struggled to keep up with her companions on the last part of her journey home and the small fleet gathered in the River Shannon to await naval protection for the convoy up the English Channel. Eventually they started on the last leg home but again a fierce storm blew up and the convoy was scattered. Captain Ogilvie must have decided to try and make for shelter at St.Peter Port in Guernsey, but sadly, she was unable to make it. As darkness fell on 16 November 1779, with a gale blowing through her tattered sails, she struck the rocks off the little island of Brecqhou. Her crew and passengers were able to get ashore safely so thankfully there was no loss of life. For several weeks the ship herself was broken up by the waves and her cargo was looted.[96]

Shipwrecks have been fairly common down the centuries around Guernsey, with the strong currents and rocky outcrops, but a ship of this size went down in local folklore. Some of the canon were dragged ashore and can still be seen in Sark today. In 1976 a young local diver, Richard Keen, explored the wreck site and later, with a team of divers, small items were recovered from the seabed. What there is to find is still attracting interest and maybe a new team of divers will investigate the site one day with more modern technology.

Sir Charles Raymond of Valentines and the East India Company

In September 1778, a year before the loss of the *Valentine*, Charles signed charterparty agreements for three new ships *Atlas (1)*, *Earl of Oxford* and *Earl Talbot (1)*, the first he had commissioned since 1771.[97] He continued as PMO of these three ships but otherwise his involvement with EIC dwindled.

More Family Matters

While the *Valentine (2)* was on her last voyage Lady Sarah Raymond died, on 14 April 1778 at their home above the bank in Birchin Lane.[98] The reason for her death is not known but Charles and Sarah had made at least two visits to Bath in February 1773 and February 1775.[99] Possibly the visits were to enjoy the social life in this most fashionable city, but maybe they also felt the need to seek the medicinal benefits of the mineral waters. Sarah's death may have been the reason that Charles ordered the three new ships – throwing himself into a busy schedule so that he didn't have so much time to think about her loss.

The Pump Room, Bath, in the year 1784 with the Characters of that Day, by Humphry Repton
© Victoria Art Gallery, Bath and North East Somerset Council/ Bridgeman Images

City Gentleman

Sarah was fifty-six when she died, Charles was a few days from his sixty-fifth birthday, and they had been married for thirty-five years. The meaning of his life at Ilford had gone, and within a few weeks, on 28 May 1778, the *Gazetteer and New Daily Advertiser* carried the following advertisement:

> To be LETT, furnished or unfurnished, eight miles from Whitechapel Church, the seat of Sir Charles Raymond, Bart. called VALENTINE HOUSE, with between 50 and 60 acres of land adjoining. May be entered upon directly, and fit for any Nobleman or Gentleman of fortune that requires a residence near town. Every thing requisite is thereunto belonging, such as hot houses, pineries, canals, &c.

> N.B. May be viewed with tickets, which may be had by applying to Mr. Cameron, at the Banking House of Sir Charles Raymond and Co. in George-street, Mansion-house; or Mr William Dearsley, attorney, at Romford, in Essex. A person at the house will attend to shew the premises.

It is not known whether a tenant took the house that summer as Charles continued to pay the rates himself for some time, but by May 1780 Lord Talbot had taken Valentine House. He had previously been living at the house at Aldborough Hatch which had been the home of John Williams and his family before his death in 1774. By this time Charles was paying the rates on Highlands, having moved in with his sister-in-law Elizabeth some time after her husband, William Webber, had died on 25 April 1779. Perhaps he felt his youngest daughter, Anna Maria, needed a lady as a companion now her sisters were married and her mother had died.[100]

William, Earl Talbot, came from Glamorganshire, which he represented in Parliament before he succeeded to the peerage on the death of his father in 1737. He was appointed Lord Steward of the Household to George III and played a leading part in his coronation in 1761. Walpole said of him 'He was strong, well-made, & very comely; but with no air, nor the manners of a man of quality.' He died at his house in Lincoln's Inn Fields on 27 April 1782, so he probably spent just a couple of summers actually living at Valentines, enjoying the country air and the local social scene.[101] Interestingly Charles had been PMO of a new ship called *Talbot* in 1762 and he named a new ship *Earl Talbot* in 1778.

The next tenant was William Raikes (1738- 1800) brother of Robert Raikes (1736-1811) who achieved recognition as the promoter of Sunday Schools in the 1780s. William became a merchant in London, a Director of the South Sea Company and one of the Commercial Commissioners under the Income Act for the City. He lived at Valentine House for some years from 1783/4 as the tenant of Charles and later Donald Cameron, but he was registered as the owner of The Rookery in George Lane, Woodford by late 1795 and was buried at St Mary's.[102]

121

Sir Charles Raymond of Valentines and the East India Company

William Raikes had a nephew, Col. William Raikes (1785-1854), son of Robert Raikes, who married Louise Boulton, granddaughter of Sir Charles Raymond, in 1820. This must just have been a coincidence as her parents, Juliana and Henry Bolton, had been living at Leatherhead since before Louise was born. Louise was a sister of Emma, wife of Sir John Henry Pelly.

On 29 June 1781 Charles's youngest daughter Anna Maria married Thomas Newte Esq, Batchelor of St Martins in the Fields, at St Margaret's church in Barking. The witnesses were her sisters Sophia Burrell and Juliana Boulton and, like her eldest sister, she married a man who was her second cousin. Thomas Newte's grandmother was Isabella Tanner, a sister of Charles's mother Anna Maria Tanner, and he had been brought up near Tiverton in Devon. He was also a retired EIC captain.

Thomas Newte started with the East India Company as servant to Captain Edward Lord Chick on *Anson (3)* 1763/4, PMO Charles Foulis. Chick had his first voyage twenty years earlier when he joined the crew of *Wager (2)* 1743/4 under Captain Charles Raymond. He had been taken on as a replacement third mate while they were in Calcutta, three weeks after Charles's brother-in-law, Thomas Webster, had died of fever along with a number of the crew. Chick would have been grateful to Charles for giving him such a good start, and he later served as first mate of the *Wager (2)* 1750/1 under PMO Charles Raymond. It is very likely that Charles had been asked by his cousin Samuel Newte to assist young Thomas, so Chick had agreed to take the lad under his wing. In the event this was to teach Newte far more than expected. The *Anson* was loaded with additional cargo of lead, iron, cannon, shot and copper (valued at £1,164) in Madeira Road and Chick was dismissed the service for smuggling.[103]

Newte's next voyage was as midshipman on *Anson (3)* and he then served on three voyages under PMO Charles Raymond before becoming captain of the *Ceres (1)* 1773/4 and 1776/7 for PMO John Raymond. He returned home from his last voyage in August 1778 and two years later he signed the charterparty agreements as PMO for *Asia (3)* and then for the *Earl of Chesterfield*, both with Donald Cameron as his second signature. He continued as a PMO for a total of eight ships, working with Cameron and John Raymond, until they had both died. In 1784 he offered himself to stand for parliament for Tiverton, but although encouraged by certain members of the corporation for several years, this came to nothing.[104]

Charles must have felt quite lonely by this time. His wife and his best friend, William Webber, had died and his daughters were married. His cousin, John Raymond, was still active and Charles may have spent time with him at his home in Chigwell. Charles made visits to Bath in December 1780 and again in March 1782, his arrival being noted in the newspapers as he was a baronet.

City Gentleman

Then on 9 August 1783 his arrival at the 'Hotwells' in Bristol was announced, but this time it was neither for social reasons, nor his own health. Sadly, Anna Maria died at Bristol Hot Wells ten days later. Her body was taken back for burial at Barking where there is a memorial to her inside St. Margaret's church.[105]

Broadstairs

Towards the end of his life Charles built a house near Broadstairs in Kent. It was described as 'a small pleasant seat for his summer residence' and was located a little to the south of the North Foreland lighthouse.[106] From his windows Charles would have had a wonderful view of the ships passing by, with nothing between but the roadway and grassland to the cliff edge. Perhaps he took comfort from the closeness of the sea which must have reminded him of his childhood at Withycombe Raleigh and the camaraderie of his younger days aboard ship.

Between his house and Broadstairs was the hamlet of Stone Street which had grown up inland from a natural cut in the cliffs, giving access to the beach. Should he wish to meet with his captains before the start or end of a voyage, he was ideally placed for them to row between the beach and the ship. Alternatively, he had a short journey should he decide to make contact with his ships when they anchored off Deal to deliver the EIC's mail and important packets to the Agent who would send them on to London. The location was close enough to London should business demands become urgent, but not as far away as Bath which was a social attraction from October to June.

By the 1780s Broadstairs, less than a mile from Charles's house, was becoming a fashionable place for sea-bathing and had accommodation for visitors in two large hotels, with a library and reading room for their additional amusement.[107] Being immersed in sea water was considered to be almost as beneficial as drinking spa water and it was becoming just as fashionable. Catherine Tylney-Long of Wanstead House, the young heiress to a vast fortune, took lodgings at Broadstairs in October 1811. Ramsgate was developed around the turn of the century and it was here the Duke of Clarence stayed in an effort to court her, though his proposal was refused.[108] Had she accepted she would have become Queen when the Duke was crowned as King William IV in 1830.

However, Margate had been established in the social network much earlier and was little more than four miles from Charles's new house. Whether or not he wanted to try sea-bathing, this was the place most likely to draw him should he need company. A guide book to Margate published in 1801 describes the facilities in some detail:

Sir Charles Raymond of Valentines and the East India Company

> The Bathing Rooms are seven in number, and situated near the harbour, on the western side of High Street: they are contrived on a plan so commodious and convenient, as to form an agreeable lounge to those who do not bathe, some of them being well supplied with the daily papers and have grand piano fortes kept for the use of the subscribers. These rooms are mostly resorted to in a morning by the company who mean to bathe; a slate is affixed in the lobby for the insertion of names, and every one, in his regular turn, is driven in the machines any depth into the sea, under the conduct of careful guides; at the back of the machine is a door through which the bathers descend a few steps into the water, and an umbrella of canvas falling over, conceals them from public view. Upwards of forty of these machines are frequently employed in a morning; their structure is at once both simple and convenient, and the pleasure and advantage of bathing may be enjoyed in so private a manner, as to be consistent with the strictest delicacy. ....
>
> Exclusive of these conveniences for cold sea-bathing, here are also four marble warm salt-water baths, upon a good construction, which being filled from the sea, are heated to any degree of temperature required, at a few minutes notice.[109]

Quite when the house near Broadstairs was built and how often Charles used it is not known. However, around his seventy-second birthday he decided he no longer needed it. On 13 April 1785 the *Morning Chronicle & London Advertiser* carried the following notice:

> ISLE OF THANET   To be Sold, completely furnished, or Let for a term, a most elegant modern FREEHOLD HOUSE, with an exceeding good stable, coach-houses, and a compact garden; beautifully situated on a pleasing eminence, in full and perfect view of the ships in the Downs, Channel, &c. and so near to the Sea as to be separated only by a lawn of a few hundred yards that gradually descends from it. The distance nearly equal between Margate and Ramsgate, and very contiguous to Broad Stairs. This House is well known, being built by, and late in the possession of Sir Charles Raymond, Bart.
>
> N.B. Convenient bathing close to the premises.
>
> Enquire of Mr. Woble, carpenter, Charles-street, Westminster.
>
> The payment of a great part of the purchase-money will be made convenient to the purchaser.

The last years

For many years, certainly from 1773, Charles had been among the many Governors of Christ's Hospital in the City, and this continued until he died. He also continued as Governor of Bridewell and Bethlem Hospitals and is mentioned as attending the Court in January 1782. His philanthropy was also evident when in 1775 a charity was set up in Old Street to give inoculation against smallpox to the poor of London 'by a few men of

City Gentleman

benevolent minds'. Sir Charles Raymond was the first of five Vice-Presidents listed in an advertisement in 1777.[110]

On 29 August 1782 whilst undergoing minor repair work at Spithead, the Royal Navy ship *Royal George* began to take on water. She capsized and sank very quickly with the loss of about 900 lives. Charles soon subscribed to the relief fund:

1782, September 26, Thursday *Morning Herald & Daily Advertiser* (London)

Subscription raised for the benefit of the sufferers by the loss of his Majesty's ship the *Royal George* are desired to apply, with full information of their circumstances... to the Committee appointed at Portsmouth... Subscriptions already received include ...

Lowe, Vere and Williams	£10 10s	
Wm. Deacon, of Portsmouth	£10 10s	
Sir Charles Raymond and Co	£10 10s	(This seems the standard amount)

Charles was now a well-known figure in the City and also, apparently, in Court circles:

Extracts from *Public Advertiser* (London) 1782, June 5, Wednesday

The KING'S BIRTHDAY. The Drawing Room was uncommonly crowded.... at St James's... the Queen was magnificently attired, the King in a Dress that was plain. The Prince of Wales was very splendid....

The Lady Waldegraves were among the most beautiful Women in the Room: They were *not* with Lord Egremont...

Also present were Lady Salisbury, Lady Harrington, Lady Lincoln, Miss Harland, Miss Cheap, Miss Woodley, Lady Duncannon, Lady Aylesford, Miss Campbell, Miss Cruikshank, &c. &c. But what are all these to the Charms of Devon's Duchess!

Lord Chesterfield was at Court, but *not* with Sir Charles Raymond.

Five years after the hanging of William Dodd the animosity between Charles and the Earl of Chesterfield was still apparent! It is worth noting that fourteen months after the hanging Thomas Newte had been PMO for the newly built *Earl of Chesterfield*, with Charles's brother-in-law and banking assistant, Donald Cameron, as his second signature.[111]

Perhaps Charles's last remaining friend from his days at sea was Gilbert Slater of Stepney who died in 1785.[112] He had served as fifth mate on Charles's first voyage as captain when all the other officers died, and then as third mate on the second voyage of the *Wager*. As already mentioned, his son, Gilbert Slater junior, was passionate about collecting new plants from abroad and had an extensive garden with stoves, greenhouses and conservatories at Knotts Green, Leyton. He was credited with introducing at least seventeen new species of plant into this country, mainly from China, including camellias, magnolias, hydrangeas etc. Charles probably enjoyed visiting him

Sir Charles Raymond of Valentines and the East India Company

at Knotts Green and seeing the new plants from abroad. He may also have visited Robert Preston at Woodford where he also had a stove and greenhouses for his plants.

His daughters were now living some distance away but Charles would have been able to spend time with Donald Cameron and his wife Mary and also to visit his cousin John Raymond, either at his home at Bedford Square, or at Chigwell. When John died unmarried in 1800 he left the majority of his wealth to three nieces, unmarried daughters of his sister Lydia Snow who were living with him. They were all a little older than Sophia and Juliana, and may also have been happy to spend time with Charles. The house may actually have been in present-day Buckhurst Hill, which was part of Chigwell at that time. John Raymond was buried at St Mary's, Chigwell, on 11 September 1800.[113]

An article in the *Gazetteer and New Daily Advertiser* (London) dated 1 December 1787 giving an account of the Burrell family, mentioned that 'Mr William Burrell, now Chancellor of Worcester, married the beautiful daughter of Sir Charles Raymond...

Sir Charles Raymond is himself a remarkable instance of the happy effects of industry, integrity, and perseverance: he has served in all capacities on board an Indiaman.... is now a banker and ship's husband, in both which characters he does so many acts of benevolence, that he is universally respected. His manners are so humble, placid, and unaffected, that the ladies call him Sir Charles Grandison.' This compares Charles with the principal character, a morally good man, in a popular novel written in 1753 by Samuel Richardson.

At the end of 1787 Charles again dabbled in property, this time purchasing the Manor of Knepp in Shipley, West Sussex. Altogether he acquired the manor, 9 farms and 1,600 acres of rich arable, meadow and pasture, with woodland. It also had a large lake, so Charles could have enjoyed both fishing and shooting had he lived there, but, as with the property he had sold earlier in 1787 at Woodham Ferrers, this was just an investment as there was no habitable manor house at that time.[114]

Sir Charles Raymond died on 24 August 1788 and was buried at St. Margaret's, Barking. His obituary in the *Gentleman's Magazine* reported that on 24 August Sir Chas.Raymond, bart., banker died at Highlands, his house near Ilford, and that he left his whole fortune equally divided between his two daughters, independent of their husbands, and afterwards to their children. The baronetcy passed to his son-in-law William Burrell.

The *Gentleman's Magazine* first reported that 'This gentleman is supposed to have died worth £200,000.' This was later corrected to 'Sir Charles property may amount in the

City Gentleman

whole to £150,000 though he met with a great loss just before his death in consequence of his having imprudently suffered himself to be exhibited to the world as partner in the banking-house of Allen, of Manchester, and being therefore answerable for the payment of their debts.' Even so, £150,000 would be close on £20m today.[115]

The will of Sir Charles Raymond was obviously drawn up by a trusted legal adviser and ensured that his daughters, rather than their husbands, would inherit from their father. Although a long and detailed document, it names very little property and is unhelpful to the historian.[116] As both the girls were now settled in their own family homes they must have decided to sell Valentine House. Presumably they took some of the family heirlooms and personal treasures, but many of the contents remained to be sold with the house, which was mentioned in *The Times* of 19 September 1788:

> Valentine House, a country seat, adjoining Epping Forest, the elegant erection of Sir Charles Raymond's taste and liberality, sharing the common fate of all his possessions, will probably come to the hammer in the course of the ensuing Winter: at present it is rented by Mr. W. Raikes.

In the event, the Valentine property was purchased by their uncle, Donald Cameron, so presumably no auction took place. In 1789 Juliana sold her share of the Knepp estate to her brother-in-law, and the whole property came into the control of the Burrell family. Sophia and William's son, Sir Charles Merrik Burrell, commissioned John Nash to build a house at Knepp and it is still in the family of his descendents, the owner in 2013 being Charlie Burrell.[117]

Elizabeth, widow of Charles's friend William Webber, had died in the spring of 1787. The Highlands estate was purchased by Sir James Tylney-Long and became part of the Wanstead estate.[118]

With the lack of family archives, newspapers have provided some insights to colour the bald facts about Sir Charles Raymond. The newly established *Times* newspaper reporting his death on 27 August 1788 further illustrates his kindness and integrity and is a fitting memorial:

> We cannot help paying our tribute to the memory of SIR CHARLES RAYMOND, who died full of years, and left a character for the living to imitate. As a servant of the East India Company, he was highly in esteem; as a ship's husband, a man revered for his integrity; a friend of mankind in general, and to the poor in particular, a benevolent example of philanthrophy. From a desire of serving others, he forfeited that ease, which would have followed him into retirement, and interrupted the calm attendant on the felicity of friendship, and the heartfelt pleasure of rendering others happy.

CONCLUSION

On 31 December 1600 Queen Elizabeth signed a charter for the East India Company; 218 men of the Merchant Adventurers were given exclusive rights to trade with the East Indies. These were men who risked their wealth in financing voyages to unknown seas. Others risked their lives by sailing into the wide and little known blue yonder to carry out the trade. For both, the risk was immense but the rewards could be beyond their wildest dreams. By the eighteenth century there were still many serious risks to the sailors who ventured across stormy seas, often with danger from pirates or enemy action, and it was never a foregone conclusion they would return and their investors would be rewarded.

Sir Charles Raymond started by risking his life and then risked his wealth in voyages for the EIC. He had earned the trappings of success but seems to have enjoyed the City buzz. He still needed a challenge, an adventure! It was men such as Charles who brought the riches of the East to England, and with them came prosperity. Their cargoes included the beautiful oriental objects we see today in country houses, as well as cottons and silks, chinaware, tea, spices and other commodities which did not survive. The cargo also included more mundane items such as salt petre (necessary for gunpowder manufacture), dyewood and other perishable goods. However, none of this could have been brought to England without the bravery and skill of the captains and crew. The EIC came to influence the whole world but it could not have done so without the men who transported its cargoes.

Charles Raymond was born into an affluent West Country family with many links to the sea. Encouraged and nurtured by his relations he made his own way in the world of the EIC, rising rapidly to the rank of captain. He appears to have been a man of intelligence who learned quickly. Perhaps he had a charismatic charm which helped him as a leader, taking command of his ship and forging trading links in India.

Although fortunate in his own career at sea, and in managing voyages with so few ships lost, his life was not without sadness. The deaths of the infants born to Charles and Sarah in the first ten years of their marriage must have been a personal tragedy, making the three daughters who followed all the more loved. Charles must have been delighted by the husbands chosen by Sophia, Juliana and Anna Maria and proud to see them married. This would have been marred only by the fact that his dear wife Sarah died five years before Anna Maria married Thomas Newte.

When he retired from the sea it was on the grounds of ill health, and with his trips to Bath in later years perhaps Charles suffered from some ailment throughout his life. During the time spent in India he must have encountered many diseases. If that is the

City Gentleman

case, it makes his success in the City and his placid manner all the more remarkable. He earned the respect shown him in later life.

Charles's success at a young age meant that he started on a career in the City while many of his contemporaries were still at sea. As they retired as captains he drew them into his commercial world. Charles attracted them to live in houses near him and welcomed some as his relations. Having risked these hazardous voyages, the captains had a bond far stronger than most and could trust one another in the truest sense. They did not doubt the ability or integrity of someone they knew so well. The fact that they settled together in East London, married each-other's sisters or sisters-in-law, and worked together in the City is extremely relevant. They were a Band of Brothers in the truest sense and a significant force in the East India Company in the eighteenth century.

THE PORTRAIT OF SIR CHARLES RAYMOND

The image of the portrait was reproduced on a Christmas card printed in the late 1930s for Williams Deacon's Bank, a predecessor of The Royal Bank of Scotland (RBS). An image of the portrait was later reproduced in *Williams Deacon's 1771-1970,* published in 1971 to commemorate the 200th anniversary of the founding of William Deacon's Bank, which on 25 September 1970 had become part of Williams & Glyn's Bank. At the time of the merger Williams Deacon's main London office was still based at 20 Birchin Lane, EC3.[119] The image appeared more recently in *The Bank and the Sea: The Royal Bank of Scotland Group and the Finance of Shipping since 1753* by David Souden, published by RBS in 2003.

Unfortunately, in spite of the efforts of one of the bank's archivists, Philip Winterbottom, who has been extremely helpful, the original painting has not been traced in recent times and the artist is not known. There are no surviving records to indicate whether the portrait was ever in the possession of Williams Deacon's Bank, or to indicate the source of the image which was used on the Christmas card and to illustrate the bank's history. Indeed, this may not be the complete painting. The portrait is quite a conundrum as the fact that it was reproduced by Williams Deacon's might suggest that it was painted either when that bank was founded by Charles Raymond and others in 1771, or in 1774 when he became a baronet (aged 61). However, the National Portrait Gallery points out that the wig and clothes suggest an earlier date. It is difficult to guess the age of the sitter. A portrait of Thomas Ripley painted by Joseph Highmore in 1746 shows him in similar fashion, so could it have been painted when Charles retired from the sea (aged 34)?

129

Sir Charles Raymond of Valentines and the East India Company

Another puzzle is the background to the sitter. One might expect this to show his country seat (Valentine House) or the means of his fortune (an East Indiaman) but instead there is a tree. It has been suggested that the overall colours depict a hot country and that the tree could be the redwood tree *Pterocarpus Santalinus*. Could the picture have been painted in India? The wood was brought back from India and used in dyeing cloth red (several of Charles's contacts were involved in the cloth trade) and also in medicine.

Interestingly John Smeaton drew up plans to remodel the windmill at Barking and install machinery for the sawing and chipping of dyewood between 1753-80, but although it was on his list of 'mills executed' nobody is shown paying rates on the mill after 1747 when, presumably, the old mill ceased working and no rate was required.[120]

Was Charles the first person to grow this tree in England, in his garden at Valentine House? *Pterocarpus Santalinus* is not growing at Kew now, although a specimen was introduced by Joseph Banks in 1800 and it was listed in *Hortus Kewensis; or a Catalogue of the plants cultivated in the Royal Botanic Garden at Kew* by the late William Aiton (published 1810-13). The National Trust doesn't have a specimen listed on any of their properties now.

There is no known line drawing of Sir Charles Raymond, but the National Portrait Gallery does have a record of a miniature by James Smith being exhibited at the Royal Academy in 1772 (no.353) but its present location is not known. Neither the Royal Academy, the Victoria & Albert Museum nor the Courtauld Institute of Art can throw any light on the miniature.[121]

The portrait is unusual in showing the sitter with a slight smile, and the face looks kind so it does fit with what little is known of Sir Charles Raymond.

City Gentleman

[1] Foundling Museum, London, exhibition

[2] *Complete London Guide* 6th edition 1755

[3] Sir John Fielding's *description of London* (1776) p.11

[4] F G H Price. *A Handbook of London Bankers; with some account of ... the early Goldsmiths. Together with lists of bankers, from ... 1677 to ... 1876* (1890) p.79, 177-8

[5] *Whitehall Evening Post or London Intelligencer* 1750, September 20

[6] William Burney, ed., *Falconer's New Universal Dictionary of the Marine* (London, 1815), p.62

[7] Thomas Cole *A Plan for the better carrying on the British white herring fishery, humbly offered to the consideration of William Beckford, Esq...* 31 January 1754.

[8] Ann Saunders *The Royal Exchange* (London 1991) p.31

[9] P G M Dickson *The Sun Insurance Office 1710 – 1960* (OUP 1960) p.265; Records of the Sun Fire Office are kept at the Guildhall in London. MS 11931 Vol.5 p.67 General Quarterly Meeting 8 April 1756

[10] Lucy Sutherland *A London Merchant 1695-1774* (Frank Cass/OUP 1962) p.10-11; P G M Dickson *The Sun Insurance Office 1710 – 1960* (OUP 1960) p.278

[11] Arthur Norman Harrisson *The family of Godfrey of Woodford, Essex, and of East Bergholt, Suffolk* Woodford Historical Society Transactions Part XII (1966), David Sanctuary Howard *Chinese armorial porcelain* Vol.I page 172 A5

[12] Naish affair see page 12; BL, IOR/B/61 EIC Court Book p.375-6 18 August 1731

[13] BL, IOR/B/93 EIC Court Book p.379 30 October 1777

[14] Records of the Sun Fire Office are kept at the Guildhall in London. Ms 11931 Vol.6 1766-83; P G M Dickson *The Sun Insurance Office 1710 – 1960* (OUP 1960)

[15] Scotch Mines Co. archives are part of the Royal & Sun Alliance Insurance Group Collection (CLC/B/192-36) held at the London Metropolitan Archives, MSS 12031-1 Journal 1755-72; MSS 12033-1 Ledger 1755-71

[16] Georgina Green *Robert Surman of Valentines* (Friends of Valentines Mansion 2005)

[17] BL, Add. MS 25494-25584 Minutes of the Court of Directors of the Governor and Company of Merchants of Great Britain Trading to the South Seas and other Parts of America and For Encouraging the Fishery, from 7 Sept. 1711 to 10 Apr. 1856. (Add MS 25517 Vol. xxiv. 1 Feb. 1763-23 Jan. 1766 ; Add MS 25518 Vol. xxv. 29 Jan. 1766-23 Jan. 1772.)

[18] *The Family Circle and Career of William Burrell, Antiquary* by John H. Farrant (*Sussex Archaeological Collections*, 139 (2001), p.169 – 185)

[19] *Morning Post & Daily Advertiser* (London) 1777, June 11

[20] *The Life of Dr. Archibald Cameron* (London, 1753)

[21] Essex Record Office D/P 167/1/7 St Mary the Virgin, Woodford, Essex (SEAX Image 21)

[22] Reginald H Nichols & F A Wray *The History of the Foundling Hospital* (OUP 1935); the Foundling Hospital archives are kept at London Metropolitan Archives (microfilm X041/010)

[23] Jonathan Andrews et al *The History of Bethlem* (Routledge 1997) pp.152 – 164; Fiona Haslam *From Hogarth to Rowlandson: medicine and art in the eighteenth-century* (Liverpool UP 1996) p.149-159

[24] Minutes of the Court of Governors are available on line at www.Bethlemheritage.org.uk

[25] Hogarth (Tate exhibition catalogue, 2006) p.83 & 93; Provenance from Cincinnati Art Museum (letter dated Nov.11th 1797)

26 Conservation Plan by Richard Griffiths Architects (2003) p.19 suggests the orangery was built by Surman; p.21 for details of Raymond's changes

27 *The Diary of Sylas Neville, 1767-1788* Edited by Basil Cozens-Hardy (OUP 1950) p.325, April 24, 1785

28 P.Muilman, *A New and Complete History of Essex by a Gentleman*, Vol.IV, (Chelmsford, 1771), pp.276-279.

29 *The Lethieullier Family of Aldersbrook House* by C H Iyan Chown, *Essex Review* Vol.XXXVI (1927) p.16

30 Guildhall Library, Sun Fire Office policy registers, MS 11936 Vol.188 policy no.269293 p.504, 21 April 1769

31 *St James's Chronicle or the British Evening Post* (London) 1797, September 7

32 Patrick Conner *The China Trade 1600 – 1860* catalogue of an exhibition at the Royal Pavilion, Brighton in 1986, p.9, 71 & 89. David Sanctuary Howard *Chinese armorial porcelain*. Vol.I p.34-5 and private correspondence with him

33 Royal College of Physicians of London MS-MANUS/197

34 *Admiral's Wife: being the life and letters of the Hon Mrs Edward Boscawen from 1719-1761* edited by Cecil Faber Aspinall Oglander (1940).

35 Essex Record Office D/DB/B7

36 "A Georgian Garden" exhibition catalogue (1997) nos. 21, 24 & 36

37 Copped Hall information from *Country Life* 5 November 1910 p.652 and Alan Cox, Architect to the Copped Hall Trust; National Trust information from Emile de Bruijn

38 *The Lion and the Rose* by Ethel M Richardson (Hutchinson) Vol 2, p.463, 477, 478, 482 etc

39 Julian Litton *The English way of Death* (Hale 1991)

40 Thesis study of Valentines Park by Stephen Smith, 2002, (p.49-50) and private exchanges with him

41 National Library of Ireland, Dublin MS 248 A Journal by Wm Robertson. Architect, 1795, p.121 Robertson's book *A Collection of various forms of Stoves, used for forcing pine plants, fruit trees, and preserving tender exotics* was published in 1798.

42 From display at Hampton Court and *Notes and Queries* for 24 November 1855. See also William Gilpin *Remarks on Forest Scenery and other woodland views...* (1791) p.149

43 *The Botanical Cabinet consisting of coloured delineations of plants from all countries with a short account of each* (1819) Vol. IV no.329

44 Andrew MacHugh *Two Hundred years of Camellias* (Hortus 24, Winter 1992)

45 Private communications.

46 *Shipbuilding on the Thames* Edited by Dr Roger Owen (Proceedings of the forth symposium, 28 Feb 2009) p.47

47 Essex Naturalist Vol.XXVI, parts III & IV (1938) *A Forgotten Essex Gardener-botanist, Gilbert Slater (c.1753-1793)* by Charles Hall Crouch

48 Letter to Royal Society from George Edwards, in Philosophical Transactions Vol.61 (1771) p.55

49 BL, L/MAR/B/499A Journal of *Granby* 1767/8

50 Conservation Plan by Richard Griffiths Architects (2003) p.22

51 W Hayes and family *Portraits of rare and curious birds, with their descriptions, from the Menagery of Osterley Park* (1794) Vol.I, plate 19 Secretary Bird, plate 30 Mandarin Duck

City Gentleman

52 Barking Rate Books held at Valence House Local Studies and Archives (Ref. 2/3/1, etc). No relationship has been traced to William Harvey of Rolls Park, Chigwell, who died unmarried in 1779, leaving that estate to his brother, later Admiral Sir Eliab Harvey (1758 – 1830)

53 *Victoria County History of Essex* Vol.V p.198, p.205, p.211, p.214

54 *Victoria County History of Essex* Vol.V p.198

55 Lucy Sutherland *A London Merchant 1695-1774* (Frank Cass/OUP 1962) p.146; P G M Dickson *The Sun Insurance Office 1710 – 1960* (OUP 1960) p.278

56 George Tasker *Ilford Past and Present* (1901) p.88-91; Haldon Belvedere, near Exeter, was built in 1788 by Sir Robert Palk (Governor of Madras 1763-67) to honour his friend Major-General Stringer Lawrence of the East India Company. It is strikingly similar to Raymond's tower which was demolished in 1923.

57 Port of London Authority Recreation Ground, Ilford, Conservation Statement (Nov 2005)

58 Essex Record Office D/DU 539/1 p.16-7, 28 & 29; Barking Rate Books held at Valence House Local Studies and Archives (Ref. 2/3/1, etc)

59 *Victoria County History of Essex* Vol.V p.208, Vol.VII p.11-13, 67-69; http://blogs.ucl.ac.uk/eicah/englefield-house-berkshire/

60 *London Evening Post* 1770, November 10*; Bingley's Weekly Journal or the Universal Gazette* 1771, February 16

61 W R Fisher *The Forest of Essex* (Butterworths, 1887) p.381-384

62 Both Lady Sophia and Sir William Burrell have entries in the Dictionary of National Biography; *Sir William Burrell - A Great Sussex Antiquarian and his Wife* by John Playford, in Sussex County Magazine (1938)

63 Harleian Society Registers No.31 Parish records of St.Helen's, Bishopsgate

64 Anthony Farrington *A Catalogue of East India Company Ships' Journals and Logs 1660-1834* (British Library 1999) p.766

65 Leatherhead & District Local History Society Proceedings Vol.6, No.1 pp.10-13; Sun Fire Office policy register MS 11936/267 policy no. 399344

66 Kent's 1771 London Directory

67 *Lloyd's Evening Post* (London) 1768, September 9

68 Records of the Sun Fire Office are kept at the Guildhall in London. Ms 11931 Vol.6 1766-83, General Quarterly Meeting 8 July 1773; Essex Record Office ref. D/DGe/P15; Valence House Local Studies ref. E295; *Gazetteer and New Daily Advertiser* (London) 1787, July 18

69 NA Will of Sir Charles Raymond of Highlands, Essex, 29 August 1788, PROB 11/1169; Emily J. Climenson *The History of Shiplake* (1894)

70 David Souden *The Bank and the Sea* p.32-5; John Carswell *The South Sea Bubble* , Sutton Publishing, Stroud, (2001) p.25; private correspondence with Philip Winterbottom, RBS

71 F G H Price *Handbook of London bankers* (1890) p.177, p.79

72 *Williams Deacon's 1771-1970,* p.4-7; David Souden *The Bank and the Sea* p.44-6, p.82; W.G.Hammock *Leytonstone and its History* p.12

73 J G Parker *The Directors of the East India Company, 1754-1790*

74 Various newspapers e.g. *Morning Post & Daily Advertiser* 1781, April 9; *St.James's Chronicle or the British Evening Post* 1775, December 7; *Morning Chronicle and London Advertiser* 1776, January 30

Sir Charles Raymond of Valentines and the East India Company

[75] A R J Ramsey et al "Luxborough" in "Robert Knight and Luxborough" p.29. (Woodford Historical Society 1987); VCH Essex IV (Chigwell) p.28

[76] P A Fitzgerald *A Famous Forgery, being the story of "the Unfortunate" Doctor Dodd* (1865); contemporary newspaper accounts; http://www.exclassics.com/newgate/ng343.htm

[77] *Morning Post & Daily Advertiser* (London) 1777, September 25

[78] E.J.T. Acaster "Partners in Peril: The Genesis of Banking in Manchester" in The Three Banks Review June 1983 pp.50-60

[79] http://www.bankofengland.co.uk/education/Pages/resources/inflationtools/calculator/index1.aspx shows £50,000 in 1788 = £6,578,000 in 2013

[80] Wiltshire Record Office, The Estate Papers & Records of Viscount Long. 947:2114 Lord Tylney's letter from Florence 20 Aug 1765

[81] Sheffield Archives: Wentworth Woodhouse Muniments :Letter from Charles Raymond, Bath, to Rockingham - ref. WWM/R/1/1426 - date: 13 Feb 1773

[82] Correspondence of King George the Third with Lord North, letter from the King 10 Oct 1774; P H Stanhope. 5th earl (Lord Mahon) *History of England, 1713-1783* (1851) Volume VI p.28-30

[83] Transactions of the Devonshire Association, Vol 62, p.206-7

[84] BL, IOR/B/78 EIC Court Book p.118, 11 August 1762

[85] Jean Sutton *Lords of the East: The East India Company and its Ships (1600 – 1874)* (Conway Maritime Press, new edition 2000) see pages 41-47 for ship building; ship size from Anthony Farrington *A Catalogue of East India Company Ships' Journals and Logs 1660-1834* (British Library 1999)

[86] R P Crowhurst *The Voyage of the Pitt – a turning point in East India Navigation* (Mariner's Mirror Vol.55 (1969) pp.43-56)

[87] Antony Clayton *London's Coffee Houses, a stimulating story* (Historical Publications 2003) p.63-6; Lucy Sutherland *A London Merchant 1695-1774* (Frank Cass/OUP 1962) p.146;

[88] F G H Price. *A Handbook of London Bankers; with some account of ... the early Goldsmiths. Together with lists of bankers, from ... 1677 to ... 1876* (1890) p.177; Ann Saunders *The Royal Exchange* (London 1991) p.31

[89] Proceedings of the Old Bailey Ref: t17741019-63 (www.oldbaileyonline.org) theft from Sir Charles Raymond and Co. warehouse

[90] NA Will of John Williams of Barking, Essex, 09 August 1774, PROB 11/1001

[91] Guildhall Library, London, Sun Fire Office records MS 11936/267 policy no. 399344

[92] Devon Archives, Parish registers, christened at St Olave's in Exeter on 12 July 1720; There is no obvious family relationship with Peter, Edmund and Joseph Godfrey but it is possible they shared a great-grandfather as Thomas Godfrey (1585-1664) had eighteen children by his second wife and a link is suggested by the choice of children's names down the generations. Equally there is nothing to connect Benjamin with Shearman Godfrey.

[93] Dictionary of National Biography

[94] BL, OIR/L/MAR/B/577B Journal of *Lord Clive (3)* 1766/7; BL, IOR/B/82 EIC Court Book p.414-5, 4 March 1767 and many subsequent entries in BL, IOR/B/83

[95] Charles Daggett with Christopher (Kris) Shaffer *Diving for the Griffin* (Weidenfeld and Nicholson, London, 1990, ISBN 0 297 81063 4) The salvage of what remains of the *Griffin* is featured in a fascinating exhibition at the French East India Company Maritime Museum at the Citadel of Port-Louis, near Lorient in Brittany.

[96] BL, OIR/L/MAR/B/452F Journal of *Valentine (2)* 1776/7; private research

[97] BL, IOR/B/94 EIC Court Book p.218 & 235, September 1778

[98] Gentleman's Magazine Vol.48 (1778) p.190

[99] Charles wrote to Lord Rockingham from Bath on 13 February 1773 (see ref.81); *Middlesex Journal and Evening Advertiser* (London) 1775, February 7

[100] Valence House Local Studies, Overseer's Valuation books for Parish of Barking (1779 – 1780)

[101] Collin's Peerage of England by Sir Egerton Brydges (1812); The Official Baronage of England by James E Doyle (1886) Vol.III p.506 quotes Walpole Mem. Geo III Vol.I p.47

[102] Essex Record Office D/DU 539/1 p.30-31; J W S Litton and F R Clark *St Mary's Church, Woodford, Essex* (Passmore Edwards Museum 1977) p.29-30

[103] H V Bowen *Privilege and Profit: Commanders of East Indiamen as Private Traders, Entrepreneurs and Smugglers, 1760-1813* (International Journal of Maritime History, Vol XIX No.2 (December 2007) p.65

[104] Thorne, R. G. *The House of Commons 1790-1820.* 5 vols. The History of Parliament. London: Secker and Warburg.

[105] *Felix Farley's Bristol Journal* (Bristol) 1783, August 9

[106] Edward Hasted *The History and Topographical Survey of the County of Kent* (1800) Vol.10 p.356-7. By comparing maps dated 1769 (by Andrews, Dury & Herbert) and *c.*1792 (by Hall) it seems likely the house called St.Stephen's is on the site of Raymond's house.

[107] The New Margate, Ramsgate and Broadstairs Guide, 1801, p.95 (Broadstairs Library)

[108] *The Correspondence of George, Prince of Wales, 1770-1812* Edited by A Aspinall (Cassell 1971) Vol.VIII p.205

[109] The New Margate, Ramsgate and Broadstairs Guide, 1801, p.52-3 (Broadstairs Library)

[110] *Gazetteer & New Daily Advertiser* (London) 1777, October 14

[111] BL, IOR/B/96 EIC Court Book p.729, 21 March 1781

[112] NA Will of Gilbert Slater, PROB 11/1129/72

[113] Rev. Philip Morant *The History and Antiquities of the County of Essex* (1763-68) Vol.I p.170 (not confirmed by the Victoria Country History Vol.IV p.29); *Gentleman's Magazine* Vol.70 Pt.2 p.908; ERO D/P 166/1/6 Chigwell Parish church, burial register

[114] http://www.knepp.co.uk/pages/history/estate_history2.asp

[115] Gentleman's Magazine Vol.58 (1788) p.758 & p.834 http://www.bankofengland.co.uk/education/Pages/resources/inflationtools/calculator/index1.aspx shows £150,000 in 1788 = £19,734,000 in 2013

[116] NA Will of Sir Charles Raymond of Highlands, Essex, PROB 11/1169

[117] http://www.knepp.co.uk/pages/history/estate_history2.asp

[118] *Bath Chronicle* 1788, November 6; Victoria County History of Essex Vol.V p.205

[119] Compliment slip given with the book on publication.

[120] Roy Gregory *The Industrial Windmill in Britain* by Roy Gregory (Phillimore 2005) p.49-50; Barking Rate Books held at Valence House Local Studies and Archives, Dagenham (Ref. 2/3/1, etc)

[121] I am grateful to Paul Cox of NPG (22 April 2008), Andrew Potter of RA Library (17 July 2008), Katie Coombs of V & A (21 July 2008) and Hollie Williams of Courtauld Institue (9 December 2011) for their assistance

Sir Charles Raymond of Valentines and the East India Company

Appendix 1 – The family of John Raymond

From the Parish Registers of Withycome Raleigh unless otherwise stated:

John Rayment [sic], Esq, (Senior) buried 21 December 1686

The children of John Rayment Esq and Bridget

Francis, daughter, baptised 20 June 1667, buried 10 June 1707

John, son, baptised 29 August 1668 (*see below*)
> married Anna Maria Tanner on 15 January 1702/3 at Farringdon
> She was the daughter of Samuel Tanner of Clyst St.Mary. Her sister Isabella
> Tanner married Samuel Newte of Tiverton on 12 September 1716

Elizabeth, daughter, baptised 29 August 1669, buried 9 June 1671

Kathren, daughter, baptised 17 September 1670, buried 8 October 1670

Charles, son, baptised 19 January 1671/2, not buried at Withycombe Raleigh
> No further information has been found about him, but he may have been the
> father of John Raymond, Captain of the *Dawsonne,* who died at sea April 1719.

William, son, baptised 7 April 1673, buried 18 September 1696

Hugh, son, baptised 30 January 1674, died 10 July 1737, buried at Beckenham, Kent
> *See Appendix 2 for further family details*

Baynham, son, baptised 23 July 1676, died at sea *c.*1719 while Captain of the *Royal Prince*
> married Mrs Lydia Hicks on 31 January 1708/9 at Stoke Damerel, Devon
> their children: **John (*c.*1713-1800)** unmarried (EIC PMO and Director)
>   Lydia married Raymond Snow
>   Their son Raymond Snow became EIC captain

The children of John Raymond Esq and Anna Maria

Anna Maria, daughter, baptised 22 June 1704,
> married John Penneck of St.Thomas's Parish (Exeter) 23 January 1730/1

Frances, daughter, baptised 25 April 1707, buried 10 June 1707

John, son, baptised 22 September 1709, buried 26 June 1710

John, son, baptised 18 September 1711, buried 15 March 1711/2

Charles, son, baptised 23 April 1713 *See Appendix 3 for further family details*

John Raymond, Esq, of Marpole, buried 15 May 1725

Anna Maria Raymond buried 27 October 1731

Appendices

Appendix 2 – The family of Hugh Raymond

Hugh, son of John & Bridget Rayment, was baptised 30 January 1674

married Dynah Jones, daughter of Captain Samuel Jones of Stepney and his wife Amy.

> Two of her sisters married captains who sailed for the East India Company[1]:
>
> > Sarah was the wife of Matthew Martin who sailed as Captain of the *Tavistock* 1699/1700, 1702/3 & 1707/8, and Captain of the *Marlborough* 1711/2, 1715/6.
> >
> > Their sons Samuel, Mathew, Thomas, George also served with the EIC
> >
> > Amy was the wife of James Osborne who sailed as Captain of the *New George* 1708/9, and as Captain of the *Hanover* 1712/3, 1716/7.

Hugh Raymond died 10 July 1737 and was buried at St.George's, Beckenham, Kent.

Dynah, his wife, buried 20 May 1717 at St.Dunstan & All Saints, Stepney

Children of Hugh & Dynah Raymond

Amy, no baptism found but she died 16 August 1789 aged 89

> married Peter Burrell Esq of Kelsey, Beckenham, Kent. He was born in 1692, became a sub-governor of the South Sea Company, Sheriff of for the County of Kent 1722; M.P. for Haslemere 1727-1747 and for Dover 1755; and died 16 April 1756.[2]
>
> Their eldest son, Peter Burrell, married Elizabeth, daughter of John Lewis of Hackney. He was Surveyor-General of Crown Lands and M.P. for Launceston.[3]
>
> Their third son **William** (born 10 October 1732) afterwards LLD and fellow of Doctors' Commons; appointed Chancellor to the diocese of Worcester 1764 and of Rochester in 1771; MP for Haslemere 1768-1774; a Director of the South Sea Company 1763-75 and the Sun Fire Insurance 1773-95; appointed a Commissioner of the Excise 1774. He married 1773 **Sophia, daughter and coheir of Sir Charles Raymond of Valentine House,** Co. Essex, Bart. He died 20 January 1796 at The Deepdene, Dorking in Surry.[4]

Dynah / Dinah Raymond baptised 20 February 1705/6 at St Dunstan & All Saints, Stepney

Jones, baptised 29 December 1706, aged 23 days, at St John, Wapping; died 23 March 1768, unmarried, leaving the Beckenham estate to his sister Amy.

Bridget, was the second wife of William Glanville, the fifth son of George Evelyn of Nutfield, by Frances his wife, daughter of Andrew Bromhall of Stoke Newington.

Susannah

---

[1] Will of Amy Jones, Widow of Stepney, Middlesex, ~ 08 November 1721, PROB 11/582

[2] Guide Book to the Parish Church of St George, Beckenham (1995) p.33-4

[3] Guide Book to the Parish Church of St George, Beckenham (1995) p.39

[4] Oxford Dictionary of National Biography

Sir Charles Raymond of Valentines and the East India Company

Appendix 3 – The family of Charles Raymond

Charles Raymond was the son and heir of John Raymond of Marple in Devon and his wife Anna Maria. He was baptised at Withycombe Raleigh, Devon, on 23 April 1713

22 Jan 1743 Charles Raymond, of Washecomb Rayleigh, Devon,
married Sarah, 1st daughter of John Webster of Bromley, Kent, born 5 January 1722.
at St. Stephen and St.Benet Sherehog, London. He was knighted in 1774.

The children of Charles and Sarah Raymond

Anna Maria (1) buried at St.John's, Wapping, in the chancel, 12 October 1743

Anna Maria (2) baptised 1 Aug 1747 at St. John's, Wapping aged 28 days
        buried 14 Aug 1748 at All Saints, West Ham

Anna Maria (3) baptised 10 April 1749 at All Saints, West Ham
        buried 27 April 1749 at All Saints, West Ham

Burial of Charles Raymond 6 April 1751 at West Ham, but nothing to confirm he was related

Sophia born 11 April 1753, baptised 6 May 1753 at West Ham and married

(1) William Burrell on 13 April 1773 at St Martins in the Fields, Westminster
        He died 20 January 1796. *For their children see page 141*

(2) Rev.William Clay
Sophia died 20 June 1802, Isle of Wight

Juliana baptism not found
She married Henry Boulton of Leatherhead on 3 Nov 1774 at St.Helen's, Bishopsgate
        For their children see page 141
Juliana was buried on 20 December 1813, aged 60, at Leatherhead

Anna Maria (4) baptised 20 Jan 1756 West Wycombe
She married Thomas Newte on 29 June 1781 at St.Margaret's, Barking
Anna Maria died at Bristol Hot Wells, 19 August 1783, buried at Barking 27 Aug 1783

Lady Sarah Raymond died 15th April 1778 aged 55, and was
        buried at Barking 20 April 1778
Sir Charles Raymond died 24th August 1788 aged 76, and was
        buried at Barking 29 Aug 1788

Appendices

Appendix 4 – The family of Sarah Raymond (née Webster)

Sarah Webster (buried at St.Leonard's, Shoreditch, 14 April 1735, aged 92 years) wife of John Webster. They were the parents of

John Webster (baptised 1 February1679 and buried 3 December 1724) who had children by his friend Judith Cooke (*c*.1695 – 1759).

> John baptised 20 Nov 1720 (In 1753 John Webster, brewer of St.Leonard's, Shoreditch)
>
> **Sarah baptised 5 Jan 1721/2 married Charles Raymond on 22 Jan 1743**
>
> Thomas baptised 27 Feb 1722/3 died of a malignant fever 10 July 1745 on the *Wager*
>
> Robert baptised 13 May 1724   (had died by 1743)
>
> **Elizabeth** baptised 16 July 1725, married William Webber on 20 Feb 1755

In December 1734 Sarah Webster (senior) made a will leaving all her estate to William Guy, a Salter of Wapping, in trust for the benefit of John, Thomas, Robert, Sarah and Elizabeth, the children of her late son John Webster, and Judith, their mother, now the wife of William Guy.

Marriage of William Guy of Stepney, Batchelor, and Judith Cooke of Bromley in Kent, Widow 16 August 1726, at St Clement Danes (in The Strand*)*

Step-siblings of Sarah Raymond née Webster, children of William & Judith Guy

> Edward baptised [a] 1 November 1726, buried 4 January 1726/7, St Dunstans etc
>
> Susanna baptised [a] 8 December 1727, buried 18 February 1736/7, St Leonard's,
>
> Mary Baptised [a] 20 June 1729, buried 3 July 1729, St Dunstans etc
>
> **Ann** baptised [b] 27 July 1734, married John Williams in 1754
>
> William baptised [b] 16 March 1735, buried 24 July 1736, St Peter & St Paul, Bromley
>
> **Mary** baptised [c] 30 September 1737, married Donald Cameron on 12 July 1763 at
> St Mary's Woodford

>> (a)   Baptism at St Dunstans and All Saints, Stepney
>> (b)   Baptism at St George in the East (Tower Hamlets)
>> (c)   Baptism at St Botolph, Aldgate

William Guy, Well Close Square, buried on 19 April 1755, aged 70 years, at St.Leonard's, For many years he was a contractor with the EIC, supplying their ships with provisions.

Judith Guy, Well Close Square, buried 27 November 1759 aged 64, at St.Leonard's, Shoreditch.

Sir Charles Raymond of Valentines and the East India Company

Appendix 5 – The Crabb – Boulton family

Thomas and Hester Crabb[5] had children:

Henry Crabb (1709-73) baptised in Stepney, 12 Sept 1709.
Clerk in East India Co from 1729, paymaster and clerk to Committee of Shipping 1737-52.
In 1745 Richard Boulton, who had been 40 years with EIC, Director EIC 1718-36, died
      leaving his estates to his cousin Henry Crabb.
Henry took the name **Henry Crabb Boulton**
1752 resigned and went into business with his brother
From 1755 he is listed in London directories as a merchant of Crosby Square, Bishopsgate
Director EIC 1753-6, 1758-61, 1763-5, 1767-70, 1772- *d.*;
Dep. chairman 1764-5; chairman 1765-6, 1768-9, 1773- *d.*
1754 became MP for Worcester, until he died.
Bought Thorncroft at Leatherhead in 1763 and died 8 October 1773, unmarried.

Richard Crabb (d.1777) brother of Henry Crabb Boulton (1709-73)
Fourth mate EIC 1730, Captain 1736/7
married Frances Heames 13 Feb 1739
1750 became PMO
1773 inherited his brother's property, calling himself **Richard Boulton** formerly Crabb Esq.

Richard and Frances had children:

    Richard Crabb born 1746, alive when father made will in 1764 but died before his father.

    Henry Crabb born 20 August 1752, later took the surname **Boulton**
    married **Juliana Raymond** 3 Nov 1774
    became PMO, Sun Fire Company, Manager *c.*1780
    Henry Boulton was buried 17 May 1828.

---

[5] Information from *The History of Parliament: the House of Commons 1754-1790*, ed. L. Namier, J. Brooke., 1964 and the *Leatherhead & District Local History Society Proceedings* Vol.6, No.1 1997; Will of Henry Boulton PROB 11/1740

Appendices

Children of Henry and Juliana Boulton

Richard

Charles

Henry

Emma (d.1856) married Sir John Henry Pelly, Bt of Upton (1777 – 1852), grandson of Captain John Pelly (1711 – 1762). They had several children including Juliana who married William Storrs Fry, son of prison reformer Elizabeth Fry.

Louise (1791 – 1875) married in 1820 Col. William Henry Raikes (1785 – 1854), son of Robert Raikes (1736-1811).

and others

Children of Lady Sophia and Sir William Burrell, 2nd Bt of Valentine House, brought up at 71 Harley Street, Marylebone, London:

Sir Charles Merrik Burrell, (1774 – 1862) 3rd Bt of Valentine House, M.P. for New Shoreham between 1806 and 1862 and was known as the 'father' of the House of Commons. He inherited property from his uncle, Jones Raymond.
In 1808 Charles Merrik Burrell married Frances Wyndham (1789-1874) the eldest daughter of 3rd Earl of Egremont and Elizabeth Iliffe, and they lived at Knepp castle near Horsham.

Walter Burrell Esq, (1777 – 1831) MP for Sussex in five Parliaments, inherited property from his great uncle Sir Merrick Burrell, Bt.

Percy (1779 – 1807)

Two daughters

Two sons died in infancy.

For the family of Sir William Burrell *see* http://www.knepp.co.uk/ Estate history

Sir Charles Raymond of Valentines and the East India Company

Appendix 6 – Cargoes

The information given in a simplified format below is from the East India Company Commercial Ledgers which provide more detail.

The Indian coinage was the Rupee (2s 6d) i.e. 8 = £1.

The Chinese currency on page 144 was converted as 3 = £1.

Wager 1737/8 (Madras and Bengal) : value of cargo out

February 1737/8 London

Factory at Fort St George [Madras] to Sundry Accounts £36028 13s 10d. being the amount of a Cargo laden on the Ship *Wager,* burthen 480 tons, Captain Charles Raymond Commander.

To Lead 747 Pigs wt per 1000 . 1 . 21 at 15 . 6 per	£ 775 – 6 –9
To General Merchandise* Each item priced and totalled	£ 1,093 – 15 –
To Broad Cloth 159 Bales	£ 5,447 – 7 – 3
To Long Ells 5 Bales	£ 193 – –
To Silver 30 Chests	£28,340 – –
To charges Merchandize for charges to Shipping	£ 179 – 4 –10
	£36,028 13s 10d

* e.g. Iron guns, Ironmongers ware, gun flints, anchors, match lines, twine, cordage tin ware, tar, tanned leather.

General merchandise on other ships also included white lead, grindstones, blocks and tackle, top masts, yards, 50 barrels of pitch, 50 ashen oars, cochineal, scales and weights and 847 elephants teeth.

February 1737/8 London

Factory at Bengal [Calcutta] to Sundry Accounts £6849 4s 7d ...

To Lead 726 Pigs wt per 1000 . 2 . 17 at 15 . 6 per	£775 – 10 –1
To General Merchandise* Each item priced and totalled	£882 – 1 – 2
To Copper Plates 8030	£5,157 – 11 – 10
To charges of Merchandize, for charges to Shipping	£34 – 1 – 6
	£6,849 4s 7d

Total value of cargo out to India on the *Wager* 1738/9 was £42,878.

East India Company Commercial Ledgers : OIOC L/AG/1/6/11 p.118 & 119.

Appendices

Wager 1737/8 (Bengal) : value of cargo home

August 1739 Amount of a Cargo laden by the President and Council at Bengal and received on board the Ship *Wager*, burthen 480 tons, as per Invoice dated 23 January 1738 [1739]:

	Approx
Total of 47 entries of cotton cloth	£84,752
Raw Silk (100 bales)	£ 9,781
Cotton yarn (6 bales)	£ 278
Redwood	£ 113
Salt Petre (1770 bags)	£ 1,770
Turmerick (400 bags)	£ 125
Cowries (500 bags)	£ 1,875
Handling Charges	£ 1,545
	£100,239

The *Wager* did not call in at Madras on the way home.

East India Company Commercial Ledgers : OIOC L/AG/1/6/11 p.178.

Wager 1743/4 (Bengal) : value of cargo home

August 1746 Amount of a Cargo laden by the President and Council at Bengal and received on board the Ship *Wager* as per Invoice dated 31 January 1745 [1746]:

	Approx
Total of 49 entries of cotton cloth	£117,995
Raw Silk (200 bales)	£ 22,216
Redwood	£ 169
Salt Petre (2505 bags)	£ 3,144
Cowries (300 bags)	£ 1,121
Handling charges	£ 1,980
	£146,625

Cotton cloth included Gurrahs, Humpums, Ginghams, Tepoys, Doreas, Seersuckers, Chints, Musters, Taffaties and Handkerchiefs among the 49 entries.

The *Wager* did not call in at Madras on the way home.

East India Company Commercial Ledgers : OIOC L/AG/1/6/12 p.185.

Harrington 1741/2 (Canton) : value of cargo home

September 1744 London

£75062 16s 8d the value of Cargoes laden [at Canton] by Messrs Edward Page, Richard Martyn, Jno Hodgson, John Searle and John Burrows, Supracargoes on board the Ships *Haeslingfield*, burthen 498 tons, Captain Robert Haldane Commander and *Harrington*, burthen 495 tons, Captain Charles Foulis Commander, per Invoices dated at Canton 16 January last and received here the 29th and 31st August last, viz:

Harrington   Approx.

Raw Silk		£1,254
Sago		£ 16
China Ware	(201 chests)	£2,392
Tea Bohea	(500 chests)	£3,914
Tea Sochony	(300 chests)	£1,111
Tea Singlo	(1967 tubs)	£4,537
Tea Hyson	(943 tubs)	£4,967
Gold 58 parcels (details given)		£10,812
Callico Leger for Nankeen Cloth P5840		£ 633
Taffaties	2300	£3,804
Handkerchiefs	800	£1,160
Gorgorons	200	£ 430
Poises	200	£ 550
Charges Merchandize, for Measurage & Charges		£ 2,029
		£37,609

The cargo of the **Haeslingfield** was very similar, but it included 60 Lute strings valued at £132, total value of cargo home £37453.

East India Company Commercial Ledgers : OIOC L/AG/1/6/12 p.110.

Porcelain fragments retrieved from the wreck of the Valentine East Indiaman by Richard Keen

Appendices

Items from the Wreck of the *Valentine*
from Richard Keen, diver (retrieved late 1970s)

Blue and white Chinese porcelain, loaded in Canton and brought to India by EIC country ships. Porcelain was often packed in boxes with loose tea or pepper for padding and best use of space. The cargo consisted of a range of qualities from choice items for the aristocratic tea party to thicker items for general use. The fine fragments illustrated below left are from a better quality (sugar?) bowl, decorated inside. The blue and white china was a popular design in England.

Small pieces of agate, cut and roughly shaped square or rectangular in India (company trade?) for use in signet rings etc

Agate is a very hard stone. Recently a dental drill was needed to make a hole for a necklace.

Two small metal handles, possibly from travelling luggage.

Two ground glass stoppers for decanters or medical jars, possibly for use on the voyage – although there was a significant quantity found.

Dark blue glass bottle bases (1) square base, probably a gin bottle

(2) round bottle, loaded in Madeira and would have contained fortified or non-fortified wine. Madeira wine was collected on the outward journey as the voyage improved the quality, if it wasn't drunk by officers and passengers before they got back to England!

> BL, IOR/E/1/61 ff. 35-37v : 22 Jan 1777
> Letters 18-19 - Chambers, Hiccox, Smart, Macky and Co at Madeira to the Court relating to the provision of wine for East India Company ships *Egmont* and *Valentine*.

The main cargo of the vessel was salt petre which, of course, was much in demand for the manufacture of gunpowder but would have dissolved in the sea. Another significant part of the cargo was red wood which was ballast as well as being of value for dyeing. Even after being in the sea for 200 years it has been possible to make a dye from the wood salvaged. Some silk was retrieved from the wreck and used by the people of Sark.

Appendix 7 – Summary of journeys made by Charles Raymond

The table below is from the **distance travelled each day as recorded in the journals.**

Distance covered each day	0 - 49	50 - 139	140 - 199	200+	miles

PRINCESS OF WALES 1732/3	Number of days travelling at above speeds				Total days at sea	Total Distance (miles)
London to Bombay	24	98	25	2	149	14487
Anjengo to London	40	106	22		168	14497

WAGER (1) 1734/5						
London to Madras	18	96	26	3	143	14457
Ingeli to London	28	108	20		156	14191

WAGER (1) 1737/8						
London to Madras	14	93	31	1	139	15210
Madras to London	58	108	18		184	14213

WAGER (2) 1740/1						
London to Madras	16	96	28	5	145	15280
Cuddalore to London	44	128	13		185	15174

WAGER (2) 1743/4						
London to Madras, via Batavia	47	163	32	1	243	21718
Madras to London	41	120	15		176	14499

The fastest day in all the voyages was 11 June 1735, Charles's first voyage as captain. On 15 May 1735 (87 days out) they rounded the Cape of Good Hope.

	Days from England	Distance each day
09 June 1735	112	28
10 June 1735	113	110
11 June 1735	**114**	**230**
12 June 1735	115	207
13 June 1735	116	203
14 Jun 1735	117	109

On 16 June they crossed the Tropic of Capricorn east of Madagascar.

Appendices

Appendix 8 – Careers

Career information taken from Anthony Farrington *A Biographical Index of East India Company Maritime Service Officers 1600-1834* (British Library, 1999).

PMO names are from charterparty details entered in the EIC Court Books or, after 1760, from Anthony Farrington *A Catalogue of East India Company Ships' Journals and Logs 1660-1834* (BL 1999)

Charles Raymond (1713 – 1788)

PMO	Ship	Dates	Captain	Other officer
Raymond, Hugh & Raymond, Jones	Dawsonne	1729/30	Steward, Francis	Raymond, Charles, Purser
Lock, John, Sir & Raymond, Hugh	Princess of Wales (1)	1732/3	Mead, Robert	Raymond, Charles, 3rd mate
Raymond, Hugh & Micklefield, Richard	Wager (1)	1734/5	Raymond, Charles	
Raymond, John & Salvador, Francis	Wager (1)	1737/8	Raymond, Charles	Webber, William, 3rd mate
Raymond, John & Tolson, Joseph	Wager (2)	1740/1	Raymond, Charles	Webber, William, 3rd mate
Salvador, Francis & Tolsen, Joseph	Wager (2)	1743/4	Raymond, Charles	
Subsequently PMO for 113 voyages				

147

Sir Charles Raymond of Valentines and the East India Company

William Webber (1713 – 1779) and a nephew?

PMO	Ship	Dates	Captain	Other officer
Raymond, John & Salvador, Francis	Wager (1)	1737/8	Raymond, Charles	Webber, William, 3rd mate
Raymond, John & Tolson, Joseph	Wager (2)	1740/1	Raymond, Charles	Webber, William, 3rd mate
PMO not checked	Prince William (2)	1743/4	Langworth, Thomas	Webber, William, 1st mate
Salvador, Francis & Tolson, Joseph	Prince William (2)	1746/7	Webber, William	
Raymond, Charles & Godfrey, Shearman	Harcourt (1)	1752/3	Webber, William	Webber, William, junr, 3rd mate
Raymond, Charles & Godfrey, Shearman	Harcourt (1)	1755/6	Webber, William	Webber, William, junr, 2nd mate
Raymond, Charles & Godfrey, Shearman	Harcourt (1)	1758/9	Webber, William	
Cary, Robert & Crabb, Richard	Oxford	1758/9	Webber, William, junr	
Raymond, Charles	Lord Clive	1762/3	Webber, William, junr	
Director EIC 1762-65 Subsequently PMO for 3 voyages				

Harcourt (1) 1755/6 managed by Charles Raymond and Godfrey Shearman sailed under Captain William Webber, with first mate Henry Fletcher and second mate William Webber junr.

In the same season Charles Raymond & Richard Crabb managed *Hector (2)* captained by John Williams.

Many others who later sailed as captains for the Raymond group were mentored on ships managed by them.

Appendices

John Williams (*c.*1723 – 1774)

PMO	Ship	Dates	Captain	Other officer
PMO not checked	York (1)	1743/4	Lascelles, Henry	Williams, John, 5th mate
Grantham, Caleb & Franks, Aaron	York (1)	1746/7	Lascelles, Henry	Williams, John, 3rd mate
Grantham, Caleb & Franks, Aaron	York (1)	1749/50	Ward, Edward	Williams, John, 2nd mate
Hallett, John & Wells, Abraham	Clinton	1752/3	Nansan, John	Williams, John, 1st mate
Raymond, Charles & Crabb, Richard	Hector (2)	1755/6	Williams, John	
Raymond, Charles & Crabb, Richard	Hector (2)	1758/9	Williams, John	
Raymond, Charles & Hough, Samuel	Hector (2)	1761/2	Williams, John	
Raymond, Charles	Hector (3)	1766/7	Williams, John	

He was replaced as Captain by his brother Stephen Williams.

Henry Fletcher (*c.*1727 – 1807)

PMO	Ship	Dates	Captain	Other officer
Beckford, Thomas & Elliston, Edward	Lynn (2)	1745/6	Gilbert, Charles	Fletcher, Henry, 5th mate
Egerton, William & Gilbert, Charles	Lynn (2)	1749/50	Egerton, William	Fletcher, Henry, 4th mate
Raymond, Charles & Steevens, William	Salisbury (1)	1752/3	Foot, John	Fletcher, Henry, 2nd Mate
Raymond, Charles & Godfrey, Shearman	Harcourt (1)	1755/6	Webber, William	Fletcher, Henry, 1st mate
Raymond, Charles & Crisp, Nicholas	Stormont (1)	1758/9	Fletcher, Henry	
Moffatt, Andrew	Earl of Middlesex	1762/3	Fletcher, Henry	
EIC Director between 1769 and 1783				

Sir Charles Raymond of Valentines and the East India Company

John Pelly (1684 – 1762) and John Pelly junior (1711 – 1762)

PMO	Ship	Dates	Captain	Other officer
PMO not checked	Middlesex (1)	1725/6	Pelly, John	John Pelly junr, purser
Collett, Jonathan & Barne, Miles	Middlesex (1)	1729/30	Pelly, John	John Pelly junr, 3rd mate
PMO not checked	Drake (1)	1733/4	Pelly, John	John Pelly junr, 1st mate
Collett, Jonathan & Pinnell, Richard	Prince of Wales (2)	1737/8	Pelly, John	John Pelly junr, 1st mate
Pelly, John & Hume, Abraham	Prince of Wales (2)	1740/1	John Pelly junr	
PMO not checked	Prince of Wales (2)	1743/4	John Pelly junr	
Pelly, John & Hall, Thomas	Prince of Wales (2)	1746/7	John Pelly junr	

Pinson Bonham (1724 – 1791)

PMO	Ship	Dates	Captain	Other officer
PMO not checked	Duke of Lorraine	1741/2	Wilson, Jonathan	Bonham, Pinson, 4th mate
Salvador, Francis & Mickelfield, Richard	Princess Mary (1)	1744/5	Osborne, Robert	Bonham, Pinson, 2nd mate
Mickelfield, Richard & Hunt, Thomas	Duke of Cumberland (2)	1749/50	Osborne, Robert	Bonham, Pinson, 2nd mate
Raymond, Charles & Tolson, Joseph	Scarborough (2)	1750/1	D'Auvergne, Philip	Bonham, Pinson, 2nd mate
Raymond, Charles & Crabb, Richard	Norfolk (1)	1753/4	Bonham, Pinson	
Raymond, Charles & Crabb, Richard	Norfolk (1)	1756/7	Bonham, Pinson	
Crabb, Richard & Raymond, Charles	Norfolk (2)	1759/60	Bonham, Pinson	
Subsequently PMO for 4 voyages				

Appendices

Charles Foulis (*c.*1714 – 1783)

PMO	Ship	Dates	Captain	Other officer
PMO not checked	Lynn (2)	1738/9	Gilbert, Charles	Foulis, Charles, 3rd mate
PMO not checked	Harrington	1741/2	Jenkins, Robert	Foulis, Charles, 1st mate
Chrichton, David & Page, Edward	Anson (1)	1746/7	Foulis, Charles	
Chrichton, David & Page, Edward	Lord Anson	1749/50	Foulis, Charles	
Chrichton, David & Page, Edward	Lord Anson	1753/4	Foulis, Charles	
Subsequently PMO for 38 voyages				

Robert Preston (1740 – 1834)

PMO	Ship	Dates	Captain	Other officer
Hallett, John & Wells, William	Streatham (3)	1757/8	Mason, Charles	Preston, Robert, 5th mate
Lost in Hugli river, Preston transferred 22 Nov 1759 to				
Raymond, Charles & Crabb, Richard	Duke of Dorset (2)	1758/9	Forrester, Bernard	Preston, Robert, 5th mate
Raymond, Charles & Hough, Samuel	Clive	1761/2	Allen, John	Preston, Robert, 3rd mate
Raymond, Charles & Moffatt, Andrew	Clive	1764/5	Allen, John	Preston, Robert, 2nd mate
Foulis, Charles	Asia (2)	1767/8	Preston, Robert	
Foulis, Charles	Asia (2)	1770/1	Preston, Robert	
Foulis, Charles	Hillsborough (1)	1774/5	Preston, Robert	
Subsequently PMO for many more than 20 voyages				

Sir Charles Raymond of Valentines and the East India Company

Pitt Collett (*c*.1729 – 1780)

PMO	Ship	Dates	Captain	Other officer
Raymond, Charles & Tolson, Joseph	Wager (2)	1750/1	Hindman, Josiah	Collett, Pitt, 5th mate
Pelly, John, Junior & Pelly, John, Senior	Onslow (2)	1753/4	Hinde, Thomas	Collett, Pitt, 3rd mate
Hallett, John & Wells, William	Caernarvon (2)	1755/6	Hutchinson, Norton	Collett, Pitt, 2nd mate
Hallett, John & Wells, William	Calcutta (1)	1758/9	Willson, George	Collett, Pitt, 1st mate
Raymond, Charles & Hough, Samuel	Clive	1761/2	Allen, John	Collett, Pitt, 1st mate
Raymond, Charles & Moffatt, Andrew	Clive	1764/5	Allen, John	Collett, Pitt, 1st mate
Raymond, Charles	Clive	1767/8	Allen, John	Collett, Pitt, 1st mate
Raymond, Charles	Duke of Richmond	1770/1	Hindman, Thomas	Collett, Pitt, 1st mate
Foulis, Charles & Preston, Robert	Hillsborough (1)	1777/8	Collett, Pitt	
Foulis, Charles & Preston, Robert	Hillsborough (1)	1779/80	Collett, Pitt	

Note Robert Preston was third mate and second mate on the voyages of *Clive* 1761/2 & 1764/5.

Appendices

Appendix 9 – Principal Managing Owners managing 5 or more voyages
for the East India Company, in 5 year periods.   This excludes Company ships.

1750/1 - 1754/5	TOTAL	%
Hallett, John	18	20.5
Raymond, Sir Charles	**13**	**14.8**
Braund, Samuel	7	8.0
Lockyer, Thomas	5	5.7
Pelly, John, Junior	5	5.7
Rogers, Simon	5	5.7
Salvador, Francis	5	5.7
21 Others	30	34.1
Total ships sailed	**88**	

1755/6 - 1759/60	TOTAL	%
Raymond, Sir Charles	**27**	**29.3**
Hallett, John	16	17.4
Braund, Samuel	6	6.5
23 Others	43	46.7
Total ships sailed	**92**	

Data from a spreadsheet compiled by the author from Anthony Farrington *A Catalogue of East India Company Ships' Journals and Logs 1660-1834* (British Library 1999) and from Court Books.

1760/1 - 1764/5	TOTAL	%
Raymond, Sir Charles	**20**	**18.7**
Durand, John	15	14.0
Hallett, John	10	9.3
Boulton, Richard (Crabb)	9	8.4
Foulis, Charles	7	6.5
29 Others	46	43.0
Total ships sailed	**107**	

1765/6 - 1769/70	TOTAL	%
Raymond, Sir Charles	**24**	**17.8**
Durand, John	22	16.3
Foulis, Charles	11	8.1
Boulton, Richard (Crabb)	10	7.4
Raymond, John	7	5.2
Moffatt, Andrew	6	4.4
Slater, Gilbert, Sen	6	4.4
Willson, George	6	4.3
29 Others	43	31.9
Total ships sailed	**135**	

1770/1 - 1774/5	TOTAL	%
Raymond, Sir Charles	**10**	**8.8**
Durand, John	9	8.0
Foulis, Charles	9	8.0
Willson, George	9	8.0
Boulton, Richard (Crabb)	6	5.3
Moffatt, Andrew	6	5.3
Raymond, John	6	5.3
Slater, Gilbert, Sen	6	5.3
Nixon, William	5	4.4
34 Others	47	41.6
Total ships sailed	**113**	

1775/6 - 1779/80	TOTAL	%
Willson, George	8	7.27
Durand, John	8	7.27
Raymond, Sir Charles	**7**	**6.36**
Hume, Alexander	6	5.45
Raymond, John	6	5.45
Moffatt, Andrew	6	5.45
Foulis, Charles	5	4.55
34 Others	64	58.2
Total ships sailed	**110**	

Sir Charles Raymond of Valentines and the East India Company

Appendix 10 – Principal Managing Owners
EAST INDIA COMPANY, COURT BOOK No. B/82 *Extracts for season 1766/7*

The following owners were approved to sign the charterparties of the undermentioned ships, viz:

p.175   12 September 1766

Charles Raymond)
Andrew Moffatt) of London Esq^{rs}

for the *Hector*, Captain John Williams Commander
for the *Latham*, Captain James Moffatt Commander
for the *London*, Captain Thomas Mottley Commander
for the *Earl of Middlesex*, Captain Henry Fletcher* Commander
for the *Bute*, Captain Patrick Maitland Commander

> * Henry Fletcher resigned the command of the *Earl of Middlesex* on 19 Sept 1766 and was replaced by John Hasell.

Charles Raymond of London Esq
Henry Hinde of London Merchant
for the new ship, Captain Henry Hinde Pelly Commander [*Europa (1)*]

p.228   17 October 1766

Richard Crabb)
Charles Raymond) of London Esq^{rs}

for the *Worcester*, Captain Richard Hall Commander and
for the *Norfolk*, Captain John Sandys Commander

p.232   22 October 1766

Charles Foulis of London Esq
Andrew Moffatt of London Merchant
for the *Earl of Elgin*, Captain Thomas Cooke Commander

Charles Foulis)
Charles Raymond) of London Esq^{rs}

for the *Northumberland*, Captain John Mitford Commander

p.266   12 November 1766

William Webber of London Mariner
John Wells of Deptford in Kent Shipwright
for the *Egmont*, Captain Charles Mears Commander

p.269   13 November 1766

John Raymond)
Charles Raymond) of London Esq^{rs}

for the *Lord Clive*, Captain Barnaby Bartlett Commander

A total of 25 ships sailed for the EIC in the 1766/7 season, one of them being a Company owned ship. Charles Raymond signed as either first or second charterparty for ten of them.

Appendices

EAST INDIA COMPANY, COURT BOOK No. B/91 *Extracts for season 1775/6*
The following owners were approved to sign the charterparties of the undermentioned ships, viz:

p.337 & 338   5 December 1775

Sir Charles Raymond Bart
Robert Williams of Bow Street Covent Garden Gentleman
for the *Nassau*, Captain Arthur Gore and
for the *Granby*, Captain John Johnston

John Raymond Esq
Sir Charles Raymond Bart
for the *Shrewsbury*, Captain Benjamin Jones

Richard Boulton Esq
Sir Charles Raymond Bart
for the *Duke of Cumberland*, Captain Augustus Savage

EAST INDIA COMPANY, COURT BOOK No. B/92 *Extracts for season 1776/7*
The following owners were approved to sign the charterparties of the undermentioned ships, viz:

p.374   23 October 1776

Richard Boulton Esq   )
Sir Charles Raymond Bart)   *Worcester*

Pinson Bonham Esq   )
Sir Charles Raymond Bart)   *Duke of Portland*

John Raymond Esq   )
Sir Charles Raymond Bart)   *Ceres*

John Raymond Esq   )
Sir Charles Raymond Bart)   *Duke of Kingston*

EAST INDIA COMPANY, COURT BOOK No. B/96 *Extracts for season 1780/1*
The following owners were approved to sign the charterparties of the undermentioned ships, viz:

p.31   Charles Foulis   )
              Robert Preston   )   of London Esq[rs]
        for the ship *Hillsborough*, Captain Pitt Collett

p.327   Henry Boulton of London Esq
              Sir Charles Raymond of London Bart
        for the *Essex*, Captain Arthur Morris

p.382   Donald Cameron of George Street Mansion House, Banker
              Thomas Newte of the Adelphi Esq
        for the *Valentine*, Captain James Ogilvie

155

Sir Charles Raymond of Valentines and the East India Company

Appendix 11 – Two poems by Lady Sophia Burrell (1753 – 1802)

Poetess and daughter of Sir Charles Raymond of Valentines

See also http://www.archive.org/details/poemsburrell02burriala

The School for Satire (1793)
How oft we see the female sex
Themselves with jealous fancies vex!
With envy, which they cannot smother,
They tell the failings of each other;
Or if a dear, provoking creature
Has not one blemish in her nature,
A mole, an eyelash can supply
The means for female industry.
(A spider clinging to a thread
Can soon the web of mischief spread.)

Black-eyed Narissa cries, 'Tis true
That Celestina's eyes are blue!
But can we find expression there? –
Besides, the fool has flaxen hair.'

I see *brown* Amarilla sneer,
Because Polyxena is *fair*;
'Tis mighty easy, she avers,
To wear a skin as white as hers; –
But, for her part, she'd rather be
From artificial fairness free.

Cynthia, whose teeth Dumergue has made,
Follows the same censorious trade;
Cries, 'What d'ye mean by Flavia's youth?
You see that she has lost a tooth!'
Tall Lucy rails at little Dy,
Who only measures four feet high;
Fat Bell detests her cousin Prue,
Since she so thin and airy grew;
And snob-nosed Chloe hates a woman
Whose nose but borders on the Roman.

Doris the saucy, free and rude,
Rails at Myrtilla for a prude;
And Galatea says, with spite,
Dorinda's eyebrows are too light,
When it is known to half the town
That Galatea makes her own.

Ah why, ye fair! this cruel rage?
Do ye not all adorn the stage?
Decreed to charm in different ways,
Do ye not all create a blaze?
And, after all that has been said,
Ye can but sparkle, bloom and fade.

Then be contented with your lot,
Nor covet charms your friends have got;
And learn that candour and good-nature
Act like a charm on every feature,
Restoring to Medusa's face
Composure, harmony and grace.

On the Right Honourable Earl Talbot (1781)
When, noble Talbot! we behold in thee
True greatness join'd with affability,
The kindest manners undefil'd by art,
The clearest head, and the most perfect heart,
That gracious liberality of mind
Which reaches to the meanest of mankind,
That steady genius, that expression strong,
Which marks the virtuous lessons of thy tongue,
That firm integrity, that conduct wise,
That honesty which loathes all mean disguise
We gaze delighted on a life so rare,
A mind so virtuous, amiable, sincere.

If we regard thee as the tender Sire,
Still more thy gentle manners we admire;
We honour thy affectionate address,
Thy placid temper, ease, and cheerfulness;
If as a FRIEND, we see thee faithful, just,
If as a subject, steady to thy trust;
Thy heart with sensibility is blest,
And honour rules the helm in Talbot's breast;
A thousand blessings on his steps attend,
The poor man's patron! and the good man's friend!
A thousand grateful hearts revere his name,
A thousand tongues his generous deeds proclaim;
What more remaineth for the Muse to tell,
But that his character is *sans parei*

INDEX

Ajax 1758/9 captured by the French   53, 115

Aldborough Hatch   44, 73, 121

Allen, John, Captain   64, 67

Allen, William   110

Angria family   13, 17, 58, 59

Anjengo massacre   13

Anson (1) 1746/7   53, 60-1

Anson, George (1697-1762) Captain, later
   Admiral Lord Anson   21-2, 59-60

Balchen, John (1670-1744) Admiral Sir   20

Bank Buildings   81, 84

Bank of England   3, 78, 80, 108

Banking   107-11, 127

Barking, St Margaret's church   65, 102, 106,
   122, 123, 126

Batavia (Jakata)   26, 65-6, 112

Bath   110, 120, 122, 123

Battles at sea and enemy action   52-3, 54, 57,
   61, 63, 66-7, 68, 69, 117-9

Beckenham, Kent   24, 105, 137

Benyon, Richard (1698-1774)   46, 102, 113

Bethlem Royal Hospital (Bedlam)   87-8, 124

Birchin Lane   78, 79, 106, 120, 129

Bird, Joseph   113, 114

Birkhead, Charles, Captain   32

Black Hole of Calcutta   65-6

Black, William   47, 85

Blackwall   38, 44, 106, 114

Bombay   13, 56, 58, 61, 117

Bonham, Pinson (1724-1791) Captain and PMO
   38, 46, 69-74, 150

Bookey, Edward and William   45

Boscawen family   85

Boscawen, Edward (1711-1761) Admiral   67

Boscawen, Frances, wife of the Admiral   93

Botany and introduction of new plants to
   England   56, 97-8, 125-6

Boulton, Emma (died 1856)   115, 122, 141

Boulton, Henry (1752-1828)   47, 106, 114, 122,
   140, 141

Boulton, Juliana (1754-1813) see Raymond,
   Juliana

Boulton, Louise (1791-1875)   122, 141

Boulton, Richard, see Crabb, Richard

Boyce, William (1711-1779) composer   94

Braddyll, Dodding   28

Braddyll, Hon. Thomas Esq   28

Braund, Benjamin, Captain   82

Braund, Samuel   6, 47, 82

Braund, William   82

Bridewell Hospital   87-8, 124

British Library, East India Company archives
   ix, xiv, 7

Broadstairs, Kent   123, 124

Bromley, Kent   24, 139

Burrell, Amy (*c*.1700-1789) see Raymond, Amy

Burrell, Peter   24, 85, 137

Burrell, Sophia (1753-1802) 103-5, 126, 127,
   137, 138, 141, 156
   see also Raymond, Sophia

Burrell, William (1732-96) Dr later Sir   85, 86,
   103-4, 107, 126, 127, 137, 138, 141

Byrom, Edward   110

Cabinet of Curiosities   90-1

Caernarvon (2) 1755/6   65-7

Calcutta (Fort William)   10, 11, 17, 19, 26, 28,
   53, 63-4, 65

Calcutta (1) 1758/9   62-3, 67

Camellia japonica, variegata   97

Cameron, Dr Archibald   86

Cameron, Donald (*c*.1740-1797)   38, 44, 87,
   91, 97, 102, 108, 121, 122, 125, 126, 127,
   139

Cameron, Mary (baptised 1737) 87, 102, 139
   see also Guy, Mary

Canals and grottoes at Valentines   40-1, 96

Canton and the Pearl River   59-60, 112-3

Cape Verd, Senegal   54, 69

Cape, Jonathan (died 1747) Captain   29

Cape Town & False Bay, South Africa   26, 53,
   68, 99

Index

Cargoes carried by East Indiamen 11, 13, 16, 28, 60, 117, 128, 142-5

Castle at Highlands 100, 101

Castle Rising 45

Cedar of Lebanon at Valentines 96

Centurion, Captain George Anson 22, 59-60

Charterparty Agreement 6

Chick, Edward Lord, Captain 122

Chigwell xiv, 28, 82, 109, 126

Child, Francis (1735-63) of Osterley 46

Child, Sir Caesar (*c*.1678-1725) of Claybury 55-6

Child, Sir John (*c*.1638-1690) of Surat 55, 56

Child, Sir John (1712-1784) of Wanstead see Tylney, Earl

Child, Sir Josiah (*c*.1630-1699) of Wanstead 56

Chinese porcelain 91-2, 102, 144-5

Chinese trade see also Supercargo 59

Chinese wallpaper 92, 95

Chinese watercolour book 92

Christ's Hospital, City of London 124

Christmas Isle 19

Clay, William Rev 104, 138

Claybury, Woodford Bridge 56

Clive, Robert (1725-1774) Lord Clive of India 114

Coaches at Valentine House 91

Collett family of Barking 25, 65

Collett, Pitt, Captain (*c*.1727-1780) 38, 57, 65-9, 152

Combrune, Lewis 82

Company's candle 31

Conyers, John (1717-1775) of Copped Hall, Epping 94-5

Conyers, Matilda (1753-1803) 95

Cooke, Judith (*c*.1695-1759) married William Guy 24, 25, 88, 139
see also Guy, Judith

Corsellis, Nicholas Caesar, of Woodford Bridge 55

Crabb Boulton family 106, 140

Crabb, Henry (1709-1773) 31, 106, 140

Crabb, Richard (died 1777) Captain and PMO 33, 43, 45, 46, 47, 48, 106, 140

Cranbrook House, Ilford 100, 101

Crichton, Elizabeth, and family 60, 101

Crichton, Katherine 101

Crisp, Nicholas 46, 48

Darling, Richard, captain's steward 16, 32

Dawsonne, East Indiaman 3, 5-11

Deal, Kent 49-50, 123

Derby (2) 1729/30 9, 10

Derby (2) 1734/5 17

Dinely, Thomas 84

Diving on a wrecked ship by EIC 62, 72

Dodd, Rev Dr William 109-10, 125

Dovecote at Valentines 99

Downs 16, 50

Drake 1728/9 11

Duke of Cumberland (2) 1749/50 53, 54, 69-72

Duke of Dorset (2) 1758/9 62-4, 67

Duke of Kingston (2) 1782/3 23, 53

Durand, John, PMO 47-8, 153

Dutch East India Company 7, 10

Dyewood 11, 128, 130, 145

Earl of Chesterfield 109, 125

Earl of Oxford 1782/3 23

Earl Talbot, East Indiaman 97, 121

East India Company archives at the British Library ix, xiv, 7

East India Company (in London) 2, 6, 14, 15, 85, 128

East India House 14, 78, 79-80

East Indiaman, accident on board ship 10, 17, 23, 50-1, 60

East Indiaman, cargoes 11, 13, 16, 28, 60, 117, 128, 142-5

East Indiaman, crew 8, 15, 29, 30

East Indiaman, damaged repaired at sea 16

East Indiaman, description and size 6-7, 112

East Indiaman, enemy action see Battles at sea

East Indiaman, fire risk and destruction 23, 52, 53, 54

East Indiaman, journals 7, 18, 19, 27, 65, 71

Sir Charles Raymond of Valentines and the East India Company

East Indiaman, lost at sea 52, 53, 62, 70-2, 116, 119

East Indiaman, punishment on board ship 16-7

East Indiaman, speed and distance travelled 13, 146

Edwards, George 98

Englefield House, Berkshire 102

Exchange Alley 81, 106

Exeter xx, 2, 4, 11, 111, 115

Expedition (4) sloop 1749/50 72

Finance of sailing for the East India Company 30-3

Fisher, Brice 82, 84

Fletcher, Henry, Sir (*c.*1727-1807) 38, 44-5, 48, 102, 109-10, 149

Forrester, Bernard, Captain 48, 63-4

Foulis, Charles (*c.*1714-1783) Captain and PMO 38, 46, 47, 57, 58-61, 64, 68, 83, 103, 115, 151

Foundling Hospital 87, 88

Foundling, The, a play by Edward Moore 94

Free British Fishery 81, 113

Freeman, William George 61

Gamage, William Dick, Captain 61

Gambia, Royal Africa Co. 71-2

Gardens at Valentines 40-1, 96-9

Gascoigne, Sir Crisp 82

George & Vulture tavern 106

Gidea Hall, Romford 102

Gilbert, Thomas, Captain 12

Glynn, Sir Richard 86

Godfrey, Benjamin (1720-1765) Captain 47, 114-5

Godfrey, David (1738-1798) 83

Godfrey, Edmund (1696-1765) 40, 83

Godfrey, Joseph (1700-1765) 82, 83, 84

Godfrey, Michael (1625-1689) 82

Godfrey, Peter (1662-1724) 83

Godfrey, Peter (1695-1769) 40, 47, 82, 83, 84

Godfrey, Shearman (1699-1766) 46-7, 48, 63, 113, 114

Godfrey, Thomas (1693-1772) 83

Godfrey, William (*c.*1728-1802) 83

Goodwin Sands 50

Granby 1767/8 99

Grandison, Sir Charles 126

Grantham (2) 1749/50 69-73

Griffin 1758/9 116

Guernsey 20, 119

Guy family 139

Guy, Ann (baptised 1734) married John Williams 24, 43, 139
see also Williams, Ann

Guy, Judith (*c.*1695-1759) 25, 139
see also Cooke, Judith

Guy, Mary (baptised 1737) married Donald Cameron 24, 87, 139
see also Cameron, Mary

Guy, William (*c.*1685-1755) 24, 25, 40, 139

Gwynne House, Woodford Bridge 55

Haeslingford 1741/2 60, 144

Hallett, James 48

Hallett, John (died 1765) PMO 47, 48, 153

Halsewell 1785/6 53-4

Hankey, Joseph 114

Harcourt, Captain William Webber 21, 41, 44

Hardwicke (2) 1757/8 62-3, 67

Harrington 1741/2 58-60, 144

Harrison, John (1721-94) of Chigwell Row 82

Harts House, Woodford 56, 57, 74

Harvey, William 101

Hayes, William "Portraits of Rare and Curious Birds .... Osterly Park" 99

Heathcote, East Indiaman 22, 29

Hector, East Indiaman 43

Herrings 81

Herringston, Dorset 43

Higham Hills (Highams), Woodford Green 56

Highlands, Ilford 41, 42, 100-1, 121

Hillsborough, East Indiaman 64, 65, 68

Hinde, Elizabeth see Pelly, Elizabeth

Hinde, Henry, of Upton 25, 38, 39, 52, 115

Hindman, Josiah (died 1775) Captain 16, 28, 92

Hindman, Thomas, uncle of Josiah 28

Hogarth, William (1697-1764) artist 88-9

Holt, Adam 40

Hornby, William (1723-1893) Governor of Bombay 56

Hugli River (Calcutta) 10, 17, 53, 62

Hunt, Mary 55

Hunt, Thomas, Captain and PMO 19, 54, 55, 116

Hunt, William (1743-1826) Captain 55

Hunt, William (died 1767) Governor of the Bank of England 55

Hutchinson, Norton, Captain 65, 67

Ilford xiv, 38, 40, 74, 101, 114

Ilford Lodge 102

India 1748, map xix

Ingleby, Dr Clement Mansfield (1823-1886) xv

Insurance of shipping 64, 113

Insurance of Valentine House 40, 91

Jackson, Elizabeth 97

Jackson, Jeffrey (*c*.1730-1802) Captain 56-7

Jacobite Rebellion (1745) 86

Jenkins, Robert (died 1742) Captain 58

Jerusalem Coffee House 106-7

Johanna, Comoro Islands 13, 58

Jones, Samuel, Captain of Stepney, and family 2, 137

Keen, Richard, diver ix, 119, 144-5

King's birthday at St James's 1782 125

Knepp, West Sussex xiv, 126, 127

Knotts Green, Leyton 97, 125-6

Latham (2) 1769/70 19

Lead-line to establish depth 13

Lethieullier, Smart, of Aldersbrook 90

Letters of Marque 46-7

Livesey, Hargreave & Co. 110

Livesey, John 110

Lloyds coffee house 113

Lock, John, Sir 12, 13

Lockyer, Thomas 46, 47

Log-line to establish the speed 13

London in the 1750s 78-81

Lord Clive 1766/7 53, 116

Lowe, Richard 110

Luxborough, in Chigwell 28, 109

Lyttleton, Sir Richard 46

Madeira 68, 122, 145

Madras (Fort St George) 9, 10,17, 19, 53, 69, 117

Main, James 8-10, 50-1, 98

Manchester bank 110-11, 127

Mansion House, London 78, 80

Margate 123-4

Marlborough, East Indiaman 54

Martin, Matthew, Captain 2, 46, 54, 137

Master Keeper of Epping Forest 103

Mausoleum at Highlands, Ilford 100-1

Mead, Robert, Captain 13, 16

Menageries 99

Mickelfield, Catherine 54

Mickelfield, Richard, Captain and PMO 15, 19, 46, 54, 116

Mickelfield, Richard, jun. (died 1743) 54

Middlefield Farm, Ilford 101

Moffatt, Andrew (*c*.1730-1780) of Cranbrook House 33, 38, 47, 61, 101, 103, 115

Moffatt, Andrew & John & Co., insurance 84, 113

Moffatt, James, Captain and EIC Director 101

Moffatt, John 83, 101

Moffatt, William 47, 101

Molineux, Crisp (1730-1792) 45

Music and dancing at Valentines 93-4

Naish, James 12, 83

Navigation 13, 19

Newte, Anna Maria (1756-1783) see Raymond, Anna Maria

Newte, Samuel, of Tiverton 2

Newte, Thomas (*c*.1747-1806) 33, 47, 122, 125

Norfolk (1) 1756/7 owners 46

Odyssey Explorer (2009) 36 no.54

Ogilvie, James, Captain 117-9

Old Bailey 113

Osborne, James, Captain 2, 3, 137

Osborne, Robert, Captain 69-7

Ostend Company and ships 7, 10

Sir Charles Raymond of Valentines and the East India Company

Osterley (1) 1757/8 owners 46

Osterley House and Park, Hounslow 46, 99

Page, Edward 46

Patagonia, Chile, *Wager* shipwreck 22

Peach, Samuel (1725-1790) 109-10

Pelly, Elizabeth 25, 39

Pelly, Henry Hinde (1744-1818) 115

Pelly, John, Captain junior (1711-1762) Captain and PMO 25, 65, 115, 150

Pelly, John, Captain senior (1684-1762) Captain and PMO 25, 38, 115, 150

Pelly, Sir John Henry (1777-1852) 115, 122

Penneck, John, of St.Thomas's xx, 4, 11

Perry, John 113, 114

Pinnell family 48

Pitt (1) 1757/8 112-3

Politics 111

Pondicherry 117-8

Pratten, Edward, Captain (Royal Navy) 72

Press Gang 17, 19, 43, 51

Preston, Robert (1740-1834) Captain and PMO 38, 47, 57, 61, 62-4, 68, 97, 126, 151

Prince of Wales (3) 1764/5 52

Princess Mary (1) 1744/5 53, 54, 69

Princess of Wales 1732/3 12-13

Principal Managing Owner 6, 33, 45, 47, 153-5

Private trade, financial reward 30-2

Purser's role 8

Radcliffe, Edward, of London 31

Raikes, William (1738-1800) 121-2, 127

Raymond family 33, 136, 137, 138

Raymond, Amy (*c.*1700-1789) daughter of Hugh, married Peter Burrell 4, 24, 85, 137

Raymond, Anna Maria (died 1731) mother of Charles 2, 4, 11, 122, 136

Raymond, Anna Maria, sister of Charles 2, 4, 11, 136

Raymond, Anna Maria, baby of Charles buried 25, 39, 138

Raymond, Anna Maria (1756-1783) daughter of Charles, married Thomas Newte 43, 94, 121, 122, 123, 138

Raymond, Baynham, Captain (died 1719) 3, 33, 136

Raymond, Bridget 93 fn, 137

Raymond, Charles, aged 40 39

Raymond, Charles, aged 60 103

Raymond, Charles, baptised 23 April 1713 2

Raymond, Charles, benevolence 87-8, 109, 124, 125, 126

Raymond, Charles, burial at West Ham, 1751 39, 138

Raymond, Charles, created a baronet 105

Raymond, Charles, death 24 August 1788 126, 127

Raymond, Charles, family 136, 138

Raymond, Charles, ill health 28, 128

Raymond, Charles, London homes 79, 80, 106, 113, 120

Raymond, Charles, marriage 22 January 1743 23-4

Raymond, Charles, politics 111

Raymond, Charles, portrait ii, 129-30

Raymond, Charles, PMO 28, 33, 39, 45-7, 48, 54, 111-2, 153-5

Raymond, Charles, property 11, 39, 101, 102, 107, 123, 124, 126

Raymond, Charles, summary of career at sea 147

Raymond, Charles, summary of voyages 146

Raymond, Charles, *Times* obituary 127

Raymond, Harley, Lloyd & Cameron bank 108

Raymond, Harley, Webber & Co. bank 108

Raymond, Hugh (1674-1737) 2-4, 6, 11, 14, 15, 19, 22, 25, 31, 33, 54, 85, 137

Raymond, John (died 1719) Captain 3, 6, 136

Raymond, John (1668-1725), father of Charles 1-2, 4, 136

Raymond, John (*c.*1713-1800) son of Baynham 15, 19, 22, 23, 31, 33, 38, 40, 46, 47, 53, 86, 113, 114, 116, 122, 126, 136

Raymond, Jones (1706-1768) son of Hugh 6, 11, 15, 22, 54, 137

Raymond, Juliana (1754-1813) daughter of Charles, married Henry Boulton 43, 94, 106, 115, 127, 138, 140, 141

Index

Raymond, Lydia, widow of Baynham 4, 136

Raymond, Lydia, daughter of Baynham
  see Snow, Lydia

Raymond, Sarah (1722-1778) wife of Charles
  25, 39, 40, 92, 93-4, 103, 120, 138, 139
  see also Webster, Sarah

Raymond, Sir Charles, and Co. Bankers 110

Raymond, Sophia (1753-1802) daughter of
  Charles, married William Burrell 39, 94,
  95, 103-5, 138
  see also Burrell, Sophia

Raymond, Williams, Vere, Lowe and Fletcher
  bank 108, 110, 125

Repton, Humphry (1752-1818) landscape
  gardener 97, 120

Rising Castle, Ilford 45

Robertson, William 96

Rockingham, 2nd Marquess, Charles Watson-
  Wentworth (1730-1782) 111

Roe, Sir Thomas (1580-1644) 55, 56

Rogers, Simon (died 1752/3) PMO 40, 47, 81

Ropeworks 44, 114

Rowe, Lady Elianor [sic] wife of Sir Thomas
  Roe 55, 56

Royal Exchange 80-81, 113

Royal George, 1782, Royal Navy ship 125

Saling Hall, Essex 4

Salter, Sir John (died 1744) 56

Salvador, Francis 19, 26, 29, 31, 46, 54

Salvador, Joseph 28, 46, 54

Salway, Richard (*c.*1701-1775) 85

Sandwich 1753/4 40

Sark, Channel Isle 119, 145

Scarborough (2) 1750/1 73

Scotch Mines 84

Sea bathing 123-4

Seahorse, Royal Navy frigate 117-9

Secretary bird 98

Sedgwick, Roger 110

Sheriff of Essex 103

Shiplake, Oxfordshire 107

Shoreditch, St Leonard's church 44, 139

Silver and Company's treasure 12, 16, 30, 70

Silver or Spanish treasure 21-2, 30, 59, 60

Slater, Gilbert (1712-1785) Captain and PMO
  16, 47, 97, 125

Slater, Gilbert, junior (*c.*1753-1793) 8, 38, 50,
  97-8, 125

Small, Charles, Captain 12

Smallpox inoculations 124-5

Smith, William 65-6

Smuggling from East Indiamen 12, 32, 122

Snake-eater 98

Snow, Lydia (daughter of Bayham Raymond)
  33, 126, 136

Snow, Raymond, Captain 33, 136

South Sea Company xv, 3-4, 85-6, 103

South Woodham Ferrers, Essex see Woodham
  Ferrers

Southwark Fair by Wm. Hogarth 88-9, 91

Spanish Galleon *Covadonga* 21-2, 59

St Helena 17, 19, 20, 28, 43, 58, 60, 66, 107

St Stephen's, Walbrook 23-4

Steward, Francis (died 1751) Captain 8, 32

Steward, Gabriel (died 1744) Captain 8, 11,
  13, 32, 114

Steward, Gabriel, junior 114

Streatham (3) 1757/8 62

Suffolk 1775/6 (picture) 52

Sun Fire Office 82, 83, 84, 106, 107

Supercargo (or Supracargo) 12, 32, 59, 70, 83,
  92, 116

Surman, Robert (*c.*1693-1759) xv, 40, 84-5,
  93-4, 95, 96, 101

Sykes, Sir Francis, of Basildon House 92

Talbot, East Indiaman 121 see also *Earl Talbot*
  East Indiamen

Talbot, Lord William (1710-1782) 96, 121,
  156

Tanner, Anna Maria see Raymond, Anna Maria,
  mother of Charles

Tanner, Isabella, aunt to Charles Raymond 2,
  122, 136

Tanner, Samuel, of Clyst St. Mary xx, 2, 136

Tea tax 111

Tellicherry 13

Theft of cordage   113
Theft of lead from Valentine House   110
Thorncroft, Leatherhead   106, 115, 140
Tilbury, East Indiaman   55
Tillotson, Elizabeth (died 1702)   xv
Tolson, Joseph (died 1752) Captain and PMO
   22, 26, 28, 29, 45, 46, 73
Turtles   59, 106
Tylney, Earl, Sir John Child (1712-1784) of
   Wanstead   95, 111
Tylney-Long, Catherine (1789-1825) of
   Wanstead   123
Tylney-Long, Sir James (1736-1794) of Draycot
   and Wanstead   102, 127
Upton   25, 39, 114
Valentine, East Indiaman   48, 53, 91, 116-9,
   144-5
Valentine House and park   xiv-xv, 40, 42, 89-
   99
Valentine House, theft of lead   110
Valentine House to let, 1778   121
Valentine House sale advertisement, 1797   91
Valentine House renamed 'Valentines Mansion'
   xv
Valentines Mansion websites   xvii
Valleyfield, Scotland   64, 97
Vere, Charles   110
Verelst 1769/70   53
Vernon, Edward, Admiral Sir   117-8
Victory, Royal Navy flagship   20, 36 n.54
Vine at Valentines   96
Wager, Charles, Admiral Sir   21
Wager, East Indiaman   14, 19, 22, 26, 46, 142-
   3, 146, 147
Wager and Anson's voyage   21-2
Wanstead   xiv
Wanstead House   40, 56, 95, 96, 102, 111, 123,
   127
Warehousing at Blackwall   114
Warner, Richard (1713-75)   38, 56

Webber, Elizabeth (1725-1787)
   see Webster, Elizabeth
Webber, William (1713-1779) Captain and
   PMO   xx, 21, 38, 40, 41, 43, 48, 83, 101,
   108, 122, 139, 148
Webber, William, junior   41, 148
Websites for Valentines Mansion   xvii
Webster family tree   139
Webster, Elizabeth (1725-1787) married
   William Webber   24, 41, 121, 127, 139
Webster, John (1679-1724) father of Sarah
   Raymond   24, 40, 88, 139
Webster, Sarah (1722-1778)   23-4, 40, 139
   see also Raymond, Sarah
Webster, Thomas (1723-1745)   24, 26, 139
Wellclose Square, Wapping   4, 25, 29, 78
Welstead, Charles (1768-1832)   89, 90
West Ham, All Saints church   25, 39
West Wycombe, Bucks   43
Whampoa,China   60, 66
Wilkes, John (1725-1797)   111
Williams Deacon's Bank   108, 129
Williams, Ann (baptised 1734) 43, 87, 139
   see also Guy, Ann
Williams, John (*c*.1723-1774) Captain   38, 43-
   4, 48, 108, 114, 139, 149
Williams, Robert (1734-1814)   43, 47, 108,
   109, 114
Williams, Stephen (1739-1805)   43, 109
Wilson, William, Captain   112-3
Wine cellar at Valentine House   91
Withycombe Raleigh   xx, 1, 21, 123, 136
Woodford   xiv
Woodford Bridge   55, 56
Woodford, East Indiaman   64
Woodford Hall   55
Woodford, St Mary's church   28, 55, 61, 83, 85,
   87, 121
Woodham Ferrers   107, 126
York (1) 1743/4   43

Lightning Source UK Ltd.
Milton Keynes UK
UKOW04f1351050217
293630UK00001B/16/P